# Writing and Editing for Digital Media

*Writing and Editing for Digital Media* teaches students how to write effectively for digital spaces—whether writing for an app, crafting a story for a website, blogging, or using social media to expand the conversation. The lessons and exercises in each chapter help students build a solid understanding of the ways that digital communication has introduced opportunities for dynamic storytelling and multi-directional communication. With this accessible guide and accompanying website, students learn not only to create content, but also to become careful, creative managers of that content.

Updated with contemporary examples and pedagogy, including examples from the 2016 presidential election, and an expanded look at using social media, the third edition broadens its scope, helping digital writers and editors in all fields, including public relations, marketing, and social media management.

Based on Brian Carroll's extensive experience teaching a course of the same name, this revised and updated edition pays particular attention to opportunities presented by the growth of social media and mobile media. Chapters aim to:

- Assist digital communicators in understanding the socially networked, increasingly mobile, always-on, geomapped, personalized media ecosystems;
- Teach communicators to approach storytelling from a multimedia, multi-modal, interactive perspective;
- Provide the basic skill sets of the digital writer and editor, skill sets that transfer across all media and most communication and media industries, and to do so in specifically journalistic and public relations contexts;
- Help communicators to put their audiences first by focusing attention on user experience, user behavior, and engagement with their user bases;
- Teach best practices in the areas of social media strategy, management, and use.

**Brian Carroll** is Professor of Communication and Chair of the Department of Communication at Berry College, where he has taught since 2003. A former reporter, editor, and photographer, he is also the author of *When to Stop the Cheering? The Black Press, the Black Community, and the Integration of Professional Baseball* (2007) and *A Devil's Bargain: The Black Press and Black Baseball, 1915–1960* (2015). You can find him on the web at cubanxgiants.com.

# Writing and Editing for Digital Media

## Third Edition

Brian Carroll

Routledge
Taylor & Francis Group

NEW YORK AND LONDON

Third edition published 2017
by Routledge
711 Third Avenue, New York, NY 10017

and by Routledge
2 Park Square, Milton Park, Abingdon, Oxon OX14 4RN

*Routledge is an imprint of the Taylor & Francis Group, an informa business*

First edition published 2010 by Routledge
Second edition published 2014 by Routledge

*Library of Congress Cataloging-in-Publication Data*
Names: Carroll, Brian, 1965– author.
Title: Writing and editing for digital media / Brian Carroll.
Other titles: Writing for digital media
Description: Third edition. | New York : Routledge, 2017. | Includes bibliographical
   references and index.
Identifiers: LCCN 2017002788 | ISBN 9781138635982 (hardback) | ISBN 9781138636033 (pbk.)
Subjects: LCSH: Online authorship. | Online journalism.
Classification: LCC PN171.O55 C37 2017 | DDC 302.23/1—dc23
LC record available at https://lccn.loc.gov/2017002788

ISBN: 978-1-138-63598-2 (hbk)
ISBN: 978-1-138-63603-3 (pbk)
ISBN: 978-1-315-20626-4 (ebk)

Typeset in Warnock Pro
by Apex CoVantage, LLC

Printed and bound by CPI Group (UK) Ltd, Croydon, CR0 4YY

Visit the companion website: www.routledge.com/cw/carroll

# Contents

# Introduction

As the first edition of *Writing for Digital Media* went to press in summer 2009, Apple had just unveiled its first iPads, and the company's latest iPhone was the iPhone 3. As this third edition goes to press, it is affordable, portable virtual reality making headlines, as well as the digitally enabled profusion of "fake news" in what is being called a "post-truth" world. Technology's pace of change is breathless, and that makes a book on writing and editing for digital media a bit like chasing the wind. The continuing growth of social media, digitally native forms of storytelling, mobile-first design, and big data are just some of the changes reshaping the digital landscape, and making income and sustainable business models elusive and user-bases unpredictable.

This latest revision of *Writing and Editing for Digital Media* is a response to these changes, as well as an attempt to expand the applicability of its best practices well beyond journalism into the pedagogies and practices of public relations, social media management, and marketing. Examples and case studies have been updated to take a broader view, one more applicable to these varied industries. The book continues, however, to teach the basic skill sets of the digital writer and editor, skill sets that transfer across all media and most communication and media industries. The approach remains essentially journalistic, especially in terms of craft excellence, because the journalist's skill set is also the basic skill set of most communication professionals. The journalist's objectives of collecting evidence and crafting a story, too, are shared across communication industries. The Internet has brought communication professionals speed, immediacy, interactivity, boundless capacity, and global reach, as well as new ways to gather, report, and distribute information. It has also brought confusion and a blurring of fact and fiction that bewilders and befuddles.

## PEDAGOGICAL GOALS

With these considerations in mind, the aims of this revised edition are to help writers and editors:

1. Better understand the implications of a communication world that is socially networked, geomapped, personalized, mobile, and always on.
2. Put their audiences first by focusing attention on user experience, user behavior, and engagement with their user bases.
3. Allow the story, the content, to determine form and media choices rather than the other way around.
4. Become more experimental and adaptable in a fast-changing media ecosystem by providing them with trends, tools, techniques, and technologies.
5. Start, shape, and sustain conversations, user participation, and "spreadability."

An important assumption of this book is the blurring of roles, responsibilities, and job titles in an era of disruption, one in which we all are consumers and producers, readers and publishers, leaders and followers. The Internet has made it possible for anyone to publish digitally, as well as to engage even a global audience. New rhetorical possibilities have brought with them both unprecedented opportunity *and* daunting challenges. Thus, this book attempts to guide students and working professionals through this new converged ecosystem, pointing them toward the best practices and techniques of writing, editing, and storytelling.

Understanding what are increasingly fragmented audiences and exploring how different media behave—their unique limits and possibilities—will help students to develop smart content. With this book, students will analyze the technical and rhetorical possibilities of digital spaces, including interactivity; immersive, visual narratives; non-linear storytelling; and user participation and contribution. Embracing change is rarely easy, but it can be exciting and empowering. And the stakes have never been higher.

## ON WRITING WELL

First and foremost, this book is about writing—clearly, precisely, accurately, with energy and voice, and for specific audiences. Fortunately, good writing is still valued in digital spaces, even in environments that are primarily visual. And it is still just as hard to find good writing in the digital era as it was when legacy media ruled the roost. Though the premium on good writing has not changed, the activity of reading has, and dramatically so. People accessing information today are not so much reading as they are scanning, surfing, moving, selecting, and adding their own perspectives. Notice the verbs just mentioned. Digital writers are engineers of spaces, in addition to being communicators with and through their words and visuals.

Regardless of the field or industry, irrespective of the medium or platform, at some level we *all* are storytellers. Throughout history, humans have taught, learned, entertained, and communicated with stories, and this has held constant across media. Stories transmit information and transfer experience. This book, therefore, emphasizes digital storytelling and upholds the value of narrative. The value of a journalistic approach to information gathering, writing, editing, and publishing should, therefore, make sense. Journalism serves the journalist and non-journalist alike, especially in digital terra incognita, where the democracy of production and publishing is threatening the relevance of such distinctions. Building on a sound foundation of good writing, this book scaffolds on top new skills and sensitivities specific to digital spaces and places, which typically are also populated with graphical content, multimedia, and hypertextual, interactive elements. Learning how to achieve a smart balance of these elements is, therefore, a primary goal.

Structurally, this book begins in Chapters 1 and 2 with the fundamentals of good writing and editing. Next, Chapters 3 and 4 build on this solid foundation with the special skills and techniques needed to create compelling content for digital environments. Chapters 5 and 6 train our attention on mission and purpose by focusing first on credibility and, second, on the needs of our audiences, with special attention paid to ethics and ethical decision-making. Chapters 7, 8, and 9 look at specific digital contexts, including blogging, journalism, and public relations, before an exploration in Chapter 10 of the ways digital publishing has changed media law. Finally, an appendix identifies and describes the core values of digital journalism. A number of pedagogical features appears in each chapter to encourage students to further explore and build upon the lessons of the book:

- *chapter objectives* that establish the learning goals for each chapter;
- *chapter introductions* that outline the major topics in the chapter and how they connect to chapter objectives;
- *chapter activities* that ask students to apply the skills, critical perspectives, and best practices introduced in each chapter; and
- *digital resources* that connect students to relevant resources where they can learn more about the topics discussed in each chapter.

By way of acknowledgments, the author would like to thank Diane Land and Allie Crain for help finding typos and other copy demons; the students of JoMC 711, Writing for Digital Media at UNC Chapel Hill, whose collective intelligence and wisdom of the crowds heavily influenced this work; and Hisayo and Mary Arden Carroll for their tolerance of the many late nights at the office and the coffee shop.

# Writing for Digital Media

*I sometimes think that writing is like driving sheep down a road. If there is any gate to the left or right, the readers will most certainly go into it.*

—C. S. Lewis

*My goal as a writer is to make you hear, to make you feel—it is, before all, to make you see.*

—Joseph Conrad

*If, for a while, the ruse of desire is calculable for the uses of discipline soon the repetition of guilt, justification, pseudo-scientific theories, superstition, spurious authorities, and classifications can be seen as the desperate effort to "normalize" formally the disturbance of a discourse of splitting that violates the rational, enlightened claims of its enunciatory modality.*

Homi K. Bhabha, Professor of English, Harvard University, "Of Mimicry and Man"

## INTRODUCTION

Whether a person is writing a news story, novel, letter to the editor, or advertising copy, the principles of good writing are essentially the same. Different media place different burdens and responsibilities on writers, but the reason behind writing is always to communicate ideas in your head to an audience through (mostly) words. Does Professor Bhabha's sentence above clearly communicate his ideas? Can you understand what he means by efforts to normalize the disturbance of a discourse of splitting? This sentence was awarded second prize in an annual "Bad Writing Contest." Bad writing obfuscates and confuses, and it promotes misunderstanding and perhaps even apathy. This chapter provides a foundation for good and better writing, including sections on writing's history, grammar, and orthography (spelling and punctuation). The chapter aims to help students identify weaknesses in their writing, then to offer help and resources to improve in those weak areas.

## THE MEDIUM IS THE MESSAGE: A BRIEF HISTORY OF WRITING

The writing tools of today are a far cry from the caveman's stone. Think about how the innovation of clay tablets, the first portable writing artifact, altered the written record of human history. Now think about the modern-day communicative practices of texting, Snapchatting, and Facebooking, and the ways in which these and other digital technologies and formats are changing the way people communicate today. The tools that we use to communicate affect *how* and *what* we communicate; the medium is an intrinsic part of the message. To better appreciate this truth, let's look to the beginning of writing.

In around 8500 BC, clay tokens were introduced to make and record transactions between people trading goods and services, leading to the emergence of a sort of alphabet. A clay cone, for example, represented a small measure of grain. A sphere indicated a larger amount, while a cylinder signified the transaction of an animal. Notably, only humans traffic in symbols, creating them to make meaning. Thus, these few primitive symbols contributed to the genesis of writing by using abstract forms to communicate discrete human actions.

The alphabet we use today developed around 2000 BC when Jews in Egypt collected 27 hieroglyphs, assigning to each one a different sound of speech. This phonetic system evolved into the Phoenician alphabet that is called the "great-grandmother" of many Roman letters used today in roughly 100 languages worldwide (Sacks, 2003). At about the same time, around two millennia BC, papyrus and parchment were introduced as early forms of paper. The Romans wrote on papyrus with reed pens fashioned from the hollow stems of marsh grasses, a type of pen that evolved into the quill pen around 700 AD. Though China had wood fiber paper in the second century AD, it would be the late 14th century and the arrival of Johannes Gutenberg before paper became a widely used technology in Europe. From this brief history so far, it's clear that what we think of as writing's primary utility—communication through language—in actuality proved a relatively low priority for a long time. Low literacy rates also contributed to this slow development. Until Gutenberg, there was not much for the average person to read beyond inscriptions on buildings, coins, and monuments. When Gutenberg began printing books, scholars estimate that there were only about 30,000 books in all of Europe. Fast forward only 50 years and Europe could count between 10 million and 12 million volumes, which fueled increases in literacy. Democratization of knowledge always spawns advances in reading and writing.

In 286 BC, Ptolemy I launched an ambitious project to archive all human knowledge, producing a library in Alexandria, Egypt, that housed hundreds of thousands of texts. None survive today. Invaders burned the papyrus scrolls and parchment volumes as furnace fuel in 681 AD. So, some of history's lessons here with respect to writing should be obvious:

- make a copy;
- back up your data; and
- beware of invaders.

Although making multiple copies of a work first occurred in Korea, Gutenberg gets most of the credit in histories of printing. In 1436, he invented a printing press with movable, replaceable wood letters. How much Gutenberg knew of the movable type that had been first invented in 11th-century China is not known; it is possible he in effect "re-invented" it. Regardless, these innovations combined to create the printing process and led to the subsequent proliferation of printing and printed material. They also led to a codification of spelling and grammar rules, though centuries would be required to allow for agreement on most of the final rules. We are still arguing, of course; language is fluid, malleable, and negotiated.

New communication technologies rarely eliminate those that preceded them, as Henry-Jean Martin pointed out in his *The History and Power of Writing*. They do often alter and in many cases replace the primary purposes of pre-existing technologies. New technologies also redistribute labor and can influence how we think. The early technologies of pen and paper, for example, facilitated written communication, which, like new communication technologies today, arrived amid great controversy. Plato and Socrates argued in the fourth century BC against the use of writing altogether. Socrates favored learning through face-to-face conversation, viewing writing as anonymous and impersonal. For his part, Plato feared that writing would destroy memory. Why make the effort to remember or, more correctly, to memorize something when it is already written down? (Why memorize a phone number when you can store it in your smartphone?) In Plato's day, people could memorize tens of thousands of lines of poetry, a practice common into Shakespeare's day, in the late 16th and early 17th centuries.

Think of for a moment: What have you memorized lately? How many poems can you recite from memory? Bible verses? Play scenes?

Plato also believed that the writer's ideas would be misunderstood in written form. When communication is spoken, the speaker is present to correct misunderstanding and has control over who gets to hear what. If you have ever had an email or Facebook post misunderstood—or read by the wrong person—these ancient concerns might ring true still.

Another ancient Greek, Aristotle, became communication's great hero by defending writing against its early detractors. In perhaps one of the earliest versions of the "if you can't beat them, join them" argument, Aristotle argued that the best way to protect yourself and your ideas from the harmful effects of writing was to become a better writer yourself. Aristotle also saw the communicative potential of writing as a means to truth, so for him, writing was a skill everyone should learn. He believed that because in writing it is truth that is at stake, honesty and clarity are paramount. Like so much of what Aristotle believed (and wrote down!), such values are every bit as important and just as rare in the 21st century as they were in the fourth century BC.

Aristotle was also the first to articulate the notion of "audience," a concept that has been variously defined ever since. He instructed rhetoricians to consider the audience before deciding on the message. This consideration perhaps more than any other distinguishes communication from expression for expression's sake, a distinction perhaps best understood by comparing visual communication to art, or journalism to literature.

While the development of printing proved a boon to education in many ways, perhaps the game changer was printing's capacity to produce multiple copies of the same text. Readers separated by time and space could refer to the same information without waiting years for a scribe or monk to copy a fragile manuscript being diminished by time and use.

The printing press soon fostered the proliferation of the book, which changed the very priorities of communication. Like any communication technology, the book has attributes that define it:

- **Fixity.** The information contained in a text is fixed by existing in many copies of the same static text.
- **Discreteness.** The text is experienced by itself, in isolation, separated from others. If there is a footnote in a book directing a reader to a reference or source material, the reader has to go get that source, physically, expending time and perhaps money.
- **Division of labor.** The author or creator and the reader or audience perform distinctly different tasks, and the gulf between them cannot be crossed. The book is written, published, distributed, and then, in separate, discrete activities, it is bought or borrowed and read.

- **Primacy for creativity and originality.** The value set embodied by books does not include collaboration, community, or dialogue—values impossible in a medium that requires physical marks and symbols on physical (paper) surfaces.
- **Linearity.** Unless it is a reference book, the work is likely meant to be read from front to back, in sequence, one page at a time. After hundreds of years of familiarity with this linearity, non-linear forms have found it difficult to gain acceptance.

Compare the book's fixed attributes to the raw materials of digital content: lines and lines and more lines of computer code, a source code that allows, say, webpages to be static or dynamic. Text might increase or decrease in size, switch typeface and color, or even adjust according to a geo-located audience. In fact, web "pages" aren't even pages; such terminology is metaphorical. What we are viewing onscreen is more a picture or image of a page.

Digital spaces are also non-linear, so the sequence of content is manipulable, by both creator and reader or viewer. Unlike a book, the web is scalable and navigable, a space we move through rather than a series of pages read in a particular, technology-ordained order. Digital readers can easily subvert planned sequences by accessing information in any order they wish. Digital spaces are also typically networked. Think about how the search function alone has changed how we access and use documents, with search engines allowing a viewer to navigate directly to page 323 of a "book." Technology changes the ways in which texts are used or read, stored, searched, altered, and controlled. While innovation doesn't ensure progress (think about what's happened to attention spans due to social media and the smartphone), it is what we expect. And, to repeat, the medium carrying or delivering the ideas will in important ways affect even what those ideas can be.

The idea that a technology is not inherently good or evil, or that its virtues and liabilities evolve as its contexts change, is an important assumption that this book makes, one that underpins many of the book's other assumptions. It is not true that the technology of the book is somehow natural while new digital spaces are somehow unnatural, though this is a commonly held view. Gutenberg's printing press was revolutionary as a technology; the Internet, too, as the product of hundreds of technologies, has also proven revolutionary.

## PRINCIPLES OF GOOD WRITING

When asked what he would do first if given rule over China, Confucius is believed to have said:

> To correct language. . . . If language is not correct, then what is said is not what is meant. If what is said is not what is meant, then what ought to be done remains

undone. If this remains undone, morals and art will deteriorate. If morals and art deteriorate, justice will go astray. If justice goes astray, the people will stand about in helpless confusion. Therefore, there must be no arbitrariness in what is said. This matters about everything.

This next section aims to help students better understand the principles of good writing, principles important no matter the medium and no matter the audience. Because writing is (or should be) a multi-phase process (pre-writing, writing, editing, revising, editing again, revising again, evaluating), each of the principles that follow is paired with an exercise or two to demonstrate the instructional point. These exercises are designed to help you think increasingly like a writer.

## Be Brief

*It is my ambition to say in ten sentences what others say in a whole book.*

—Friedrich Nietzsche

Writing should be clear and concise. Readers need little reason not to read further, and this is especially and painfully true with smartphone-delivered information on ever-smaller screens. So prune your prose.

---

### EXERCISE 1.1

Here are some samples of cluttered writing. Re-write the sentences to convey the same meaning in fewer words, perhaps using a sentence or phrase you have seen somewhere else.

*Problem:*

The essential question that must be answered, that cannot be avoided, is existential, which is, whether or not to even exist.

*Solution:*

To be or not to be, that is the question.

Now, try these:

- People should not succumb to a fear of anything except being fearful in the first place, and we should stick together on this so we can't be defeated.

- The male gender is so different from the female gender that it is almost as if the two genders are from completely different planets.
- There were two different footpaths in the forest, one that had been cleared by foot traffic and another that obviously fewer people had used. I decided to take the one that fewer people had used, and it really made a big difference.

## EXERCISE 1.2

Hemingway supposedly once wrote a short story in six words. "For sale: baby shoes, never worn." He called it his best work.

The task in this exercise is to do what Hemingway did: Write a short story in just six words. This will force you to be judicious and deliberate choosing your words. (This should be an easy, fun exercise for active tweeters.)

Here are some examples, from *Wired* magazine:

- "Failed SAT. Lost scholarship. Invented rocket." (William Shatner);
- "Computer, did we bring batteries? Computer?" (Eileen Gunn);
- "Vacuum collision. Orbits diverge. Farewell, Love." (David Brin); and
- "Gown removed carelessly. Head, less so." (Joss Whedon)

## Be Precise

> *When I use a word it means exactly what I say, no more and no less.*
> —Humpty Dumpty, from Lewis Carroll's *Through the Looking-Glass*

We strive to use exactly the word that our meaning requires, not one that is close or, worse, one that merely *sounds* like the right word. A dictionary and a thesaurus should never be far away (and online or with an app or two, they don't have to be). Here are a few examples:

- "A sense of trust was **induced**." >> No, trust is enabled, rewarded, or encouraged, it is not induced. Labor in a pregnant woman? That can be induced.
- "Put into **affect** . . ." >> No, put it into *effect*, though A might *affect* B.
- "She was **surrounded** by messages." >> Perhaps she was inundated with messages, or drowning in information, but surrounded by a ring of messages? Unlikely.

- "He was **anxious** to go to the game." >> He was probably eager, not anxious, unless he was playing in the game, in which case it is possible he was, in fact, nervous or worried.
- "He watched a **random** TV show." >> Perhaps he arbitrarily chose a show to watch, but it likely wasn't *random* at all; a broadcaster determined with great precision what to air and when. Random has a specific meaning, which is that each and every unit or member of a population has an equal chance of being selected.
- "In **lieu** of this new information, we should. . . " >> No, in light of the new information. . . *in lieu of* means *in place of*.
- "The two courses were **complimentary**." >> No, they were *complementary*. If the courses were good, the students who took them might say *complimentary* things about them.
- "His **conscious** told him he should go to bed." No, his *conscience* told him to lie down and fall asleep, or become *unconscious*.

## EXERCISE 1.3

Write a sentence for each of the words in the pairings of words below. The sentences should illustrate the differences in meaning or nuance in each pairing.

*Example:*

deduce: From the blood on the single glove, he deduced that the murderer was left-handed.
infer: By leaving her bloodstained glove on the table, she inferred her guilt.

- ambiguous
- ambivalent
- healthy
- healthful
- apprise
- appraise
- disinterested
- uninterested
- accept
- except
- adverse
- averse

- allusion
- illusion
- lightning
- lightening

## Be Active

*Just do it.*

—Ad slogan for Nike

Though some passive voice is inevitable, too much yields writing that is boring and life-less. Habitually writing in the passive is what we want to avoid. In the passive, which uses a form of the verb "to be" and a past participle, the subject is acted upon. An example:

- The ball was fielded by the baseball player (passive).

Inject energy into the sentence by flipping it structurally and making the player the subject doing the action:

- The baseball player fielded the ball (active).

You'll also notice that the active voice sentence is shorter and more readily understood.

## EXERCISE 1.4

Re-write the following sentences to make them active and more descriptive.
First, here's an example:

*Problem:*

I was tired, so I finished my work and went up to bed.

*Solution:*

Exhausted and bleary-eyed, I somehow negotiated the winding staircase, spilling me into my bed. Work would have to wait for a fresh day.

- The labor leaders were frustrated by the latest offer, which forced them to go through with the strike.
- She walked into the room without saying a word, sat down, and looked at me.
- The shoplifter was tackled in the store aisle by my superhero brother, Mick.

## Be Imaginative

*You have to try very hard not to imagine that the iron horse is a real creature. You hear it breathing when it rests, groaning when it has to leave, and yapping when it's under way . . . Along the track it jettisons its dung of burning coals and its urine of boiling water . . . its breath passes over your head in beautiful clouds of white smoke which are torn to shreds on the track-side trees.*

—Novelist Victor Hugo, describing a train

Analogies, similes, and metaphors are like sutures and scalpels, which is, of course, to use an analogy. In expert hands, they can transform. In the hands of quacks, however, somebody is going to get hurt. The reader can decide whether the surgery metaphor here is an apt one or not, but make no mistake: metaphors are powerful. Understanding and communicating experience in terms of objects allow writers to pick out parts of their experience and treat them as "discrete entities," as Lakoff and Johnson argued (1993, p. 35). Once a person has made his or her experiences concrete in some way, they can be referred to, compared, classified, quantified, and reasoned about. And they can be visualized or seen. Metaphors are not merely language, therefore, but ways of seeing and understanding. Once expressed in language, metaphors begin to structure thoughts, attitudes, and even actions. Because experience is diffuse, fragmented, and isolated, a good analogy leaps across a wide terrain of experience to reveal connections between domains that we wouldn't have thought had anything to do with one another. In so doing, the analogy brings us up for air, elevating us into a broader expressive context that allows us to see a given phenomenon in the light of another.

For the poet Maya Angelou, social changes have appeared *"as violent as electrical storms, while others creep slowly like sorghum syrup."* For French novelist Colette, the skyscrapers of Paris resembled *"a grove of churches, a gothic bouquet, and remind us of that Catholic art that hurled its tapered arrow towards heaven, the steeple, stretching up in aspirations."* Dorothy Parker, a riotously funny writer, once declared, *"His voice was as intimate as the rustle of sheets."* (She also wrote that *"brevity is the soul of lingerie."*) Irish poet Seamus Heaney avoided *"the fishy swivel of his housekeeper's eye."*

The trick or skill is to see analogies and metaphors in your mind's eye when writing them and visualize the images they conjure. Are they apt and effective in conveying your intent? Are you mixing metaphors? Mixed metaphors are not only inaccurate, they distract the reader and discredit the writer. *"He smelled the jugular."* ESPN broadcaster Chris Berman actually said this describing a playoff football game. (To hold a broadcaster to the standards of the written word is perhaps unfair, but it underlines how easily metaphors can go tragically awry.) Because of cultural and language differences, global audiences might struggle getting the point of metaphors and analogies, so great care should be exercised. We use metaphors only where they *help* to communicate an idea, not where they might *hinder* understanding, offend, or alienate.

Berman's example points to another danger, which is that posed by the use of clichés. It is easy to settle for a cliché, but in writing terms, this is like arriving a day late and a dollar short, like taking candy from a baby, like picking some low-hanging fruit. And at the end of the day, when all is said and done, when the chickens have all come home to roost, laziness is perhaps the writer's greatest enemy. So, avoid these clichés *like the plague*:

- last but not least;
- they gave 110 percent;
- he suffered an untimely death (think about this one for a minute; when would it have been *timely*?);
- she was brutally raped (a *friendly* rape is not possible);
- they were few and far between;
- just stick to the game plan; and
- he fell off the wagon, or maybe on the wagon, or maybe he's circling the wagons.

## EXERCISE 1.5

Think of some additional clichés, because the more the merrier. If you need inspiration, or a list of more clichés than you can shake a stick at, visit the American Copy Editors Society website, www2.copydesk.org/hold/words/cliches.htm.

## EXERCISE 1.6

We use analogies for rhetorical reasons: to illuminate, to explain, to reveal a new aspect of something, to draw out something unseen, to drive home a point. As Wittgenstein wrote, "A good simile refreshes the mind." Describe the technological innovation of your choice in two sentences, each using a different analogy, and each with a different emphasis in meaning.

*Example:*

As an information superhighway, the Internet too often resembles a Los Angeles cloverleaf during rush hour.

## Be Direct

*I am hurt. A plague o' both your houses! I am sped.*
—Mercutio in Shakespeare's *Romeo and Juliet*

Shakespeare knew how to deliver a verbal punch with a stab of brevity. A short sentence, especially when paired with a long one, can provide energy and pop, as Ernest Hemingway shows here: *"He knew at least twenty good stories. . . and he had never written one. Why?"* For another example of this sort of rhetorical one-two punch, here's another master, the Reverend Dr. Martin Luther King, Jr. *"This is our hope. This is the faith with which I return to the South to hew out of the mountain of despair a stone of hope."*

In King's quote, the brief introductory sentence sets up the sentence of normal length that follows. In Hemingway's, the abrupt question, "Why?" adds emphasis to the character's flaw that is under examination. The short sentence (Hemingway's was one word) can also be used for transition. For Shakespeare, Mercutio's words are his last, like final, choking gasps for air.

## Be Consistent

Verb tenses should not mysteriously change mid-sentence. The singularity or plurality of subjects or objects should not vacillate or change in the same sentence. If a list begins with a verb modified by an adverb, all of that list's items should begin with a verb modified by an adverb. Parallel structure is a challenge for many writers, but fidelity to it is a hallmark of good writing. Here are examples of some of the common ways parallel structure breaks down:

*Problem:* One cannot think well, have love, and fall asleep, if dinner was bad.
*The solution:* One cannot think well, love well, and sleep well, if one has not dined well.
In this example, the verbs tenses should match: think, love, sleep.

*Problem:* Jane likes to hunt and fishing.

*The solution:* Jane likes to hunt and to fish. This sentence corrects the problem of mismatched direct objects. The writer combined the infinitive, "to hunt," with the present tense verb form of "to fish." The solution put both direct objects in the infinitive.

## EXERCISE 1.7

Re-write the following sentences to correct problems with parallel structure.

- Delta Airlines promises a bounty of international flights that are on time, have convenient connections, and offer a well-balanced, in-flight meal.
- Homicide detectives in movies are cynical, chain smoke cheap cigarettes, wear trench coats, and usually arrive at the scene about two minutes after the bad guy has left.
- Telephones in older movies are always knocked over after waking the character, ring three times before getting answered, and get manhandled when the character frantically taps on the cradle, shouting, "Hello? Hello?"

## Be Aware

Even experienced writers can inadvertently fall into any number of other common pitfalls, such as:

- **Stereotyping**—"Journalists are cynical." And "Lawyers are sharks."
- **Generalizing**—"Videogame players struggle with addiction." Really? All of them? This problem is similar to stereotyping, and you can avoid it by being wary of words such as all, none, nobody, always, never, and everything.
- **Plagiarizing**—You wouldn't intentionally plagiarize, but it is easy to mistakenly commit this writer's sin by failing to cite a source or credit an idea to its originator.
- **Oversimplifying**—Rarely is a choice or position or stance either/or, and rarely does a question or issue have only two sides. Strive for comprehensiveness, attempting to represent as much of the spectrum of views or positions as you can.
- **Jumping to conclusions**—During summers in New York City, surveyors noted that sales of ice cream jumped. They also noted a spike in violent crime. But ice cream doesn't cause violent crime, right? A hasty conclusion might be to find causality where there is only correlation. It is likely that the cause of increases in both violent crime and sales of ice cream is the summer heat.
- **Applying faulty logic or circular arguments**—Using the Bible or Qur'an to *justify* one's faith is an example of a circular argument, though citing the Bible or Qur'an is fine when *explaining* one's faith.

- **Overusing pronouns and articles**—Very common and easy to catch, this problem manifests in an abundance of mentions of "this," "these," "those," "he" or "she," "they" and "them," and "it." Though the writer knows who or what is being referenced, the reader is left to wonder. Scrutinize your pronouns, then replace at least half of them with the specific referent.

## Good Writing

Although George Orwell wrote his essay, "Politics and the English Language," more than 70 years ago, it is as timely now as the day the essay was published, and in it you will find echoes of some of the themes of this chapter. The most common problems in writing in 1946, as Orwell saw them, were:

- staleness of imagery;
- lack of precision or concreteness;
- use of dying (or dead) metaphors;
- use of "verbal false limbs" such as "render inoperative" or "militate against";
- pretentious diction (words like phenomenon, element, individual); and
- use of meaningless words.

Orwell wrote that a scrupulous writer asks himself at least four questions in every sentence he or she writes:

1. What am I trying to say?
2. What words will express it?
3. What image or idiom will make it clearer?
4. Is this image fresh enough to have an effect?

And he will probably ask himself two more, especially in a digital age:

1. Could I put it more succinctly?
2. Is my meaning accessible across cultures?

In cautioning against "prefabricated phrases" and "humbug and vagueness generally," Orwell's essay provides writers with several points of advice:

- Never use a metaphor, simile, or other figure of speech that you are used to seeing in print.
- Never use a long word where a short one will do.

- If it is possible to cut a word out, always cut it out.
- Never use passive voice where you can use active.
- Never use a foreign phrase, a scientific word, or a jargon word if you can think of an everyday equivalent.

To Orwell's last point, let's take a look at a concurring judicial opinion written by Supreme Court Justice Jackson in a First Amendment case from 1945, *Thomas v. Collins*. Revel in Jackson's directness, and appreciate how accessible his language is compared to most judicial opinions and legal documents generally, rife as they are with legal jargon. The court case had to do with the constitutionality of a Texas law requiring labor organizers to register with the state before soliciting memberships in a union. From page 323 of the decision:

> As frequently is the case, this controversy is determined as soon as it is decided which of two well established, but at times overlapping, constitutional principles will be applied to it. The State of Texas stands on its well settled right reasonably to regulate the pursuit of a vocation, including—we may assume—the occupation of labor organizer. Thomas, on the other hand, stands on the equally clear proposition that Texas may not interfere with the right of any person peaceably and freely to address a lawful assemblage of workmen intent on considering labor grievances.
>
> Though the one may shade into the other, a rough distinction always exists, I think, which is more shortly illustrated than explained. A state may forbid one without its license to practice law as a vocation, but I think it could not stop an unlicensed person from making a speech about the rights of man or the rights of labor, or any other kind of right, including recommending that his hearers organize to support his views. Likewise, the state may prohibit the pursuit of medicine as an occupation without its license, but I do not think it could make it a crime publicly or privately to speak urging persons to follow or reject any school of medical thought. So the state, to an extent not necessary now to determine, may regulate one who makes a business or a livelihood of soliciting funds or memberships for unions. But I do not think it can prohibit one, even if he is a salaried labor leader, from making an address to a public meeting of workmen, telling them their rights as he sees them and urging them to unite in general or to join a specific union.
>
> This wider range of power over pursuit of a calling than over speechmaking is due to the different effects which the two have on interests which the state is empowered to protect. The modern state owes and attempts to perform a duty to protect the public from those who seek for one purpose or another to obtain its money. When one does so through the practice of a calling, the state may have an interest in shielding the

public against the untrustworthy, the incompetent, or the irresponsible, or against unauthorized representation of agency. A usual method of performing this function is through a licensing system.

But it cannot be the duty, because it is not the right, of the state to protect the public against false doctrine. The very purpose of the First Amendment is to foreclose public authority from assuming a guardianship of the public mind through regulating the press, speech, and religion. In this field, every person must be his own watchman for truth, because the forefathers did not trust any government to separate the true from the false for us. *West Virginia State Board of Education v. Barnette*, 319 U. S. 624. Nor would I. Very many are the interests which the state may protect against the practice of an occupation, very few are those it may assume to protect against the practice of propagandizing by speech or press. These are thereby left great range of freedom.

This liberty was not protected because the forefathers expected its use would always be agreeable to those in authority, or that its exercise always would be wise, temperate, or useful to society. As I read their intentions, this liberty was protected because they knew of no other way by which free men could conduct representative democracy.

Opinion available: http://supreme.justia.com/us/323/516/case.html.

The first thing you may notice is how Jackson is present with you, speaking to you right here, right now. He isn't "performing," trying to impress you with rhetorical flourishes and impressive legal diction. Jackson's intellect, voice, and method of thinking are on vivid display. He first identifies what he sees as the core issue. He presents the facts. He identifies the principles by which he will decide. He decides. Finally, he explains his decision in such a way that even non-lawyers, perhaps especially non-lawyers, can understand. In short, Jackson says what he means and means what he says, accomplishing an impressive ratio of intended meaning and interpreted meaning.

While we are on the subject of law, consider another example of conspicuously clear writing on what is an especially complex subject—libel law in America. In this example, an attorney for *The New York Times*, David McCraw, responds to a threat by then-U.S. presidential candidate Donald Trump to sue the media company for *libel per se*, or libel "on its face." His letter addresses Marc Kasowitz, the lawyer for Trump who demanded the retraction of a *Times* story about two women who said Trump inappropriately touched them.

Dear Mr. Kasowitz:

I write in response to your letter of October 12, 2016 to Dean Baquet concerning your client Donald Trump, the Republican Party nominee for President of the United States. You write concerning our article "Two Women Say Donald Trump Touched Them

Inappropriately" and label the article as "libel per se." You ask that we "remove it from [our] website, and issue a full and immediate retraction and apology." We decline to do so.

The essence of a libel claim, of course, is the protection of one's reputation. Mr. Trump has bragged about his non-consensual sexual touching of women. He has bragged about intruding on beauty contestants in their dressing rooms. He acquiesced to a radio host's request to discuss Mr. Trump's own daughter as a "piece of ass." Multiple women not mentioned in our article have publicly come forward to report on Mr. Trump's unwanted advances. Nothing in our article has had the slightest effect on the reputation that Mr. Trump, through his own words and actions, has already created for himself.

But there is a larger and much more important point here. The women quoted in our story spoke out on an issue of national importance—indeed, an issue that Mr. Trump himself discussed with the whole nation watching during Sunday night's presidential debate. Our reporters diligently worked to confirm the women's accounts. They provided readers with Mr. Trump's response, including his forceful denial of the women's reports. It would have been a disservice not just to our readers but to democracy itself to silence their voices. We did what the law allows: We published newsworthy information about a subject of deep public concern. If Mr. Trump disagrees, if he believes that American citizens had no right to hear what these women had to say and that the law of this country forces us and those who would dare to criticize him to stand silent or be punished, we welcome the opportunity to have a court set him straight.

Sincerely,
David McCraw

In this letter, which was published by a number of media outlets and, therefore, saw wide readership, McCraw deftly lays out the core legal question or issue, explains very specific legal terms, such as *libel per se*, and pre-empts legal challenges to the *Times*'s reporting by describing "diligent" work by its reporters in service to "an issue of national importance." The writing is clear while at the same time being legally precise, and it is accessible to anyone, presumably even the candidate. (It's also perhaps the first time in legal history in which "libel per se" and "piece of ass" were used in the same document.)

Letter available: nytco.com/the-new-york-timess-response-to-donald-trumps-retraction-letter/.

## GETTING STARTED: PUTTING YOUR IDEAS IN WORDS

You now have a grounding in how writing has evolved, and why. You can gain inspiration from Pascal, Hemingway, Shakespeare, and even an attorney for *The New York*

*Times*. Finally, it is time to write. The steps that follow are designed to help you get started, and to start well.

## A. Get the Idea: Determine Your Purpose

- **Freewrite:** Write down anything and everything that comes to your mind. Everything. Get it out. Clean out your mind of mental "lint" so that afterwards you can focus on the writing task.
- **Brainstorm:** Next, write down anything you think that might be related to the task at hand, even if it seems only tangentially related at the moment. There is no judgment in brainstorming, which, to use a sailing metaphor, is like producing your own wind power. As the Latin proverb goes, "If there is no wind, row!" The best way to get some ideas, at least one good idea, is to generate a lot of ideas.
- **Write a purpose statement:** Write down your thesis or purpose statement at the top of the page. What is your mission? Next, write under that statement all of the ideas that flow from that thesis, including sources, questions to pursue, and perhaps things to avoid. What will spectacular success look like?
- **Cluster:** Clustering is similar to brainstorming, but it is designed for visual learners and thinkers. To "cluster," put a main idea in the middle of the page, perhaps in a bubble or circle. Next, link to that central idea as many related ideas as you can, then ideas related to the related ideas, and so on. Your ideas should radiate out from a conceptual center, giving you a mind map to guide the writing and perhaps an outline for its form or structure.

## B. Map It Out

The previous activities have helped you to establish your purpose. You're almost ready to begin the article or project. Think, if for only a few moments, of your responses to this series of purpose-driven questions:

- What is my topic or question? Your mission statement might suffice.
- What are my main point(s) or themes? Look at your conceptual map for the big picture.
- Who is my primary audience? Do I have any secondary audiences? What do I know about them?
- What do I want this audience to take away from what I write?
- What sources will I use, and where can I find them?
- How will I gather my information and verify my facts?
- What's my deadline?

## A Word About Audience

Knowing who you are trying to serve should influence topic, tone, complexity, and presentation. To help you think through this all-important question, here are some excellent prompts adapted from a worksheet developed by long-time literary agent Laurie Rozakis:

1. How old are your readers? What is their gender?
2. How much education do they have?
3. Are they mainly urban, rural, or suburban?
4. In which country were they born, and how much is known about their culture and heritage?
5. What is their socio-economic status?
6. How much does this audience already know about the topic?
7. How do they feel about the topic? Will they be neutral, oppositional, or will this be more like preaching to the choir?

The answers to all of these questions might not yet be available, but thinking through them will help you begin systematically thinking of and even for your readers* or users* as you begin writing or even gathering information.

## BOX 1.1

### Interactors

*Surprisingly, we do not yet have a word for the people we are trying to serve in digital spaces. They are variously referred to as readers, users, consumers, and visitors, to list only a few, with the choice of referent often determined by the profession of the writer (public relations practitioner, reporter, marketer, etc.). None of these terms adequately encompasses the range of activities that people perform online and on their smartphones and tablets. They do more than read. They do more than "use" (and "users" has drug-use connotations). We need a better term. What should we call the people who visit our blogs and websites, use our apps, interact with our content, and join the conversation via social media? This book suggests the term "interactors," and it uses this term from this point forward. "Interactor" better connotes and allows for the multiplicity of activities our "readers" or users do in digital spaces, for how they behave, for what it is they want. The term's inclusion of "actor" also hints at the various identities and personas people create and express in digital spaces, from LinkedIn to Facebook to Snapchat and beyond.

## C. Outlining and Storyboarding

Outlining helped to prepare this chapter before it was written, laying out a basic architecture for the presentation of its points. So, after you've answered some basic questions about purpose and audience, it's time to organize and lay out how the content will be presented. A metaphor here might be new home construction. A blueprint (and other site maps and renderings) is used to organize the work, and it can indicate the different pieces of the project that will be done at different times by different people. The blueprint can be changed, and it does not have to be elaborate. Even generating a visual map might do the trick, and the conceptual map you generated in pre-writing can be readily adapted to achieve this purpose.

**Note:** This is a good time to recommend reverse-outlining, as well, or outlining after your writing project is complete. So few writers do this, which is a shame, because it can reveal structural flaws, redundancies, awkward or ill-fitting sections, and perhaps a better order for the information. Reverse-outlining is a learned skill; writers can quickly achieve proficiency at it, requiring only a few minutes to successfully reverse-outline even a magazine-length piece after only a few repetitions.

Before getting to work, writing students are advised to buy or borrow a writing handbook like one most of us used in English composition as first-year undergraduates. Examples include *The Everyday Writer* by Andrea A. Lunsford (this author's favorite), Longman's *Handbook for Writers and Readers*, *Rules for Writers*, or *When Words Collide*. Most every major publisher has one.

## D. Revise It—Then Revise It Again

Ernest Hemingway famously said, "All first drafts are shit." Give yourself time to fail, to polish, to revise and perfect. The *only reason* for a first draft is to have something to work from and revise, and it could be argued (and is argued here) that only after the draft has been written can the real work of writing begin. Editing and revising take patience and perseverance, but *all* good writing depends on it. Even Mozart's compositions show where he added and, more often, subtracted, re-arranged, and polished what is some of the world's finest music.

During this revision process, question hard the decisions you made writing the first draft. Reconsider, critique, and question the following:

- Your first paragraph. Even as simply an exercise, re-write your first paragraph from an entirely different perspective, then sit back and think about which beginning you like better. For that alternative beginning, try thinking sideways. Come at the subject from an entirely different angle.
- Your last paragraph. For the same reasons, try rewriting your last paragraph. Is there a better way to bring closure and give your readers a soft, satisfying landing?
- The one or two sentences you absolutely love and simply could never imagine tampering with or cutting. Now delete them. That's right, excise them. Now ask yourself, "Is my writing stronger without my precious darlings previously there preening for readers' attention?" The lesson here is the need to remove anything that is merely for effect, designed to impress, to be admired as witty or clever. Hemingway described prose not as interior decoration but as architecture.
- Your adjectives. Look for redundancy and for empty descriptives like "the long hallway," the "brilliant yellow sunflowers," or "the deep, blue ocean." Hallways are by definition long, and we know what colors sunflowers and oceans typically are.
- Your adverbs. Often one good verb is superior to a verb-adverb combination. Here's an example: "He ran briskly across the field." Try: "He sprinted in pursuit." This exercise asks you also to reconsider your verb choices.
- Ambiguity, vagueness, generalities. If you are not quite sure what a passage means, re-write it, because your reader won't have a chance. And isn't being understood why you're writing in the first place?

## E. Myths

To promote improvement in our writing, it might help to explode a few myths, or commonly shared misconceptions about the practice or skill of writing. First, know that *writer's block does not exist.* It is a fiction, a fabrication, a myth, a crutch, and an excuse. Writing is a job, so we have to go to work. Imagine being a garbage collector: "Oh, I have garbage collector's block. I'm just not feeling it. I'll wait until I am inspired, until the muses of garbage collection have spoken, singing their siren songs into my ear." You may not feel inspired, but go to work anyway. If you think you are suffering from this mythical malaise, follow what has to be one of the best single pieces of writerly advice, again from the master Hemingway: Write something that is true.

Writing is, or should be, "a rational, purposeful activity" that you can control, as Joan Acocella pointed out. She noted that neither the French nor German languages even have a term for writer's block. So writing is not inspired by muses or magically, supernaturally guided by God. If there is no wind, start rowing. If you can't think of a beginning, start in the middle or at the end. Establish habits and strategies. This book was written mostly in the mornings, 9 a.m. to noon, when energy was high and the day offered opportunity and possibility. The prolific author Anthony Trollope, writer of 49 novels, wrote 5:30 to 8:30 each and every morning. Garrison Keillor described a similar writing schedule. Hemingway wrote a workmanlike 9 to 5, at which time, of course, he began drinking. . . a lot.

Second myth: The first draft is all you need. We all want to write well right now, but don't expect too much from the first draft. In fact, expect very, very little. It is, after all, only the beginning. Allow yourself to fail.

Third myth: "I am a multi-tasker." No, you're not. Well, you might be, but it's difficult to imagine Michelangelo painting the Sistine Chapel or chiseling David with his Pandora pumping out Rihanna. Turn off all devices so you can write without distraction, disruption, or temptation. Most writers most of the time need uninterrupted peace and tranquility.

Fourth, writing is a chore. The irrepressibly funny Taylor Mali, formerly an English teacher, was asked about his favorite place to write. This is how he responded:

> *I'd love to say I have a handmade Japanese paper and a 200-year-old fountain pen. . . and every morning, after making love, for the third time. . . I go running, for about five miles. . . if I'm feeling lazy. At the top of our house, there's an old cupola, and I watch the sunrise up there, in the nude, and I write my poems longhand. I'm right-handed but I force myself to use my left hand, because I find it makes me more creative. And I write, in Latin, because it forces the brain to work in a new way—backwards, like Hebrew.*
>
> *But really I just sit in front of my computer.*

Yes, writing is hard work. If there is no wind, we row. But writing is also a tremendous privilege, a flowering of expression and even identity. So begin instead with a heart of gratitude. "Wow! I get to write! I get to maybe discover something about myself. I'm a writer." If it is or feels like a chore, the writing will probably reflect it. If it's a joy, the writing will probably reflect that, too.

## F. The Writer's Commandments

Also helpful are these "commandments"—more suggestions, really—for writing, suggestions that will help almost any writer with almost any writing project:

- The first commandment of writing: Sit your butt in the chair. Sit there daily. Write!
- Second: Thou shalt not be obscure. William Zinsser wrote that "clutter is the disease of American writing. We are a society strangling in unnecessary words, circular constructions, pompous frills and meaningless jargon."
- Third: Thou shalt show and not tell. Joseph Conrad said that his goal as a writer was "to make you hear, to make you feel—it is, before all, to make you see."
- Fourth: Challenge every adverb.
- Fifth: Challenge every adjective.
- Sixth: Challenge your first paragraph. Delete it, and read your piece again. Are you sure you need it?
- Seventh: Challenge your last paragraph. Delete it, and read your piece again. Are you sure you need it? A good ending gives the reader a lift, often by surprise.
- Eighth: Challenge every line you love. Take out anything that is purely for effect, all that is clever, all interior decoration and ornamentation. You are an architect of meaning, not a decorator.
- Ninth: Challenge every exclamation point.
- Tenth: Challenge every use of the verb "to be."
- Eleventh: Circle each and every verb. Now decide, are they the right ones?
- Twelfth: Be alert for your pet words.
- Thirteenth: Read your draft aloud. You will hear all manner of errors that silent reading will never see, and you get to hear the rhythm, pacing, and flow of your writing, as well.
- Fourteenth: Proof and proof again (grammar, punctuation, spelling, consistency and clarity, economy, architecture).
- Fifteenth: Proof for precision (It's not a tree, it's a Liberty elm. It's not a fruit, it's a kumquat. Give things the dignity of their names.)
- Sixteenth: Writing is never finished; it is abandoned. Put another way, the writing is finished when it is due. Rewriting, Zinsser wrote, is the essence of writing.

## G. A Writer's Checklist

Finally, read your writing one last time with the following in mind, a list that catalogs common writing problems the author has observed in student writing over the years. This "top ten" list is the product of decades of grading and editing undergraduate student writing:

1. Know that *media* is a plural term. *Medium* is singular. So media *are*; a medium, such as newspapers or broadcast television, *is*.

2. Avoid ethnocentric references such as "we" or "our" or "us" or "our country." These referents assume too much, and they communicate exclusivity. Many interactors might not consider themselves members of any one person's "us" or "we" or "our." What of immigrants, green card aliens, or international students? What does "us" even mean, to the writer or to the audience? Instead, be precise by using the proper noun for the population or group you mean.

3. Look for problems with singular-plural agreement, such as in the sentence, "The government is wrong when they tell us what to do." The government is an "it," singular. People who work for governments are a "they." So, "the government is wrong when it tells us what to do." Another example: "A, B, and C are a predictor of future behavior." No, together they are predictors, because there are three of them. Example 3: "The surfer is able to read the article themselves."

4. To repeat an earlier warning: Beware of imprecise, even reckless use of personal pronouns such as "they," "their," "them," and "it." Which "they" is being referenced? Most writing includes discussion of more than one group. Which "them"? What "it"? "Their" refers to ownership, but by whom? The writer knows to who or what the words refer because the sentences flowed from the writer's head. The reader, however, is left confused.

5. Be on guard against a related precision issue with adjectives. "A lot" . . . "more and more" . . . "massive amounts" . . . "very detrimental" . . . "a great deal." None of these subjective judgments tell the reader much. Massive compared to what?

6. Do your part to prevent semicolon abuse. Semicolons, colons, commas, hyphens, and dashes each have their own specific purposes, and referring to a writer's handbook often is the quickest way to discern those purposes. The comma, for example, is "a small crooked point, which in writing followeth some branch of the sentence & in reading warneth us to rest there, & to help our breth a little" (Richard Mulcaster, writing in his 1582 volume, *The First Part of the Elementarie*). A common apostrophe problem confuses "its" and "it's." "It's" is a contraction for "it is." "Its" is possessive. Hyphens hold words together, like staples, whereas dashes separate. "Twin-engine plane" gets a hyphen; "twin-engine" is a compound adjective. "She was—if you can believe this—trying to jump out of the car." This sentence, by contrast, gets dashes to separate the parenthetical phrase or interruption in the thought. Because dashes have no agreed upon rules, they are overused and can be a sign of laziness.

7. After beginning a quote, make sure you end the quote, somewhere, sometime, with close-quote marks. It is a common mistake to begin a quote but then to forget to add the close quotes, effectively putting the rest of the treatise into the quotation. This is the writing equivalent of flicking on your turn signal, turning, then leaving it blinking the rest of the way down the highway. Come on, Grandpa!

8. A related problem concerns orphan quotes. Quotes should all have parents, so be sure to identify this parentage, or who is saying the quoted words, in the text. Orphan quotes are quotations dropped into an article without identification of the speaker or writer or source.

9. Be careful of relying too much on quoted material. You are subletting your precious real estate to someone else. Too many quotations can transform your writing into a thin piece of string merely holding other people's work together, like a charm bracelet. The writer should be providing some pearls, as well, which means taking the time to integrate and weave the parts into a coherent, meaningful whole. Rarely is there benefit in merely grafting in quoted material just because it is on topic and seems worded more ably than the writer thinks he or she could accomplish.

10. Give your writing fresh eyes and ears. Regardless of how short your writing piece is, even a single blog post or discussion board comment, step away and do something else. Go to the coffee shop. Go for a run. Refreshed and renewed, return to your writing to give it one more read. You will be amazed at the problems, possible misinterpretations, and opportunities for improvement you will quickly identify.

## CHAPTER ACTIVITIES

**1** Generate a writing sample of 750 to 1,000 words, which will provide enough of your writing to identify or make manifest strengths and weaknesses. The choice of subject is entirely yours, but here are some suggestions:

- your first vivid memory of writing;
- your best (or worst) experience with writing;
- a short travelogue about somewhere you have recently visited;
- a richly detailed description of your "brush with the stars"; and
- an opinion piece on some question or issue of the day.

Whatever you choose to write about, include in your presentation:

1. a headline that distills or summarizes;
2. identification of your audience(s);
3. a one- or two-sentence abstract, which will help you to begin thinking about layers of meaning;
4. a list of key words a search engine might use to find this writing piece online, which will help you to begin thinking about search engine optimization; and
5. a tweet of 140 characters or less to drive interactors to your story.

**2** Once the writing pieces are finished, students can pair up for a writer's workshop. This exercise can be extremely valuable from both perspectives, that of being critiqued and that of (gently) critiquing. Some might be nervous or uncomfortable critiquing a classmate's work, especially early in a course, but don't fret. Just be civil and constructive, and demonstrate that you have or are (quickly) developing a thick skin. Writing improvement demands a great deal of constructive criticism and, therefore, an increasingly tough skin and short memory. And we all need an editor.

Workshop partners should have at their disposal a writing handbook. Which writer's handbook does not matter; they cover the same general topics. Each student should use the handbook to analyze his or her own writing and that of his or her workshop partner(s).

**Length:** also in the area of 1,000 words, but this target is admittedly arbitrary. Feel free to establish a conversation about the writing, which can be used to ask clarifying questions. It's also recommended that workshop partners exchange multiple versions of the writing samples.

## Digital Resources

**Arts & Letters Daily**
**(aldaily.com)**
Great resource for all writers and readers.

**Elements of Style (original 1918 edition) by William Strunk, Jr.**
**(bartleby.com/141)**
A free edition of the classic guide to writing well.

**"More Clichés Than You Can Shake a Stick At"**
**(www2.copydesk.org/hold/words/cliches.htm)**
A list of journalistic clichés compiled by Mimi Burkhardt for the American Copy Editors Society.

**Purdue University's Online Writing Lab**
**(owl.english.purdue.edu/)**
Style guides, writing and teaching help, and resources for grammar and writing mechanics.

**Writing Sample Analyzer**
**(bluecentauri.com/tools/writer/sample.php)**
This online tool takes a sample of your writing and then calculates the number of sentences, words, and characters in your sample. From these basic statistics, it calculates the Flesch Reading Ease, Fog Scale Level, and Flesch-Kincaid Grade Level—three of the more common readability algorithms.

# BIBLIOGRAPHY

Acocella, Joan, "Blocked," *The New Yorker* (June 14 2004).

Barzun, Jacques, *Simple & Direct* (New York, NY: Harper & Row, 1984).

Bhabha, Homi K., "Of Mimicry and Man: The Ambivalence of Colonial Discourse," in *The Location of Culture* (New York, NY: Routledge, 2004).

Callihan, E. L., *Grammar for Journalists* (Radnor, PA: Chilton Publishing, 1979).

Dufresne, John, *The Lie That Tells a Truth* (New York, NY: Norton, 2003).

Eisenstein, Elizabeth, *The Printing Press as an Agent of Change: Communications and Cultural Transformations in Early-Modern Europe* (Cambridge, UK: Cambridge University Press, 1980).

Elbow, Peter, "Revising with Feedback," in *Writing with Power* (New York, NY: Oxford University Press, 1981).

Esktritt, Michelle, Lee, Kang, and Donald, Merlin, "The Influence of Symbolic Literacy on Memory: Testing Plato's Hypothesis," *Canadian Journal of Experimental Psychology* (March 2001): 39–50.

Fedler, Fred, Bender, John R., Davenport, Lucinda, and Drager, Michael W., *Writing for the Media* (Oxford, UK: Oxford University Press, 2001).

Kessler, Lauren and McDonald, Duncan, *When Words Collide: A Journalist's Guide to Grammar and Style* (Belmont, CA: Wadsworth Publishing, 1984).

Lakoff, George and Johnson, Mark, *The Metaphors We Live By* (Chicago, IL: University of Chicago Press, 1993).

Landow, George P., *Hypertext 2.0* (Baltimore, MD: Johns Hopkins University Press, 1997).

Lewin, Tamar, "Informal Style of Electronic Messages Is Showing Up in Schoolwork, Study Finds," *The New York Times* (April 25 2008): A12.

Liestol, Gunnar, Morrison, Andrew, and Rasmussen, Terje (eds.), *Digital Media Revisited* (Cambridge, MA: MIT Press, 2003).

Mali, Taylor, available: www.youtube.com/watch?v=O_POEIhEXRI.

Martin, Henry-Jean, *The History and Power of Writing* (Chicago, IL: University of Chicago Press, 1994).

McMahan, Elizabeth and Funk, Robert, *Here's How to Write Well* (Boston, MA: Allyn and Bacon, 1999).

Pavlik, John and McIntosh, Shawn, "Convergence and Concentration in the Media Industries," in *Living in the Information Age*, Erik P. Bucy (ed.) (Belmont, CA: Wadsworth Publishing, 2005): 67–72.

Rozakis, Laurie, *Complete Idiot's Guide to Creative Writing* (New York, NY: Alpha Books, 1997).

Sacks, David, *Language Visible: Unraveling the Mystery of the Alphabet From A to Z* (New York, NY: Broadway Books, 2003).

Truss, Lynne, *Eats, Shoots & Leaves* (New York, NY: Gotham Books, 2004).

Vandenberg, Peter, "Coming to Terms," *English Journal* 85, no. 4 (April 1995): 82–84.

Williams, Rick and Newton, Julianne, *Visual Communication: Integrating Media, Art, and Science* (New York, NY: Lawrence Erlbaum, 2007).

Wolf, Gary, "The Great Library of Amazonia," *Wired* (December 2003): 215–221.

Zinsser, William, *On Writing Well* (New York, NY: Harper & Row, 1976).

# Editing for Digital Media

## Strategies

**2**

> I revise a great deal. I know when something is right because bells begin ringing and lights flash.
>
> —E. B. White

> An editor should tell the author his writing is better than it is. Not a lot better, a little better.
>
> —T. S. Eliot

> I made this [letter] very long only because I have not had the leisure to make it shorter.
>
> —Blaise Pascal

**CHAPTER OBJECTIVES**

After studying this chapter, you will be able to:

- understand the fundamentals of digital editing and the many roles of the editor;
- be able to optimize content for search engines;
- think strategically about how to expand your audiences; and
- understand the unique demands of freelance work.

## INTRODUCTION

Most people know or can intuit what a reporter does, or a photographer or social media manager. But what does an editor do? How does he or she fill the day? The answer, of course, depends; it varies by medium, based on where the editor is in the hierarchy of his or her organization, and on the particular priorities of the employer. While it might be difficult to categorize the roles and responsibilities of digital editors, identifying their shared skill sets is a simpler matter, and it is the focus of this chapter. Much like the term "writing," "editing" refers to a large and diverse group of activities unified by their purpose, which is to deliver or present accurate, compelling, engaging information that serves the interactor.

And these activities and skill sets aren't for the editor alone. A world-class designer who can't write a declarative sentence is of little value.

## THE DEVIL IS IN THE DETAILS

The theory of Gestalt holds that the whole is different from, and usually more than, the mere mathematical addition of the constituent parts. To ensure the quality of the whole, we have to inspect and evaluate all of the digital parts, and that, broadly speaking, is the role of the editor. Each and every element on a webpage, for example, has to be scrutinized, from the page title at the top to the copyright notice at the bottom to the key words in the metatag. Graphics and illustrations, photo credit lines, headlines and subheads—everything should get a second (or third or fourth) look. The immediacy of digital might lead us to assume that editing for digital spaces means less attention to detail, or less time spent checking, re-checking, verifying, and vetting. In fact, the complexity of digital media means that there has never been more to get wrong.

It might be more useful to think in terms of the activities, habits, and characteristics common among digital editors than to focus on job titles. Common in these activities are exercising care, showing great attention to detail, and collaborating to get things right. Also common is the editor's role of ensuring correct grammar, orthography, and style. The shift to digital has done nothing to diminish the importance of these principles, which transcend industry, medium, and context. Finally, all editing has an ethical dimension. The myth holds that ethics only come into play when there is controversy or crisis. Not true. Ethics is also about doing the small things well, treating colleagues well, and thinking about what it means to serve your interactors in the hundreds of decisions you might be called upon to make in a typical workday.

## MULTI-TASKING, CROSS-TRAINING, AND SILO-BUSTING

One medium-specific statement that should be made: digital publishing is not at all like editing for print, at least in terms of job responsibilities. In print, there are, or at least were, clear distinctions between roles and duties among writers, designers, editors, and copy editors. Media convergence has blurred and blended these roles and responsibilities, and because the job descriptions keep changing, the most valuable employees are those who prove flexible and adaptable.

To help us appreciate the diversity of roles and responsibilities of editors, let's take a look at some of the job titles common to news, just one of many communication contexts in which digital editors live and work:

**Copy editors:** This is the job title most people likely think of when they hear the term, "editor." Copy editors fact-check, clean up writing, correct grammar and punctuation, write headlines and photo cutlines, and generate key words for search engine optimization. If short bursts of copy need to be written, such as news alerts, summaries, and bulletins, often it is the copy editor charged with the task. At CNN, copy editors write the news crawls running at the bottom of the screen, as well. In newspaper sports departments, they compile and compute the box scores and agate type. In digital media, often the copy editor's duties are shared among the reporters and content producers.

**News editors, desk editors, and bureau chiefs:** These editors all have managerial responsibilities, directing coverage, managing work flow, overseeing design and layout, and supervising reporters, photographers, and copy editors. In smaller organizations, these responsibilities are shared, while in larger ones, the roles can be quite specialized. Desk editors typically are responsible for specialized reporting "beats," such as "courts and cops," sports, features, city news, and business. In local and regional broadcast news, these divisions are usually news, sports, and weather.

**Managing editors:** Like a director of a major motion picture, a managing editor is responsible for the big picture, but also for making deadlines and budgets, and for coordinating the disparate activities of the news organization. Desk editors, bureau chiefs, the copy desk chief, and many other positions report to the managing editor. Budget meetings, which in newsrooms are about assigning stories and "budgeting" space, not money, are run by the managing editor.

**Executive editors:** This is the where the buck stops for news operations. The executive editor oversees the entire news staff, with the managing editor being second in command. This role, therefore, is largely about planning, troubleshooting, supervising, administering, and working with the other departments of the organization. This person, who usually has a great deal of experience in newsgathering, spends most days in conference rooms and offices in what is a rolling series of meetings.

**Design/layout editors:** As you might expect, this editor is responsible for overseeing and usually also creating themselves the graphic content, laying out the publications and pages (print and digital), and determining the best combinations of textual and graphical information, including photography, animation, information graphics and data visualizations, and typography.

**Video, audio, photo, and multimedia editors:** These jobs are largely technical, dependent on software to select, edit, and produce video, audio, Flash, and photo packages, as well as presentations that combine these media. In digital, it's common for these editors to also fulfill the roles of copy editors, writing headlines and checking all of the constituent parts of the packages and presentations.

Because of their many job duties, digital editors and content producers typically are organized, curious, self-directed, and versatile. They are ethical and persistent, and often they have a pretty good sense of humor and rhino-thick skin when it comes to taking criticism. These attributes point to the very stark differences between the activities of writing and editing, though, of course, these activities are complementary and interdependent. Many of the editor's traits are required for the arduous processes of proofreading and copyediting, which require an eye for detail and a reservoir of patience. Editing is mostly about making choices and decisions—lots and lots of decisions. Editing well means being able to read at several different levels at the same time, from where commas should go to whether or not an online navigation scheme is working to how topics and stories are trending across social media.

Ideally, an editor is involved in page or site development, as well, even in the earliest stages of planning. As an advocate for readers, editors should be able to influence, if not direct, information design and planning rather than merely fixing or correcting problems later in the process. In fact, when and how editors are integrated into a website's or publication's organization says a great deal about that site's or publication's estimation of editors' importance or value. With these roles in mind, here are some of the responsibilities common to many if not most digital editors:

1. **Identify the audience and the purpose of the content, then serve that audience and that purpose.** The needs of interactors should guide what you do and the decisions you make. Fidelity to mission is perhaps a digital editor's top priority.

2. **Determine a scalable, sensible structure.** It's up to editors to develop a document and file structure that is suited to the content's purpose, one that is obvious and easy to navigate. Websites, sections, and even individual pages have to be largely independent within that structure, because interactors often go directly to an individual page, often deep within the site. Webpages should support non-sequential and incomplete reading, and the content should be broken up into coherent, self-contained chunks that are understandable even if read out of sequence. Though an interactor's path may be unpredictable, the structure of the documents and files should not be. A clear sense of how the site and webpages are organized should be facilitated so interactors can easily, even unthinkingly, move through them. It's the editor's job to reduce, if not eliminate, disorientation.

3. **Edit the content.** Review and edit everything, including structure and navigation, links, writing style, style consistency, and visual design. Begin early and repeat throughout. Check colors, graphics, headlines, subheads, paragraph lengths, and consistency of all elements. You might edit content chunks out of order rather than in sequence to replicate the experience of many, if not most, interactors.

4. **Proofread and test usability.** Misspelled words are an embarrassment, and they detract from credibility, suggesting that multiple copyediting steps or stages should be in place. One stage or step, for example, could focus on consistency in visual

design, another on testing links, and still another on naming conventions. Because the organization of a site is translated into file names according to certain conventions, this copyediting step is an important one, and it should include inspecting the naming conventions for pages, folders, files, graphics—anything that lives as a separate file.

5. **Copyedit some more.** While it's true that good editors can read on different levels, looking for more than one type of error at the same time is difficult and untrustworthy. When time allows, editors should read multiple times, looking each time for different things. First, read for understanding. Does it make sense? Is it clear? Is the information complete? Are there structural problems that need attention before you can read for smaller-scale issues, mistakes, and weaknesses? Here are some of these levels, or types, of readings that editors should apply:

- *Organization and focus.* Does each paragraph focus on a single idea? Are transitions clearly and simply made? Does the piece wander, or is it focused on the theme or topic? Is there a better organization?
- *Accuracy.* Names, places, dates, titles, numbers. Facts have to be checked and, when they are counter-intuitive, corroborated. Are the facts consistent with each other? Do the numbers add up? If you're not sure, look it up. Is it Adolf Hitler or Adolph Hitler? If you are sure, look it up anyway. Is the Mendoza Line for batting averages in baseball .200? Is it .180? Look it up. (It's .200, even though the term comes from a lifetime .215 hitter, Mario Mendoza.)
- *Grammar, spelling and orthography, punctuation and style,* or the little demons covered in Chapter 1. This is basic copyediting. It is in these details that the devil lives.
- *Pacing, rhythm, and flow.* Is the language clear and precise? Does it flow? Is there too much jargon?

These kinds of copyediting tasks will require a few reliable sources, whether in print, online, or via an app:

- the stylebook(s) for your organization's adopted style (for most news organizations, it is the Associated Press Stylebook);
- an all-purpose dictionary, and perhaps one specific to your field, industry, or area of specialty;
- a writing and usage handbook;
- a thesaurus;
- maps, an atlas, and a general information almanac;
- directories and perhaps biographical information, depending on topics and categories;

- an encyclopedia; and
- archives of industry-specific publications.

6. **Write headlines.** Typically it is the digital editor who writes the headlines, and because headlines in digital spaces serve different purposes than do their print counterparts, they should be written differently for digital. Searchable key words should drive how headlines are written because search engines "read" the headlines in order to create and rank their findings. In addition, headlines in digital spaces often are displayed out of context, in isolation, or as part of a list of articles, such as in a listing of findings for a search query or in a tweet, so they have to be written with this in mind. When scanning lists of stories, people frequently look only at the highlighted headlines, skipping summaries and other information. The headline, therefore, is all-important. Sadly, smartphone displays cut and conjoin headlines mindlessly, putting an even greater premium on brevity.

7. **Test usability.** Test the tasks that readers will want to perform. Check that navigation is easy and intuitive. Evaluate reading comprehension. Put yourself into the shoes of your audience.

This list indicates that digital editors wear a lot of different hats. Content developer, content strategist, producer, manager, managing editor, project manager, proofreader, usability expert, search engine optimizer, social media manager—a digital editor is a sort of content superhero. Digital editors might also be tasked with producing multimedia, moderating discussion, aggregating tweets, or going into the field to do the heavy lifting of original reporting. Media convergence has brought with it pervasive role convergence.

The list also dramatizes the many levels at which digital editors must engage with content, and the many types of error or missed opportunities for which he or she must look. A lack of resources, the pressures of immediacy and competition, and internal organizational dysfunction sometimes inhibit or even undercut many of these roles, of course, but in a healthy, productive work environment, they are valued, even treasured.

## EDITING TECHNIQUES

To systematically check the places where error likes to hide, digital editors need routines, habits, and systems of checks. For example, an editor responsible for editing a site's webpages might create a checklist for proofing and making sure that errors are searched for in their usual hideouts. These include:

- bylines and datelines;
- headlines, deckheads, and subheads;
- photo credits and cutlines;

- hyperlinks and references to other articles, places, and sites;
- grammar and orthography (spelling, punctuation, and capitalization);
- quotations (checking for missing quote marks and proper punctuation);
- hyphenation and line breaks;
- line wraps (around photos, cutlines, pull quotes, etc.);
- metatags and descriptors;
- ALT tags for images (or the text that is displayed or read by computers for the blind);
- page titles, which are different from headlines; they appear in the browser above the page; and
- copyright and "last updated" text.

There are other safe havens for error, but this list provides a useful starting point. Other steps a digital editor should take include running spell checks, doing the math for any numbers that are presented, and looking for split infinitives and faulty em dashes (—). Just as links should be checked, so too should phone numbers, addresses, Twitter handles, and hashtags. If you are listing a phone number, someone should dial the number to make sure it's still working. If the site offers multimedia, someone should click to play any videos, slideshows, or audio to ensure everything functions as it should, and he should do it in multiple browsers and view with varying screen sizes.

Someone should have the clear responsibility of applying a discipline of verification, someone who is, therefore, accountable for accuracy. Fact-checking should be a stand-alone activity or function and not something that ends up blended (and probably lost) with other editing roles and functions, though in digital, sadly, this blurring is exactly what has become the norm. Established routines and a combination of methods and steps for editing give the organization the best chance at reducing error.

Very specific steps a digital editor can take include these proven ways to vastly improve the content:

- **Read once through quickly.** This gives you a sense of what the story is about and reveals the flow and arc of the narrative.
- **Read backwards.** This focuses the brain to engage at the word level as opposed to the sentence or paragraph level. Reading backwards forces you to read individual words, which gives you the best chance of spotting typos and spelling mistakes. Yes, it makes for a nonsensical reading, but that's one reason it works. The brain isn't jumping ahead, skipping, or assuming; it's merely encountering individual words.
- **Print out a hard copy.** Ink on paper is tactile, making it physiologically easier or more comfortable to read than pixels on screens. Print, therefore, promotes closer readings.

- **Read it out loud.** You might feel a bit awkward or self-conscious at first, but reading out loud is perhaps the single most effective editing technique you can employ, and for several reasons. First, it slows you down. We speak more slowly than we read, so verbalizing what we're reading gives us more time to catch mistakes. Second, reading sentences helps us to identify problems with syntax and mechanics. We can hear the mistakes. Third, saying what we are reading allows us to hear the pacing of the writing, the rhythm, and the flow. Problems in any of these areas become discernible when they are heard rather than merely read. Finally, the method puts you in the seat of your reader, which is a good and right place to be.

- **Read to find holes in the story and to evaluate organization.** Think of the article as a building, with each paragraph serving as an individual floor or wing. Is there a better order or arrangement? If you moved the 13th floor to the 4th, would the story make more sense? If a floor disappeared entirely, would the building, in fact, be better off?

- **Cut it up and spread it out.** A professor now retired from the University of North Carolina, Colonel Don Shaw, would routinely take his journalism history students' writing into a conference room, laying out all of the pages, no matter how numerous. He would then note or mark transitions and changes in direction or theme. Next, he would physically cut up the paper with a pair of scissors, cutting at the marked breaks or transitions. In a step many of us found uncomfortable, he would ball up redundancies or tangents and toss them in the trashcan, rearranging what was left into a better, clearer order or progression. Often, he would also ball up and throw away the first paragraph and the last one, an act of bravery we writers can rarely muster the courage to do. Whatever was left, the Colonel would tape together, roll up, and hand back to the student author. Before exiting, he would say, barely audibly, "Now get to work." (Once you have a draft, he often reminded, you're ready to begin.) Try this yourself. It's an architectural-level editing technique that cannot be done well simply staring at a computer screen, and there is something visceral and exciting about physically cutting it up and piecing it back together. This might be editing's nuclear weapon.

- **Read it all again.** When you think you are finished, go get a cup of coffee. Go for a run. Walk the dog. Do something different. Then, come back and give the piece one more read, especially the headline. A fresh reading is your best and last opportunity to discover error. You'll find yourself asking, "What was I thinking?"

## One Editor's Experience

To appreciate the multifaceted roles of digital editors, let's hear from a magazine editor at a large custom publishing company that specializes in in-flight magazines. In her description, she identifies several steps or stages of editing at her company, steps any organization could implement. Her description also reveals many of the hiding places for error and carelessness:

> When I proof a layout, I use "these ten steps to perfect proofing." These steps include checking:
>
> - photo credits;
> - folios (or four-page groupings of pages);
> - throw lines (or "see p. x" lines) to other pages or sidebars;
> - grammar and orthography in all display copy;
> - byline name spelling and matching name in the biography;
> - every single line for correct or best hyphenation;
> - every line that wraps around a photo;
> - photo cutlines;
> - pull quotes, for matching body copy;
> - consistency of spelling of all names; and
> - bad breaks, widows, and orphans.
>
> On my publication, our copy editor has a baseline list that she always checks, including running a spellcheck, cross-checking any mention of a page number, [double-checking] spacing around em dashes, city/state style, split infinitives, and checking that the table of contents entries match every layout. But she adds on checklist items for each issue based on recent experience. For instance, she is known as the "hyphenated adjective ninja." [Or is that "hyphenated-adjective ninja"?] Once a client complained about our splitting his company name over a line, so now she checks for that in the magazine, as well.
>
> If a piece is intensive with service information, one round may be devoted only to phoning all numbers and testing every web link published. This may also be the time to check the spellings of proper names, places, and the like.
>
> Most of our publications have a separate, fairly early fact-checking phase for all copy. Some editors' checklists for this simply state, "Check all facts." I issue a two-page instruction memo that goes into much more detail.
>
> And before all of this happens, the story undergoes content editing—from structure and length to identifying information to put higher in the story and smoothing out awkward language. The writer may have conducted additional reporting to fill information gaps. And another editor has written a headline, deck, and subheads.
>
> By the time I'm looking at blue lines (the last phase before press time), I'm confident enough to have my checklist down to fewer than five items: looking at the display copy, quadruple checking the page numbers/folios, and reviewing the changes requested at the proof stage prior.

Another revising strategy: setting a word limit, or at least a target. I generally write long, particularly when I am quoting sources. Cutting a story down to the right length is an important part of my revising process. Why is this useful? Making a story shorter can't be done with only one method. I find it has to be a combination of line edits, substitutions of long phrases for short adjectives, and removal of entire blocks of text.

This hints a bit at my pre-writing process. I have a rough outline of topics, and I work a lot of composing in my head, but I also let myself free-write at points, which then needs to be reined in.

This experienced, professional editor describes a process and a culture of editing and of careful attention to detail. She lays out a process of established routines shared by several people in her organization. The immediacy of digital is forcing changes in these print-based processes, but not in the importance of a discipline of verification. And the editor makes another critical point: No one method can substantially edit down a story or article or check that article for errors of fact or of writing.

## SEARCH ENGINE OPTIMIZATION AND USER EXPERIENCE

An important role many digital editors are now responsible for is search engine optimization (SEO). Search engines algorithmically find and rank digital content using key words, looking especially in headlines and subheads, in tags typically listed at the beginning or end of the story, and in the HTML's metatags. When users type words or phrases into a search engine box, the search engine tries to match those words with words it has found and recorded previously, and from that matching, the engine delivers a list of findings. Though search engines change their algorithms and, therefore, the ways they rank, basically they scan webpages to find repeated words and phrases. So, in terms of search, key words are the currency of the digital realm: You want your carefully determined key words to appear in the places the search engines are looking. Using popular key words will optimize even further the likelihood of your pages coming up in searches, and it is this process of determining and using these key words that is called search engine optimization. The better your key words, especially in your headlines, the higher your content will rank in search results.

### So Let's Get Started

Take a look at the article or piece that you are trying to optimize in terms of search. Think about what people might type into a search box to find the story for which you are writing a headline. After you've written the headline, test it by entering its key words into a search engine to see what comes up. You could also test by entering your entire headline into the search box. The findings will both gauge how "optimized" your headline is for likely searches for your subject, and it will turn up similar content from which you can glean key words to refine your own search engine optimization.

The next chapter will more comprehensively cover headline writing, but here now are some techniques that will improve your headlines for search success:

- **Be brief.** Google data show that headlines of about ten words work best. Shorter is better, and important key words should appear up front. This is, of course, good advice for headlines that will appear on smartphones, the screens of which mindlessly, violently butcher headlines at the first available line break.
- **Be complete.** If you were writing a headline for a story about the terrorist attack at Istanbul's airport in June 2016, for example, you would use the key words "Istanbul," "terrorists," "Ataturk," "bombing," and "2016," among others. Some users may remember that it was in Istanbul but not when, and vice versa.
- **Be clear.** Will an interactor understand what the story is about by reading only the headline? She should, because distillation and signaling are important tasks for any headline. Most of the time, the headline is all that interactors will read. Given this punishing truth, it is amazing how few digital news organizations get this right.
- **Be proactive.** Test your key words, and there are several ways to do this. You can use Google's auto-complete feature, which prompts additional words to complete a phrase. You can also test key words using Yahoo and Google SEO resources, such as google.com/trends.

Below were the most popular news stories trending on Google News on a fall day in 2016. Notice that none of the headlines are longer than ten words, and note the proper nouns they use (proper nouns make the best key words):

Cubs win Series, end 108-year title drought
*USA TODAY*

U.S. court deals Trump a setback in poll-monitor fight
Reuters

Islamic State leader says 'no retreat' from Mosul
*USA TODAY*

Venezuela opposition gives Maduro until Nov. 11 to meet demands
*Los Angeles Times*

S&P 500 losing streak runs to 8 days
*The Wall Street Journal*

Common also to these headlines is that all are direct, clear, and straightforward in signaling the content. If a visitor is searching for the latest information on the big Christmas parade downtown, don't use the headline, "Yule procession to begin at 9 p.m." No one will ever find this story using even the best search jujitsu. While "Christmas Parade" might not be the most politically correct label to use in the headline, it is the clearest. Google has made it clear that what counts the most is the content of the webpage itself. Presenting valuable information that has some density around a subject, and doing so in a straightforward manner, is rewarded by Google's algorithms. Keeping ads from cluttering that presentation is also rewarded, so SEO is not an activity wholly divorced from maximizing the user experience (UX). Google uses machine learning to compare a page to a spectrum of similar pages ranging from dreadful to excellent, and it decides on this basis where that webpage *looks* like it belongs. If you have less than eight seconds to engage a visitor once that person has landed on your webpage, it makes sense to be direct, clear, and useful.

Meaningful SEO takes time, and Google does not reward quick fixes. When implementing SEO practices, expect to be able to measure positive results in about six months. Improving SEO is more like planning out a city than putting out a fire, and it depends on great content consistently offered for a long time. You have to establish a track record. If you offer information that people need, if you present stories that make people feel something, they will share it with their friends and colleagues.

Meaningful SEO is also at least, in part, based on substance. From a pure SEO perspective, you need a minimum of 300 words, because articles and blog posts shorter than this find it difficult getting indexed by Google. In Google's view, a piece that short cannot offer real value. Shorter articles may get more comments, but longer ones get shared more often.

Meaningful SEO avoids manipulative linking, or links created or cultivated merely to game the system. The best links in terms of Google search come from sites that have authority, that are trusted by Google. Think nytimes.com, mayoclinic.com, and yale.edu. You can evaluate your own links using tools such as Moz.com's Open Site Explorer (moz.com/researchtools/ose) and MajesticSEO (majesticseo.com/reports/site-explorer). You are still only as good as the company you keep, so acquiring inbound links of the first rate is a powerful way to boost your page ranks in the search results. Keep in mind that Google is constantly tweaking its algorithms, making an estimated 500 to 600 changes per year based on thousands of tests. The fundamentals—user experience and satisfaction, meaningful content, quality inbound links—are what will win the day.

The exception that perhaps proves many of these emergent "rules" is the popular news blog Boing Boing (boingboing.net)—a sprawling site specializing in news and interesting reads. In its presentation, it bucks conventional wisdom and breaks a lot of digital's "rules," or guidelines. For its hyperlinks, long phrases and sentences are common. The now passé "More at (insert URL here) site" kinds of referrals are also common at Boing Boing, which gets away with *how it links* perhaps because of *the integrity of its linking*: the content and usability of what it links to are consistently excellent. Boing Boing does a good, even great, job linking to other content you might actually want to read (or view).

Boing Boing also gets away with its practices because it has built up trust among its interactors. When you click on a Boing Boing link, you know it's going to be a trustworthy site that is useful in some way. If the link points to a less-than-trustworthy site or source, Boing Boing lets you know why it's being linked. The Recording Industry Association of America, for example, is not a favorite of Boing Boing writers, but they link to it anyway when it adds to the presentation.

Another useful approach to linking can be found at A List of Things Thrown Five Minutes Ago (throwingthings.blogspot.com), a blog that integrates links into the text in ways that clearly signal to what the visitor is clicking, using phrases that avoid interrupting the narrative. Both Boing Boing and Throwing Things routinely link out; yet, in spite of the trends, these two blogs' interactors keep coming back. Great content, high trust, and an awareness that there is a lot of good, relevant content outside their sites add up to high readerships.

Still another model is that offered by content recommendation companies such as Outbrain, Taboola, Revcontent, and Meebo. These content automators select headlines from elsewhere on the web to highlight with a site's own news content. A report from ChangeAdvertising.org found that 41 of the top 50 news sites use widgets from these recommenders, which trade in what is commonly referred to as "click bait." At Quest News, a Brisbane, Australia, community newspaper website, Outbrain runs a widget beneath Quest's news articles and videos. Populating what's called in web terms a "widget," Outbrain automatically feeds top headlines from a basket of other sites. Here's the interesting part: It's Outbrain that pays Quest News to run the widget, not the other way around. Outbrain makes its money from other sites for the click-through traffic, and it runs an algorithm on these headlines to see which ones generate the best click-through results. The "winners" are placed in the widget, delivering site traffic to Outbrain's paying clients. In other words, here is a third-party business model built mainly on good headline writing (and really good analytics). It is the headlines that make this

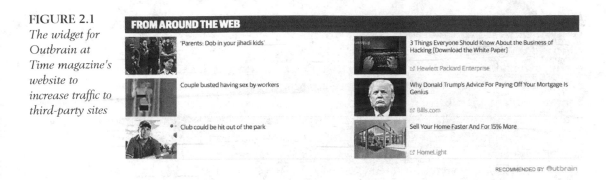

work. Though a different business model than SEO, it is based on the same principles as SEO. And like much of SEO, the Outbrain model blurs the line between human and machine readers in determining the most shareable or potentially viral content. Humans write Quest News's headlines; Outbrain's widget then ranks and displays them as a result of a complex algorithm that attempts to maximize cost per click revenue.

Because these "recommended" stories can place dubious content just a click away from otherwise credible news sites, the practice has come under fire. The revenue these companies can generate for those news sites, however, has made them difficult to resist. For some sites, these "around the web" placements are the largest single source of revenue.

## Commercially Sponsored Search Results

In 2013, the Federal Trade Commission's consumer protection staff sent out letters to search engine companies instructing them to better distinguish between commercially sponsored results (third-party ads) and non-sponsored (or "natural") results to avoid consumer deception. The distinction, according to the FTC's letter, must be "clear and prominent" when evaluated from the perspective of consumers, taking into consideration how the results appear when using various browsers, apps, devices, etc. As the FTC's announcement noted, paid search results have become less distinguishable as advertising. Failing to clearly and prominently distinguish advertising from natural search results could be determined by the FTC to be a deceptive practice. To prevent this, the FTC recommends visual cues, labels, or other techniques to effectively distinguish advertisements.

Some search companies have been doing the opposite. The shading in the top ad boxes, or boxes for paid ads at the very top of a search page, has lightened, making it more difficult for consumers to recognize them as distinct from natural search results. In addition, some search engines' results that integrate or offer specialized search options as part of the service—for example, by allowing users to refine their search to categories such as news or local businesses—are, in reality, another way of presenting paid ads. The FTC's efforts to combat the resulting confusion is good for content producers that clearly and transparently label and identify what they publish, because, as the FTC posted, readers "expect that natural search results are included and ranked based on relevance to a search query, not based on payment from a third party. Including or ranking a search result in whole or in part based on payment is a form of advertising."

For its part, Google is fighting search-finding manipulation specific to links and key words in press releases (support.google.com/webmasters/answer/66356?hl=en). Excerpting from Google's guidelines: "Any links intended to manipulate PageRank or a site's ranking in Google search results may be considered part of a link scheme and a violation of Google's Webmaster Guidelines. This includes any behavior that manipulates links to your site or outgoing links from your site." Thus, repeated words raise a red flag for Google's search monitors. Multiple postings of the same release similarly promise greater scrutiny from Google, which might see this common public relations practice as an "unnatural" boost to the popularity of a piece of content. According to Google, press release publishers must "create unique, relevant content that can naturally gain popularity in the Internet community."

Public relations practitioners are faced with a difficult dilemma, therefore. Including hyperlinks is good practice, and it helps journalists writing stories that use the press release. But these links could now be penalized by Google in its search findings for being "unnatural" in their promotion of a website. The same might apply to feature articles, columns, and posts, depending on a range of variables Google does not completely disclose. The simplest advice in this matter is to stick to the basics and conspicuously avoid attempting to game Google's or any other search engine's algorithms. Google has long been upfront about what it's looking for from site owners and publishers: great original content that serves the best interests of their sites' visitors. This imperative valorizes good writing, and it rewards honesty and straightforwardness.

## MULTIMEDIA STORYTELLING

Because, as a delivery channel, the Internet can handle text, photo, video, and sound with equal ease—they all are 0s and 1s, after all—digital editors are also determining the best or most appropriate media through which to tell the stories. Before digital distribution, TV stations showed video, newspapers ran printed articles and photos, and radio stations broadcasted music and talk. Via the web and mobile, anyone can do all these, allowing the story to drive the media choices rather than the medium determining the kinds of stories that are pursued and produced. It is this convergence as much as any other that has changed media industries in the past 20 years. Thus, knowing the capacities and limitations of different publishing environments can inform important choices even in conceptualizing stories. Further down the production line, digital editors should be able to create simple webpages and have a basic understanding of HTML and CSS, to better understand the capacities of hypertextual environments.

In the aftermath of the Paris terror attacks of November 2015, remember that TV provided breathless coverage of the chase for the one terrorist who slipped away, placing talking heads in prominent locations in greater Paris to provide live standups and to punctuate what was entirely visual coverage. Meanwhile, newspapers did what they do best, providing narratives of the fast-changing events and doing the heavy lifting of explanation, such as how the target sites were selected, how the shooters got inside, and what law enforcement was doing to secure the city. On the web and powered by mobile, news organizations could do it all. So they did, providing:

- Twitter feeds of breaking news and updates of what French and Belgian police were discovering and how Paris was dealing with the aftermath of the attacks;
- interactive maps of the path of destruction, showing the locations of the attacks and of traffic closures subsequent to the attacks;
- video, podcasts, and photo slideshows;
- links out to resources, such as Paris's mass transit system for information on disruptions in service and when service would be restored;
- a narrative with sidebars guiding readers through the major developments and explaining their significance; and
- fact-checking, revising earlier reports and correcting mistakes, which were numerous.

Editors could choose the medium best suited to a particular angle or element of the story, rather than being restricted to one medium. And editors weren't limited to the kinds of stories they could tell through or by their primary medium. "If it bleeds, it leads" is a rather well-known aphorism from TV news, explaining how news gets on television.

Editors should ensure that whatever they pursue with their coverage, it adds something and serves the reader or viewer. Local TV news, by contrast, shows an inordinate number of live camera shots because they have invested heavily in the equipment to do it. Whether a story merits a live reporter on the scene or not, often TV news will go live simply because it can. This nonsensical approach to informing a democracy isn't necessary online.

Poynter Institute's Eyetrack studies (poynter.org/tag/eyetrack) reveal that successful multimedia presentations are typically:

- short;
- interactive;
- personal (or local or hyperlocal); and
- navigable (the better the interface, the better the experience).

## Big Data

The overwhelming volume of information we produce simply going about our daily lives, including data produced by the ubiquitous smartphone, has fueled interest in mining this "big data" for meaning. Harnessing this data and analyzing it is only one part of the challenge. Figuring out how all of this data might impact people is a big question, one digital editors are usually charged with asking and answering. Finally, there is the question of how to present or publish these big data-driven answers in ways that are accessible to interactors.

One of the simpler examples of this challenge of data visualization, and one of the easier layers of information to add to a story or story package, is an interactive map. With digital mapmaking applications, digital editors can leverage the growing abundance of geomapped information about our globe. For a public armed with smartphones and an array of geomapped applications, a public that increasingly expects customized, localized information, interactive maps have become standard fare.

The geomapped data are coming from efforts such as Google Earth and Google Street View, which are comprehensively charting the surface of our globe with incredible granularity. Google offers this data freely to web and mobile app developers. Fortunately, the multiplicity of inexpensive, even free tools available online have fairly short learning curves. More importantly, a smartly developed interactive map can offer interactors a high density of information in a small space.

Some common uses of maps include plotting routes; showing directions; signifying key locations of something, such as wifi spots or public transportation; and layering spreadsheet data such as crime, voting, polling, or traffic data. Most of the online tools also offer the capacity to annotate your maps, allowing you to add clickable regions, points, or icons, as well as images, sound, and even video.

Most digital mapmaking applications generate the necessary HTML code needed to add the map to another webpage, code that can simply be dropped into a webpage's

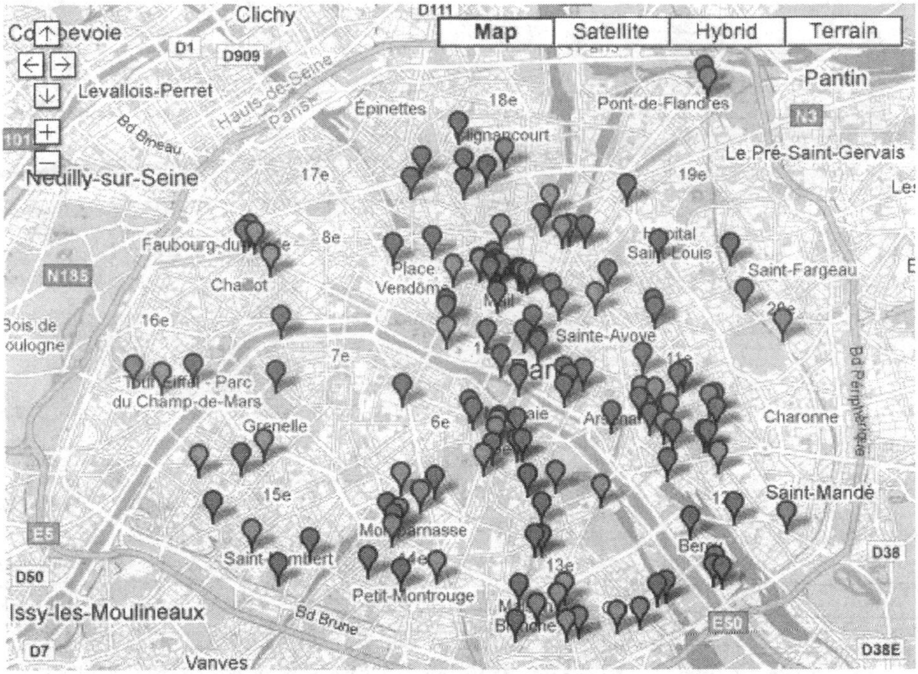

**FIGURE 2.2**

*A Google map of coffee shops with wifi in Paris. When clicked, each marker reveals additional information, such as café name, location, and hours*

coding for full interactivity. For example, the code below was generated by Zeemaps. com. The snatch of HTML shown here inserts a frame with a map of Paris with the location of the Palais Garnier opera house:

```
<iframe frameborder = 0 style = 'width:200px;height:300px'; src =
www.zeemaps.com/widget?group=618923 ></iframe>
```

The code sized the map at 200 pixels wide by 300 pixels high, and once in a webpage, the code will pull the map data from Zeemaps.com using a unique URL, zeemaps.com/widget?group=618923.

To create mashup maps, or maps that combine different types of data, such as crime statistics, school rankings, weather and climate conditions, etc., you can access free public databases such as those maintained by the Government Printing Office (gpo. gov) and the U.S. Census Bureau (census.gov). You can also solicit data from your interactors, which engages and involves them while at the same time leveraging what they know or can gather.

Interactive maps allow interactors to zoom in or rotate for a sort of magic carpet ride. In terms of the amount of information your map conveys, though, it's a good idea to be judicious. Cluttered maps risk being ignored. Maps that quickly locate significant, easily recognizable landmarks or tourist attractions are effective because they quickly orient users and avoid overwhelming with too much information.

For a model of what a map can do when combined with a dataset, take a peek at a *New York Times* map powered by Google showing major crimes in New York City from 2003 to 2011. The data represented came from police reports, news accounts, court records, and original reporting, creating a database that then generated a map presenting changes over time (projects.nytimes.com/crime/homicides/map). The dots of various colors represent the locations of major crimes. The blue dots, for example, represent homicide locations. Clicking on a dot pulls up information about the homicide, including when it occurred, the name and a description of the victim(s) and of the perpetrator, a motive, and the weapon used. This data can be categorized and represented using a range of variables, including day and time, race/ethnicity of the victim, race/ethnicity of the perpetrator, sex of either victim or perpetrator, age, weapon, or New York City borough in which the crime(s) occurred.

Smartly combining information from several credible sources produces a robust interactive data map that layers or cascades information. For example, at the top of the *Times*'s map is a timeline that can be used to show how many murders occurred each year, hiding the ones that occurred in other years, and a box into which a reader can enter a location or address to check if any homicides occurred there. This is possible because this map's developers layered the data to reveal important patterns and trends.

Another impressive delivery of complex data over time to create meaning that matters is the "Atlantic Slave Trade in Two Minutes" interactive timeline at Slate.com (slate.com/articles/life/the_history_of_american_slavery/2015/06/animated_interactive_of_the_history_of_the_atlantic_slave_trade.html). Animating 315 years and 20,528 slave trade voyages, the map places contemporary understandings of the North American slave trade into fresh perspective, showing it to be a "bit player" relative to the global slave trade over time. Designed and built by *Slate*'s Andrew Kahn, the timeline gives you a sense of the scale of the trans-Atlantic slave trade, as well as the flow of transport and eventual destinations. The dots, which represent individual slave ships, also correspond to the size of each voyage. The larger the dot, the more enslaved people on board. Interactors can pause the map, click on a dot, and learn about the ship's origin point, destination, and history in the slave trade. A graph at the bottom accumulates statistics based on the raw data used in the interactive, representing only about one-half of the number of enslaved Africans who were transported away from the continent.

To help journalists and journalism students develop map-based presentations like the *Times*'s homicide map or the slave trade timeline, the Knight Digital Media Center

FIGURE 2.3
*Slate.com's slave
trade timeline*

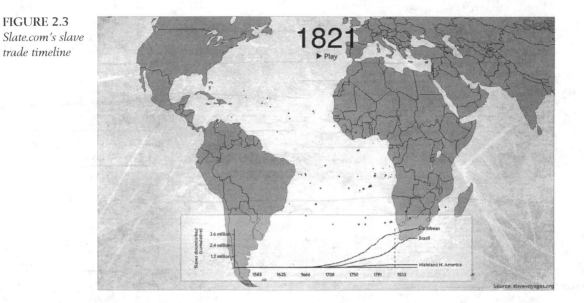

has developed a series of tutorials at multimedia.journalism.berkeley.edu/tutorials/cat/ maps. If you are ready to get started on one, you might first try one or two of these mapmaking applications online:

- **Bing Maps** (bing.com/maps/) generates maps that can be embedded in a webpage and that can include point A to point B directions. Free.
- **Google Maps** (maps.google.com/) offers the same features as Bing Maps. Free.
- **MapQuest** (mapquest.com/) offers the same features as Google Maps. Free.
- **Zee Maps** (zeemaps.com/), powered by Google, allows users to make custom maps. Free for basic maps, or users can pay to place more markers, including markers with advanced features, such as links to email, websites, audio, or video. Also enables map-makers to highlight a region of the map using a particular color, or to save as a .pdf or .jpg file.

## Content Management Systems

How an editor does his or her job is influenced, if not dictated, by the publishing environment that the editor must work within. During the last decade, the movement has been away from pure HTML environments and toward content management systems that combine coding languages with pre-fab templates and shells. Content management systems (CMSs) constrict what editors and web developers can do, but with the use of templates they also make updating and adding content fairly routine and much, much simpler than writing code.

A CMS is essentially a sophisticated software system that automates many of the processes or functions of updating, moving, and archiving copy and content. A CMS also helps digital publications to achieve and maintain a consistency in look while updating content from any number of sources both within the organization and from without. CMS software makes it easier to publish, and it erases the need for writers and editors to learn or to know more than a little HTML, CSS, or Java-Script—though, of course, for troubleshooting and customizing, it's good to be comfortable with these languages. A good content management system makes it fairly simple for almost anyone to learn how to upload content to the publication's site and to format that content using simple tags or by clicking a few buttons on a dashboard.

CMS software packages also automate how a site interfaces with databases. For example, if an online newspaper wants to allow site visitors to search and view its database of real estate listings, a CMS can be built to provide a drop-down menu or sequence of drop-down menus enabling that database to be searched by price or location, or any other data field, and to do so without leaving the CMS environment. A CMS might also be used to automatically feed a homepage with updated content, and a common utility of this function is populating a page with breaking news headlines that link out to whole stories published, also automatically, on interior pages. In short, a good CMS can perform many of the functions of print editors, freeing up human resources for the more important tasks, such as fact-checking and copyediting.

With the fast growth of mobile, CMS tools, not surprisingly, have been developed for smartphones and tablets. A company called MobileCMS, for example, offers a mobile app CMS that generates RSS (really simple syndication) feeds and manages updating of photography and video. The number and diversity of competing platforms (Apple's iOS, Android, etc.), each with its own specs and standards, makes this front in digital development expensive and slow going, especially relative to the comparatively open HTML publishing platforms. For the brave willing to develop an app, try a tool such as AppMkr, which is inexpensive and provides a relatively easy way to learn the basic characteristics of app development. If its end products aren't sophisticated enough for a final app to offer your audience, AppMkr can be used to prototype in order to pitch an app concept inside the organization, or to show a third-party developer more precisely what your organization wants.

## MAKING THE TRANSITION

"Ink-stained wretches," as veteran print writers and reporters are sometimes called, have had difficulty making the transition from analog to digital. It takes time and even moral fortitude to learn new tools, technologies, and routines, even to discern what changes need to be made and what are merely passing fads. For many professional print writers, the big leap to digital has produced a sort of crisis, both at a personal level ("Do I still have what it takes?") and at an organizational level as once-analog companies get left behind or find their business models obsolete. Print advertising has continued to drop precipitously, and newsrooms throughout the world continue with layoffs, buyouts, and downsizing. Spending on newspaper advertising in the United States fell by about 11 percent in 2016, to about $12.5 billion, while digital advertising has failed to grow quickly enough to stem the losses. The fundamental shift to mobile has forced companies big and small to reconfigure their operations such that the jobs that allow writers to focus only on writing, to work only with words, are disappearing. Necessary today are communication professionals with many skills and aptitudes. Even Clark Kent (a.k.a. Superman) ditched *The Daily Planet* in 2012 to start his own blog. Superman became a mild-mannered blogger. "I was taught to believe you could use words to change the course of rivers—that even the darkest secrets would fall under the harsh light of the sun," Kent told his newspaper colleagues. "But facts have been replaced by opinions. Information has been replaced by entertainment. Reporters have become stenographers. I can't be the only one who's sick of what passes for the news today." For a fictional fantasy, Kent's description has proven eerily accurate.

The proportion of Americans who read news on a printed page is declining, according to the Pew Research Center for the People & the Press, which found that most people who read an article on a website do not read *any other articles on that site in a given month.* Incidental readership is common. The share of Americans who get their news on legacy platforms has fallen behind most other media, and the news industry hasn't yet found a way to persistently capture that audience.

At a minimum, digital writers and editors need to know how:

- to capitalize on the new rhetorical capabilities of digital in terms of presentation;
- to monetize those presentations to pay at least some of the bills;
- to choose the media most appropriate for the story, and then to effectively utilize those media; and
- to work with others as a team, and to share their work as a whole and not as separate or disparate pieces.

This doesn't mean that every digital writer or editor has to know how to win awards with their video *and* their photography, *and* how to code a website from the ground up, *and* how to manage social media to best promote the content, *and*, oh, by the way, still write powerful prose. But, today's digital communicators do need to take advantage of the new tools for presentation and for distribution, and to embrace convergence, just as the son of Krypton did.

## HELP FOR FREELANCERS

Since the first edition of this book was published, a number of students, most of them working professionals, have asked for help navigating the fluid, fast-changing world of freelancing. The days of working for one company for 30 years are, of course, long gone. Many find themselves freelancing to make ends meet and to soften the blow of layoffs and business shutdowns. Help is here.

As anyone who has tried to freelance full time well knows, freelancing is a punishing business for all but an elite few. Your academic degree(s) don't matter all that much, even if they are journalism degrees. It is difficult to know how much you will earn month to month, producing economic uncertainty and financial instability. You have to appear to prospective clients, paradoxically, as both productively busy and available for hire at the same time. There is incredible pressure to work for low or no pay, in exchange for "exposure" in the Internet's "attention economy." You often work alone, meaning little or no access to editors who might mentor you and collaborate with you. It is easy to lose that key contact at a publishing house, magazine, or website. Your writing will be judged often by algorithms and "eyeball" counts, and algorithms care not how well written something is or how much industry went into putting it together. Finally, the democratization of digital tools has erased the barriers to entry, meaning an oversupply of citizen journalists, amateur writers, and aspiring media workers crowding you out and normalizing the assumptions publishers have about paying little or nothing for digital "content." Legions of prolific, tireless, talented writers are out there shaking the publishing trees right along with you.

To survive, therefore, is a daunting proposition, and anyone writing advice on how to do it invariably will use the word "hustle." In fact, despite the growth of digital journalism and writing, it is more difficult than ever to make it as a freelancer, because freelance writers are on the front edge of broader trends or dynamics that are conspiring to de-value the labor of reporting and writing, trends that began before the Internet but that digital has accelerated and exacerbated. On top of everything else, freelancers lack the solidarity of, say, unions or the strength in negotiating that more formal labor arrangements offer. How is a freelancer to know what a fair fee or wage is, or to what degree he or she is being exploited?

### Writing the Pitch

To get someone interested in publishing or running your story, you have to pitch it, and this, too, requires skill and industry. Once you've identified a potential publication or website or app, you should read it. Become familiar with its presentation, its sensitivities and style, and, most importantly, the audience. Learn the types of stories that publication likes to run. Once you've edited your story to fit that publication's style of writing, find out whom to send it to. Search the publication's masthead or online staff listing. Email and/or reach out via social networks such as LinkedIn or Facebook. (And you absolutely must spell the name and title of the person you are contacting accurately; a misspelling here and your story will never get read.)

In a cover letter or message, (very) briefly introduce yourself with just a little about your background. The key words here are "briefly" and "just a little." Autobiographies and breathless listings of academic honors are door-closers. The editor doesn't care, at least not yet. Then, quickly get to your pitch. What is your story about? Why is it a good story? Why is it a good story to run now? Why would the publication's audience be interested in it? Finally, include all of your contact information. Make it easy for the editor to contact you.

Just as you learned when searching for a job, follow-up is important, but don't overdo it. Editors are busy, and they are as busy and overworked as never before. Give them grace. Follow up once or twice, but no more than that. Give editors a week or so to respond. If two follow-ups or two weeks roll by without response, it's time to move on. If you do find interest, be flexible. Rarely—almost never—does a story get published just as it was submitted. Some rewriting is likely, a lot is possible, and sometimes all an editor is interested in is the basic story idea or concept.

Your story might be accepted on spec, which means you can write or re-write the story and, if the publication likes and runs it, you get paid. If the publication rejects the piece written on spec, you can take it elsewhere, but you don't get payment unless a "kill fee" was negotiated up front. A kill fee is typically a fraction of the amount that would have been due upon publication, and it compensates at least some for the effort required to put it together, even though it was "killed." Writing on spec is a way for both the publication and the writer to try each other out.

Here's a sample cover message for an article submission, to give freelancers some help starting out:

*Dear Ed Etoor,*

*I'm Silas Crain, a veteran sports journalist who has published in a number of national and regional newspapers, magazines, and websites. I've written an in-depth feature on the Chicago Cubs' Anthony Rizzo's recovery from cancer last October, before the Cubs' historic World Series win, a feature written after several interviews with the first baseman. I have attached that story to this email. I also have several images for which I own the copyright, if you are interested in running those, as well. If you're interested in running the story, please let me know. I can be reached at. . . .*

Another method is to offer yourself as an expert on a topic, with the hope or aim of being contacted for stories on that topic. Here is a form of press release announcing a person's expertise and availability:

> Sports training expert and CEO of BodyImpact.com, Gerry Toome (headshot and bio below) is available to take the mystery out of personal training by offering tried-and-true tips and tricks. Toome is available to provide insight and answer questions on sports training, fitness, and fitness programs.
>
> If you are interested in setting up an interview with Toome to discuss these topics, or to see one of Toome's many columns written on these topics, please contact him at. . . .
>
> **Bio:** *Sports training expert Gerry Toome is an industry leader in helping people maximize their physical potential. In addition to serving as both CEO and key expert for Body Impact, Gerry frequently speaks to college athletics departments, teams, and youth athletics organizations throughout the country.*

## Getting Paid

If your pitch is successful, your next task is to negotiate compensation. For digital-first organizations, freelancer rates are varied and mostly arbitrary, and often it is difficult to get paid in a timely manner. A search online for pay rates found the following:

- BuzzFeed: $0.17–0.50/word; more for investigative reporting, less for opinion pieces and news articles;
- *Fast Company*: $0.33/word for 1,500-word feature;
- Gawker: Before it declared bankruptcy following a successful lawsuit against it by Hulk Hogan, as part of its Recruits program to attract new writers, Gawker paid $5 for every 1,000 unique visitors an article attracted to the site (joel.kinja.com/introducing-recruits-1520191540); otherwise, $0.15–1.33/word;
- Hairpin: $300 for criticism 1,000 to 2,000 words;
- Mashable: $200 for reporting piece of between 500 and 1,000 words;
- *The Nation*: $2,000 for 6,000-word feature;
- *Newsweek*: $0.20/word for 2,000-word feature;
- Quartz (qz.com): $0.15/word for 1,500-word feature;
- *The Washington Post*: $100 for news story of between 500 and 1,000 words; and
- xoJane: $50 for essay of about 1,000 words.

These idiosyncratic piece rates show how little agreement there is on how to account for the capital costs of creating good "content," the value of that content in terms of generating traffic, or the market value of any one writer or reporter. They also hint at a huge shift in digital that makes each individual article a stand-alone profit center, a ticket to generating more attention de-contextualized from any larger whole. Such a shift turns good writing (and bad writing, for that matter) into a saleable commodity—content—robbing it of its dignity as an art. Where once we celebrated the arts of writing, photography, criticism, illustration, and film, each with its own notions of taste and artistic and professional standards, today digital workers are asked to produce content, as if it were sugar, flour, or barley or oats. At BuzzFeed and *Huffington Post*, the largest single source of revenue is native advertising, or branded content. This "between the banner ads" filler looks and reads as if it were independently produced journalism but is paid for by a single sponsor or brand.

Thus, much of digital writing today is treated as simply a process of commodity production for private profit. Though freelancers have great individual autonomy and control, which are the benefits of being entrepreneurs, ultimately they are also subject to capitalist production processes that often result in what can only be described as exploitation. With so many sites simply re-shuffling the Internet by aggregating and re-arranging, the freelancer's value as a knowledge worker is under great pressure. These realities aren't presented to discourage anyone from going into freelancing, but to acknowledge how difficult it is for most self-employed writers. It is also to counter the message these important writers get that it's up to them to find a way to fit into the new media ecosystem when it should also be the responsibility of privately owned media companies to figure out how to fairly pay for the labor they count on to turn a profit. "Exposure" doesn't pay the bills or send the kids to college.

## CHAPTER ACTIVITIES

1. This chapter's assignment has two parts. First, revise your Chapter 1 writing sample based on the feedback and help you receive from your workshop partner(s) and the instructor. Feel free to continue dialoguing with your workshop partner(s) and/or the instructor during this revision process. Second, begin formatting the piece for online readership. The purpose here is merely to get started, so do not worry about how sophisticated your formatting is or about the limits of your knowledge of HTML or CSS.

2. Generate a map using any web-based mapmaking software, such as Google Maps (maps.google.com/) or Map Builder (mapbuilder.net/). Use your local zip code. The map you will build will show site visitors where in the city there are wifi hotspots for wireless Internet access. So, first research where those hotspots are, then plot the location data on your map. Label the map "Wireless Access Points in YOUR CITY NAME," then publish the map to any blog or webpage. If wifi information isn't available, try instead plotting your area's coffee shops, for example, or emergency medical services.

3. Create an infographic: There are many free and low-cost tools online with which to create infographics. In this exercise, you will take freely available census data found at census.gov to create a simple graphic. Here's how:

   (a) Go to census.gov. Off the top-line navigation, choose "Data." Next, choose "QuickFacts." Use the graphical map to select your state. From the second-layer navigation line, choose or click "More STATE data sets." Next, from "Population Estimates," select "Estimates for all counties" (Excel). This will give you an Excel spreadsheet that you can download and pull from to make an infographic.

   (b) Next, go to infogr.am. You will have to register, but the service is free. Of the options, choose "New Infographic." From the Excel spreadsheet at census.gov, select three years' worth of data for the counties you wish to highlight. Copy and paste into your new infographic. Experiment with the labels and with getting the rows and columns to align correctly with the data from which you are pulling.

   (c) Experiment further by adding a map, a photo, or even a video.

4. Editing and layering: First, find a long (3,000 words or more) feature online. (If you need a suggestion, try Esquire's article, "The man who killed bin Laden is screwed": esquire.com/features/man-who-shot-osama-bin-laden-0313.) Second, re-make and edit the feature article into something more conducive for digital presentation. Use the guidelines discussed in this chapter to facilitate scanning and to make the piece interactive. More specifically:

   • Look for elements or key words to hyperlink. Be sure to indicate what you would link to, what would happen when clicked (a new tab, a new browser window, etc.), and why that's the best decision.

   • Break the article up into text "chunks." Do this by adding subheads and even sub-subheads, by looking for places to convert text into lists, and by restricting each paragraph to one idea.

   • Look for content to pull out and make its own entity, like a "how-to" box or "best of" list. This shortens the main story and helps the reader more readily use what's pulled out of the main.

   • Finally, brainstorm suggestions on how to improve the content even further to make it a more useful digital experience. For example, propose producing a video to accompany the text. Perhaps a Flash presentation or interactive graphics. Be specific, detailing the content for any of these, spelling out exactly what should be developed and how it would be experienced online.

5. Fact-checking: This exercise is designed to help you evaluate sources and to think through the fact-checking process. The following is a list of facts that you, as the copy editor of a news website, need to confirm. Sources for the information can be found on the Internet. Be sure to write the answer, your source, and the URL for that source. Remember that a URL is not a source, but rather the online address of a source.

   • Your newspaper is doing a story on the registrar of the University of North Carolina at Wilmington. Find that person's name and confirm the name and its spelling. Corroborate by finding a second source verifying the information.

- You are doing a story celebrating the establishment of the First Amendment. What is the exact wording of that amendment? List your source and corroborate by finding a second credible source with the same exact wording.
- You are doing a story on a new airline servicing the international airport in Atlanta, GA. The airline will be based out of the international concourse of that airport. What is the proper name of the airport? Which of its concourses is the one devoted to international flights? Identify your source and corroborate.
- The blog you write and edit for is working on a feature on alternative weeklies. You need to find and confirm the name of the editor-in-chief of the *Metro Pulse* in Knoxville, TN. Corroborate what you find with a second source.
- According to the Georgia Bureau of Investigation, what is the most common violent crime in the state of Georgia, and is it rising or falling?
- What is the most recent population figure for Floyd County, GA? How does this figure compare to the total for the year 2000? How does it compare for the data for Floyd County, IA?
- Your blog is doing a story on Pulitzer Prize-winning fiction. You need to confirm the 1995 recipient of that award and the name of that author's book.
- You are editing a financial story for Bloomberg News. You need to know how many employees are working for Atlanta-based Coca-Cola Enterprises. Be careful, there are several companies and divisions with the name "Coca-Cola." Find out the name of the company's highest-ranking female executive (name and title). What were the company's most recent annual total revenues (called "operating revenues") for the most recent fiscal year? (Note: the fiscal and calendar years are not always the same.) How much was the company's profit (or loss) for that year? Be careful with how you present the answers. Often they are reported with thousands assumed (US$000s), meaning that you have to add three zeroes to correctly answer the question. Provide your source(s) for your answers and rely only on credible sources, such as the Securities and Exchange Commission or the Lexis Nexis Academic Universe database.
- According to court documents, what did the U.S. Supreme Court decide in the case *Hosty v. Carter*, No. 05–377, 546 U.S. 1169; 126 S. Ct. 1330? This is a kind of a trick question, so be careful to get precisely what action (if any) the Supreme Court took. Make sure you understand your own answer. Do not rely on news accounts.
- How do modest amounts of coffee intake affect a person's risk of renal cancer, according to the *International Journal of Cancer* (published November 15, 2007, vol 121, no 10: 2246–2253)? The article, "Intakes of coffee, tea, milk, soda and juice and renal cell cancer in a pooled analysis of 13 prospective studies," was co-authored by about 28 people (J. E. Lee et al.). Make sure your answer is in layman's terms.

## Digital Resources

**"Atlantic Slave Trade in Two Minutes" (slate.com/articles/life/the_history_of_ american_slavery/2015/06/animated_interactive_of_the_history_of_the_atlantic_ slave_trade.html)**
Interactive timeline of the history of the trans-Atlantic slave trade.

**Government Printing Office (gpo.gov)**

**Inforgr.am (infogr.am)**

**Knight Digital Media Center (multimedia.journalism.berkeley.edu/tutorials/cat/maps)**
Series of journalism tutorials, including some on map-making.

**New York Times interactive map of major crimes in New York City from 2003 to 2011 (projects.nytimes.com/crime/homicides/map)**

**U.S. Census Bureau (census.gov)**

**Map-making Resources:**

- **Bing Maps (bing.com/maps/)**
- **Google Maps (maps.google.com/)**
- **MapQuest (mapquest.com/)**
- **Zee Maps (zeemaps.com/)**

## BIBLIOGRAPHY

Adler, Ben, "Piecemeal Existence: For Today's Young Freelancers, What Will Traffic Bear?" *Columbia Journalism Review* (July/August 2012), available: http://cjr.org/feature/piecemeal_existence.php.

Cagle, Susie, "Eight Years of Solitude: On Freelance Labor, Journalism, and Survival," *Medium* (March 15 2014), available: https://medium.com/@susie_c/eight-years-of-solitude-110ee3276edf#.o65za6iom.

Carr, David, "Risks Abound as Reporters Play in Traffic," *The New York Times* (March 23 2013): B1.

Cohen, Nicole S., *Writers' Rights: Freelance Journalism in a Digital Age* (Montreal: McGill-Queen's University Press, 2016).

Friend, Cecilia and Challenger, Donald, *Contemporary Editing*, 3rd edition (New York, NY: Routledge, 2014).

Hammerich, Irene and Harrison, Claire, *Developing Online Content: The Principles of Writing and Editing for the Web* (New York, NY: John Wiley & Sons, 2002).

Levy, Steven, "Can an Algorithm Write a Better News Story than a Human Reporter?" *Wired* (April 12 2012), available: www.wired.com/gadgetlab/2012/04/can-an-algorithm-write-a-better-newsstory-than-a-human-reporter/.

Lorea, Eduardo, "Improving Accuracy: Creating a Newsroom System," *Poynter Institute* (March 10 2008).

Lynch, Patrick and Horton, Sarah, *Web Style Guide 2* (New Haven, CT: Yale University Press, 2001), available: www.webstyleguide.com.

Nielsen, Jakob, *Designing Web Usability* (Indianapolis, IN: New Riders, 2000).

Parker, Roger C., *Guide to Web Content and Design* (New York, NY: MIS Press, 1997).

Price, Jonathan and Price, Lisa, *Hot Text: Web Writing That Works* (Indianapolis, IN: New Riders, 2002).

Rude, Carolyn and Eaton, Angela, *Technical Editing*, 5th edition (Harlow, UK: Longman, 2011).

Sholchet, Catherine E., "Clark Kent Quits Newspaper Job in Latest Superman Comic," *CNN.com* (October 24 2012), available: http://edition.cnn.com/2012/10/24/showbiz/superman-quits-job.

Troffer, Alysson, "Editing Online Documents: Strategies and Tips," self-published paper (August 1999), available: http://faculty.weber.edu/sthomas/3140/editing-online-documents.pdf.

Wong, Julia Carrie, "Writing, Prestige, and Other Things That Don't Pay the Rent," *The Nation* (April 7 2014), available: www.thenation.com/article/writing-prestige-and-other-things-dont-pay-rent/.

# Writing for Digital Media II

## Tools and Techniques

*Everything that is needless gives Offense.*

—Benjamin Franklin

*All I need to make a comedy is a park, a policeman, and a pretty girl.*

—Charlie Chaplin

*Each of us literally chooses, by his way of attending to things, what sort of universe he shall appear to himself to inhabit.*

—William James, psychologist

> **CHAPTER OBJECTIVES**
>
> After studying this chapter, you will be able to:
>
> - write effective headlines, deckheads, subheads, and lists;
> - organize content in layers to facilitate deep drilldowns;
> - expertly hyperlink to organize information and facilitate navigation; and
> - convert large wads of text into digital-friendly chunks.

## INTRODUCTION

Ernest Hemingway, one of our heroes in Chapter 1, re-wrote the last page of his great novel, *A Farewell to Arms*, 39 times. Writing—crafting language—takes time and persistence. The great American philosopher William James called writing a "peculiarly stubborn effort to think clearly." This chapter arms you with digital tools and techniques that will help you think, write, and present information clearly, without clutter, in service to your audience(s). These techniques include layering to facilitate drilling, surfing, and scanning; headline writing; hyperlinking; and listing. Helping you convert big text blocks into smaller packets and pieces is also a focus. Finally, we will look at what research tells us about how people use their smartphones, the web, and tablets to access information.

## EXTRA! EXTRA! GET YOUR GOOD HEADLINES HERE!

With each headline you write, you are making a wager and assuming a risk: Will the interactor read on? Because about 70 percent of your readers will read at least your headline, what you put on that top line is of critical importance. Good headlines engage and stir interest, they distill and summarize, and they lead to search engine optimization. Because interactors skim, surf, scroll, and scan, those good headlines have to do all of this important work in a few seconds. Readers have to quickly discern what the story (or infographic, or photo slideshow, video, or, really, any piece of digital content) is about, then decide to keep reading or to move on.

Brian S. Brooks and Jack Z. Sissors, authors of *The Art of Editing*, give headlines at least six tasks. They need to:

- attract attention;
- summarize;
- organize and give the content visual identity;
- help the reader to index that content (determine its importance and relevance);
- depict mood and tone; and
- provide typographic relief.

For digital spaces and places, we might add to this list the role headlines play in optimizing search, because the key words that generate headlines are the key words that the big search engines are reading to rank content. Perhaps most importantly of all, headlines help interactors decide from the overwhelming abundance of information what *not to read*. Researchers at the University of York in England determined that if we read each and every user agreement for all of the sites and apps we use, we would spend an average of 46 minutes *per day* trying to keep up. None of us has the luxury of this kind of time, nor the interest to use it in these ways even if we did. Good headlines free up interactors to move along and read something else, and this is no small thing.

Keep in mind that headlines are needed for video packages, photo galleries, press releases—any and all sorts of information presentations. Thus, the first utility Brooks and Sissors mention, arresting attention, is of premium value even within the information ecosystem of one website or app. Knowing that it is the headline that might get tweeted and re-tweeted, shared, and liked raises the stakes. Thus, you will be tempted to use your wit to get poetic, to dazzle with your wordplay. To quote the rapper Tupac Shakur, resist the temptation of these beasts, because what you thought would be heaven might turn out to be Google's equivalent of hell. Most attempts at "clever" fall far short, achieving, at best, only "cute." Better to stick to the basics and achieve the headline's primary purposes: inform and summarize. If what you write somehow entertains and amuses, when and where the tone of the story allows, then all the better. But humor is a double-edged semantic sword. Your audience, which potentially is global, likely has diverse comedic sensibilities and values. A reference or pun that might make your headline seem clever to you may be lost on your readers. Also lurking in the semantic brush is sexual innuendo, as well:

- cops bust topless dancers;
- DA eager to probe sex case;
- researcher prefers the company of mountain sheep; and
- jayhawk women like being on top.

Though the "just the facts" style won't likely win prizes for originality, it will help readers make intelligent decisions about whether to stop or keep moving, and it will keep you

## THE LATEST

NOVEMBER 7, 2016
CULTURAL COMMENT

**THE BEST SONG FOR SOOTHING YOUR ELECTION ANXIETY**
BY AMANDA PETRUSICH

---

NOVEMBER 7, 2016
SARAH LARSON

**MICHAEL FRIEDMAN'S SONGBOOK OF THE 2016 ELECTION**
BY SARAH LARSON

---

NOVEMBER 6, 2016
SARAH LARSON

**A NIGHT OF WISE, TORTURED ELECTION ANXIETY WITH JON STEWART AND FRIENDS**
BY SARAH LARSON

POP MUSIC

## MIRANDA LAMBERT'S POWER PLAY
BY KELEFA SANNEH

The country singer's sprawling concept album, "The Weight of These Wings," defies Nashville wisdom—and is one of the year's best releases.

---

BOOKS

## HOW JACK REACHER WAS BUILT
BY JOHN LANCHESTER

The novelist Lee Child knows just how to ballast wish fulfillment with earthbound details.

**FIGURE 3.1** *Sub-menu options at The New Yorker's website, newyorker.com*

out of the kind of trouble the headlines above brought their writers. A sub-menu from *The New Yorker* magazine website (newyorker.com) illustrates many of these points. The department header, "The Latest," is on the top line in larger type, which establishes a hierarchy of information. Sub-departments, such as "Pop Music" and "Books," are labeled with smaller red subheads. Individual stories are stacked, with clear, easy-to-read headline-and-deck combinations to accompany them. The headlines have energy, and they deliver the key facts. The deckheads, also called drop heads, such as "The novelist Lee Child knows just how to ballast wish fulfillment with earthbound details," takes the reader to the next logical level of information. The headlines as a group are similar in style, substance, and length, and as a set, they provide clear navigation. The standard smartphone screen clearly drove the of this page but the stacking means it will work well on desktops and laptops, as well as on tablets and e-readers.

If an article or story is longer than, say, 350 words or so, use subheads to break up the presentation, to offer visual relief, and to guide readers through the story. Like headlines, subheads should be brief, straightforward, active, and useful. Think about subhead lengths in terms of two to five words.

## HOW TO WRITE A GOOD HEADLINE

"Clutter is the disease of American writing," wrote William Zinsser, newspaper editor and author of the classic text on writing, *On Writing Well*. "We are a society strangling in unnecessary words, circular constructions, pompous frills and meaningless jargon." Zinsser would have loved the headline from *The Sydney Morning Herald* website when the actor Heath Ledger died: "Heath Ledger dies." Succumbing to the beast, the *Herald*'s competition, *The Age*, opted instead for, "Dead in bed." Is this clever? Or is it merely cute? (Or worse, simply in bad taste.) You be the judge, but remember that search engines get a vote too, and in this case they overwhelmingly voted for "Heath Ledger dies." Straightforward, simple, perhaps even a little dull, the headline generated all of the traffic because it includes the necessary key words, and only the necessary key words. Search engine optimization is a multi-billion dollar business driving how content is found (or not).

To write good headlines, then, begin by determining your key words. There are two basic steps to composing a headline:

- determine what to highlight; and
- decide how, given the limits on space.

Select the key words that you need to convey the essential meaning of the content. In our example, these words are: "Heath Ledger" and "dies" or "dead." Next, consider how the content will be indexed by Google. If by simply reading the headline, a reader is able to grasp what the story is about, as he or she readily can with "Heath Ledger dies," you've done your job, and Google will reward you.

Generating your key words can be as easy as measuring the frequency with which the story uses terms and phrases, and getting these metrics can be as easy as cutting and pasting. As one simple method, visit wordle.net. Click, "Create your own wordle." Copy the full text of an article or piece of content for which you need to write a headline. Paste the text in the Wordle template box to generate a graphical illustration of the words in that article rendered to correspond by size to the frequency with which they appear. The larger the word, the more prominently it features in the article. Figure 3.2 shows a wordle of the text of this chapter up to this point in your reading.

This simple exercise quickly reveals a handful of key words that can be used to drive headline and subhead composition, not to mention metatags, headers, webpage titles, tweets, and email subject heading lines. When choosing your key words, pay special attention to specificity or particularity. The second Heath Ledger headline, "Dead in bed," is too general and too vague to help the search engines or interactors. Similarly, the headlines "Panel re-visits damage plan" or "Congress passes bill" fail to say meaningfully what their respective stories are about. They are empty, vapid phrases incapable of inspiring interest.

Speaking of specificity, let's look at some specific rules for headline writing, rules that take a little getting used to and that sometimes bend or break the rules of grammar and style. Veteran headline writers:

- **Use present tense.**

  "Heath Ledger dies"
  Headlines about events in the recent past are written in the present tense to give readers a sense of immediacy and drama, and to underline that the news is, in fact, new. Though Ledger was dead when the headline was written and published, this one passes the test.

FIGURE 3.2 *A wordle for this chapter, generated by wordle.net*

- **Omit articles.**

  Articles such as *a, an*, and *the*, especially when starting the headline, are simply omitted in order to shorten headlines and to contribute to a "no nonsense" style.
  "~~The~~ Yankee pitcher to miss start this weekend"

- **Omit present-tense forms of the verb *to be*.**

  The verbs *is* and *are* can be assumed, so leave them out unless they really are needed for clarity.
  "Stephen Curry named most valuable player"
  Assumed in this headline is the *to be* verb *is*.

- **Replace *will* with *to*.**

  If immediate past stories are presented in the present tense, what about the future? Stories about events in the future tense use *to* in place of *will*, mostly because it shortens the headline.
  "Sales tax to increase in June"

- **Replace *and* with a comma or semicolon.**

  "Tar Heels destroy Duke, advance to title game"
  Use a semicolon if the elements joined by *and* are independent clauses with different subjects.
  "Browns finish in last place; coach's contract not renewed"

- **Use numerals rather than spelling out numbers to save space.**

  "120 killed in landslide in Myanmar"

- **Omit end punctuation.**

  Don't punctuate your headlines with periods or exclamation points; they are unnecessary. Question marks are used when in fact the headline asks a question.

- **Attribution is important, even in a headline.**

  If you are quoting someone, you need to attribute the source, regardless of where it appears. To do this economically in a headline, use either a colon or a comma. The colon is used when the source appears first:
  "Trump: Tax reform on the way"
  Use the comma when the source comes after:
  "Airlines to keep raising fares, experts say"

- **Use single quote marks.**

  When quoting in a headline, use single quotes.
  "Green Party candidate a 'dirty, rotten scoundrel,' rival candidate claims"

If you are writing headlines for multiple media, consider what might work best for each medium. Different media can accommodate different kinds of headlines. In the "Heath Ledger dies" case study, "Dead in bed" would be an excellent choice for print, where context for the headline can also be presented. Imagine a photo of the actor next to the headline and story, and perhaps a deckhead with another layer of information on the tragedy. This context is difficult if not impossible to immediately provide in smaller digital spaces, such as phone screens.

Headline writing is a skill. It can be learned, honed, refined, and even perfected. A great way to improve your headline writing is to read good, even great headlines. News organizations such as *The New York Times* and *The Wall Street Journal* employ some of the industry's most capable editors to write their headlines, editors who typically accomplish most and sometimes all of Brooks's and Sissors's purposes in a single headline. Spend some time reading the headlines at these sites to get a sense of what's possible in these tight spaces.

## THE PULL QUOTE AND THE TEASER

Another useful tool to break up text is the pull quote. By magnifying a particularly colorful, provocative, or summative quotation, you can draw attention to the story, attention that doesn't distract from the headline, and provide another entry point into the article or package. Figure 3.3 (on p. 66) shows a pullout quote from *B/R Mag*, a multiplatform sports magazine from *Bleacher Report*. The pull quote has been off-set, magnified, and presented in a yellow box to contrast with the article from which it came.

Related to the pull quote is the teaser, or a short burst of text that grabs attention, perhaps by asking a question, and leads to another layer or level of information:

### Read More: *Can Coffee Intake Reduce Cancer Risk?*

The boldfaced "READ MORE" slows a reader just enough to give the hyperlinked headline a chance. The homepage of the Association of Lighthouse Keepers (alk. org.uk/) demonstrates this function as a guidepost (or lighthouse!) for surfing and scanning:

> The **Association of Lighthouse Keepers** was formed in 1988 by a group of serving and **retired keepers**, with the aim of maintaining contact between its members and enthusiasts throughout the world who share an interest in **lighthouses** and other **coastal** and **inland** aids to **navigation**. Our aims are to forge links with other **lighthouse associations**, to act as an information exchange, to expand our growing **archive** on lighthouse-related material, and in the long term, to establish a museum/study centre to promote the growing interest in **pharology**.

FIGURE 3.3 *A pull quote from a page at B/R Mag that also uses all caps to grab attention*

"I don't know why the f--k I'm here," she screamed. "I'm not doing this."

Laurer flew home the next morning and never spoke to Kathy again. For years, though, she sent threatening messages via voicemail, postcard and fax.

*"I can't believe you deserted me."*

*"You're going to pay for this."*

*"I'm going to come get you."*

"I lived in fear of my sister for a long time," Kathy says. "I was literally scared she was going to show up at my front door with a knife or a gun."

## "I DIDN'T RECOGNIZE THE PERSON I SAW THAT DAY. IT WAS LIKE THE DEVIL HAD INVADED JOANIE'S BODY."

In Hamilton, Laurer lost not only her sister, but also her best friend, the only one who had supported her during tough times. Goodness knows, there were plenty of them.

Readers likely will scan the boldfaced words to discern the purpose of the site and its basic organization. A scanning eye can only pick up two or three words at a time, so the wording uses no long phrases in its hyperlinked text.

## THE POWER OF THE LIST

Yet another powerful tool for breaking up big text blocks is the digital-friendly list. Smartphone users have a seemingly insatiable appetite for lists: "13 Reasons Why It's Better To Travel With A Buddy," "23 Gifts People Are Buying On Amazon Right Now," "15 Reasons Why Digital Stories Should Have A List." Lists come in two basic varieties: ordered and unordered. Ordered lists are numbered; unordered lists are not. Sequential lists, step-by-step instructions, and "how to" forms of content are ideal for ordered lists, as are "Top Ten" lists and chronologies and timelines. For example, here is a list instructing a young ballplayer how to throw a curveball:

1. **Holding the ball:** Grip the ball between your thumb and middle finger, placing your middle finger along the bottom seam of the ball and your thumb along the back seam. The curves of the seams should be close to your palm, with one on top and one on bottom. Don't use your index finger to help the grip. Use that finger to point where you want the ball to go.
2. **Throwing the ball:** Your dominant foot should be on the pitching rubber in a parallel position. Lift your opposite knee and rotate your hips forward as you throw the ball. Your elbow should be level with or above your arm, bent at a 90-degree angle.
3. **Releasing the ball:** Keep your palm facing inward. Release as your arm extends and you step forward with the opposite foot. As your arm comes down from the throw, it should be headed toward your opposite hip.
4. **Practicing the pitch:** The spinning action of the throw is achieved by the hand moving as if it is turning a doorknob or snapping your fingers as the ball is released.

This ordered list judiciously uses **boldface** to lift the text ever so slightly off the page, which slows a reader just enough to command attention. To use a roadway metaphor, boldface serves as a sort of speed bump, and like speed bumps, boldface can become annoying rather quickly.

Unordered lists are for information that doesn't need to be presented in any particular order, such as lists of criteria, benefits, and requirements. Because good lists can be quickly scanned, there is less need for punctuation, as in the unordered list below, one cataloging the benefits of renting a room at the Hotel California:

- free in-room wifi;
- hot breakfast every morning;
- cable TV;
- indoor and outdoor pools; and
- wake-up service.

For both ordered and unordered lists, the key is consistency. If you begin one list item with a verb, begin all of that list's items with a verb. If you use a lead-in or teaser for one item, use a teaser for all of the items. If that first lead-in is two words, all of the lead-ins should be two words.

Other guidelines for cooking up some tasty lists include:

- **Setting up or signaling the purpose of list.** Lists shouldn't come out of thin air, so take the time to set it up. Signal to the reader what she is about to see.
- **Presenting list items consistently.** Items should be roughly equivalent in length, structure, phrasing, spacing, punctuation, cap style, and typeface. Use similar grammatical structure and syntax.
- **Keeping it brief.** The sweet spot for list lengths is six to eight items. Longer lists risk losing the reader's interest.
- **Avoiding the overuse of lists.** Too many lists threaten to erode any one's effectiveness or impact, and the aggregate impression on readers could be that the site or app lacks substance. BuzzFeed, anyone?

To demonstrate how a list can help to transform a wordy paragraph into something that can be easily scanned, take a look at these two presentations of Tokyo's top tourist attractions:

First, the "before":

Tokyo is filled with internationally recognized attractions that draw large crowds of people every year without fail. During the first six months of 2017, some of the most popular places were the Imperial Palace (1.2 million visitors), Tokyo Disneyland (1.1 million), Ueno Park Zoo (678,000), Toshugu Shrine (386,598), Tokyo Science Museum (360,000), and Yasukuni Shrine (228,446).

Rather than this text chunk, what if we presented these sites in a hyperlinked list ordered by popularity of attraction?

In the first six months of 2017, six of the most-visited places in Tokyo were:

- *Imperial Palace*;
- *Tokyo Disneyland*;
- *Ueno Park Zoo*;
- *Toshugu Shrine*;
- *Tokyo Science Museum*; and
- *Yasukuni Shrine*.

## HYPERTEXT

None of the arrows in a digital writer's quiver is more powerful than the hyperlink, the most common form of hypertext, which is simply computer-coded text capable of taking the reader somewhere else. *Hyper* is from the Greek root meaning "beyond" or

FIGURE 3.4

"over." It might be difficult to believe that when hypertext was introduced to the masses in 1989 (as a technology, hyperlinks have been around since the 1960s), it sparked controversy. Critics in English departments throughout the country questioned whether hyperlinking interferes with reading comprehension and understanding. Since then, research has shown that hyperlinks do neither. Links can actually enhance comprehension because a quick look at the links can give the reader a general sense of what the page is about.

No other medium allows a reader to jump so easily to another story, another source, or another subject altogether. Thus, we should link to related content to allow readers to further pursue a subject or interest. One of the best websites at doing this, at creating a sort of connective tissue of related information, is Wikipedia. The crowdsourced online encyclopedia layers information and links to logical and intuitive next-level sites and artifacts. The "Florence Cathedral" entry in Wikipedia for the Duomo in Florence, Italy, for example, demonstrates effective layering, with a "contents" list, hyperlinked terms, and, at the bottom, a list of other resources (Figure 3.4).

Think about term papers you have written that had footnotes or endnotes. This is the kind of information you want to link to in your digital spaces. To access resources footnoted in print, you would have to visit a library or courthouse. In digital spaces, those same resources are a click or touch away. The once solitary main text now can have a potentially infinite number of next-door neighbors.

## Hypertext Challenges

One of the navigational challenges now facing designers and producers is the fact that the "homepage" is no longer the front door for most websites most of the time. Search engine findings, Facebook "Likes," and tweeted URLs are, more often than not, giving interactors entry to specific information directly, with no thought to homepages or sequenced information. Each and every webpage, even each article, has to be designed and produced with this consideration in mind; each webpage or content piece has to stand on its own, independent and self-contained. Each and every page should prominently display a link or route back to the homepage, as well, if for no other reason than to reassure interactors about how easily they can re-orient themselves to the site's content.

While creating hyperlinks is relatively easy, maintaining them is another story. Broken, outdated links are a common problem for any site with large collections of links, and those that rely on, say, YouTube find themselves constantly chasing the content they hope to link out to as the videos get moved about. Broken links chip away at a publisher's credibility by signaling age and even neglect. Thus, hyperlinks must be periodically checked and updated. Most web authoring software does this automatically.

Though hypertext can enable non-linear and multi-linear presentations, or those that can be read or accessed through multiple pathways, digital readers still prefer traditional narrative formats. Many authors have experimented with producing elaborate, narratively complex, multilayered hypertextual writings, but the traditional story arc of beginning-middle-end still reigns supreme.

Inserting a link is also something of a risk. Once a reader has exited a site by clicking a hyperlink, she rarely returns. Determining when, how, and to what to link, then, are important decisions. A feature story on a cancer survivor, for example, shouldn't be interrupted by hyperlinks, especially in the early going, which, no matter how judiciously handled, are interruptions. A story promoting a coming event, however, very likely—and logically—could link out to that event's homepage even in the first paragraph, because putting a reader in touch with information about that event is the story's purpose.

Because links change the direction of a reader's experience, a new rhetorical style is needed, one that recognizes and even facilitates non-linearity. It's the interactor, not the author or producer, who dictates the order in which information is read or accessed, so hyperlinking should be used as an efficient way to get a reader to the most relevant information that the reader might be interested in, regardless of where it lives in cyberspace.

## To What Should We Link?

Digital writers should carefully consider how, when, and where to link. Ask what the reward will be for following that link, to prevent gratuitous linking. Reasons you might link to another article or site or source include:

- directing attention;
- attributing information, citing, and referring to sources and source documents, such as court cases, research studies, transcripts, public records, court opinions, etc.;
- providing context for your article by referring to related articles, next-layer sources, definitions, and explanations, much as Wikipedia does;
- enticing and rewarding readers with something more, with additional layers or dimension to the story, such as related or archival stories; and
- offering interactivity and allowing for personalized texts.

## How to Hyperlink

With the popular web more than 20 years old, conventions have developed to guide hyperlinking:

- **Size.** Hyperlinks should be the same type size as the main body text.
- **Differentiation.** Once almost always underlined, hyperlinks today can be any color and underlined or not. But they should stand out one way or another—boldfaced or underlined, appearing in an alternating but consistent color.
- **Intuitiveness.** Readers should be able to successfully predict what they will find by clicking or touching, enabling them to decide whether to visit now, later, or not at all.
- **Clarity.** The links should be explicit about the type of content to which they lead.
- **Goodwill.** Linking to a product or a site selling something will likely be punished; no one likes to be suckered.

Implied by this list is that hyperlinks should not merely point to content, but that they be regarded as content themselves. This is also true for headlines. "Click here" is the equivalent to a headline in print that states, "Important story below." Such a pointer fails to provide enough helpful information; it merely points to what might be good information. A few examples:

**Bad:** For more information on the Boeing 777, *click here.*
**Good:** The company has more than a dozen *Boeing 777s* in its fleet.
**Bad:** The commission's report is available by *clicking here.*
**Better:** The commission's report is available at www.report.com.
**Best:** Read the commission's *report.*

Let's look at another example of good hyperlinking, from an undergraduate student's blog:

> The news media, including journalists, editors and executives, largely agree that the core principles of journalism are getting the facts right, getting both sides of the story and not publishing rumors. Journalists increasingly agree with public criticism of their profession and the quality of their work, according to the *Pew Research Center for the People and the Press*. About half of news media executives and journalists rank *lack of credibility* with the public as a major reason for declining audiences. In 1989, only one-third of the press said this. Americans' evaluations of the news media's credibility have declined since the mid-1980s.
>
> *The poll* was conducted in coordination with the *Committee of Concerned Journalists* from November 20, 2016 to February 11, 2017. Lack of credibility is the single issue most often cited by the news media as the most important problem facing journalism today.

This short post's links:

- take readers to the supporting evidence and primary source material without interrupting the flow of the main body of text;
- help readers to predict where the links will take them;
- are only a few words long, increasing the chance they'll be read; and
- appear differently than the main text.

The specific text and link color choices are not that important, provided they are legible, but consistency and repetition are important. If one hyperlink is deep green, all of the hyperlinks should be in deep green. Because they typically are an alternate color, links are similar to boldfaced words in how they slow the reader, if ever so subconsciously.

So, when hyperlinking, ask:

- How can I assure and orient readers when they first arrive on or at the page?
- How can I help them to read efficiently and with pleasure?
- How can I help readers to retrace the steps they have taken in their reading paths, or to return to any one step or level in any one of those paths?
- How can I describe or signal the destinations for the links in the document?

## Hyperlinking Hygiene

Two more decisions for writers: whether hyperlinks should open in new windows, new tabs, or within the same browser window, and whether they should link to outside sites or keep the interactor within the same digital environment. If linked material opens up in a new, separate window, the original window and story are still there, so the reader can resume reading the main narrative after accessing the sidebar or background information. But new windows can be seen as clutter. Linking to open up in the same browser window leaves the linking page behind, however, and few interactors will return. Links that open up a new tab on the same browser are a good compromise, one that leaves the original story in one tab but that also provides access to sidebar information under a new tab within the same browser window.

The answer to the second question has shifted 180 degrees since the web's early days. From being careful not to jettison readers from a site, the current thinking is to acknowledge that readers want and even demand universal, egalitarian access. Link accordingly. This makes effective sites and apps increasingly aggregators and curators, as well as producers. The philosophy, first learned from Google, seems to be that if a site does a good enough job sending people away, they will come back for more. Journalism professor Jeff Jarvis proposed an apt golden rule for linking: "Link unto others' good stuff as you would have them link unto your good stuff."

## WWGD?

With Google in the back of their minds, writers should think in terms of key words when hyperlinking, just as they do when writing headlines or thinking about what to put into boldface relief. Use the vocabulary of your readers. Interactors are scaling mountains of information. The more key words we can provide—the more words that jut out even slightly from the rock face of all that information—the more places the reader can grab onto, step up on, and keep moving from. These key words provide Google's algorithms with the means of finding information and ranking it in its findings. Google's AdWords keyword Planner (adwords.google.com/KeywordPlanner) allows you to measure the popularity of any key word and identify suggested alternatives. As alternatives to the Keyword Planner, you could try paid services like the WordTracker app (app.wordtracker.com/) or Keyword Discover database (keyworddiscovery.com). Finally, Google Trends (google.com/trends/) provides real-time metrics on what's being searched for using Google's engine, information that can be broken down geographically and by topic.

## Types of Links

You have determined what to link and where. Next decision: what kind of hyperlink to deploy, an embedded link, inline link, or hot area. Each operates a little differently. **Embedded links** are by far the most common, and they are usually placed behind a word, a selection of words, or an object (image, button, icon). Though most embedded links are embedded in text with HTML, other elements can serve as embedded

73

links, such as buttons and icons, navigation bars, and image maps. A **hot area** typically is found in or on an image, diagram, or other graphical object in which an HTML image map has been placed. Moving the cursor over the hot area activates one or more embedded links. Below, HTML code is shown that embeds individual African country links into a larger map of Eastern Africa, a graphical file named "navbar":

```
<P>
<OBJECT data = "navbar.png" type = "image/png" usemap = "#mapA">
<OBJECT data = "navbar.gif" type = "image/gif" usemap = "#mapA">
    <MAP name = "mapA">
    <P>Navigate the map:
    <A href = "sudan.html" shape = "poly" coords =
    "0,0,118,28">Sudan</a> |
    <A href = "chad.html" shape = "poly" coords =
    "118,0,184,28">Chad</A> |
    <A href = "ethiopia.html" shape = "poly" coords =
    "184,200,60">Ethiopia</A> |
    <A href = "uganda.html" shape = "poly" coords =
    "276,0,276,28,100,200,50,50,276,0">Uganda</A>
    </MAP>
</OBJECT>
```

Moving a cursor over the section of the map labeled "Sudan," which is pinpointed on the graphic using coordinates, then clicking or touching, would take a site visitor to an HTML page file named "sudan.html," a webpage with more information on or about Sudan.

FIGURE 3.5 *This graphic shows two hot areas, one for cubanxgiants.com and one to redirect interactors to WanderingRocks.wordpress.com*

# Visual Rhetoric (COM

**FALL 2017**
**MWF 1200-1250pm | LAU 113**

**Professor: Dr. Brian Carroll**
**Office: LAU 100**
**Office phone: 706.368.6944**

**email: bc@berry.edu | web: www.cubanxgiants.com**
**bc's blog: WanderingRocks.wordpress.com**

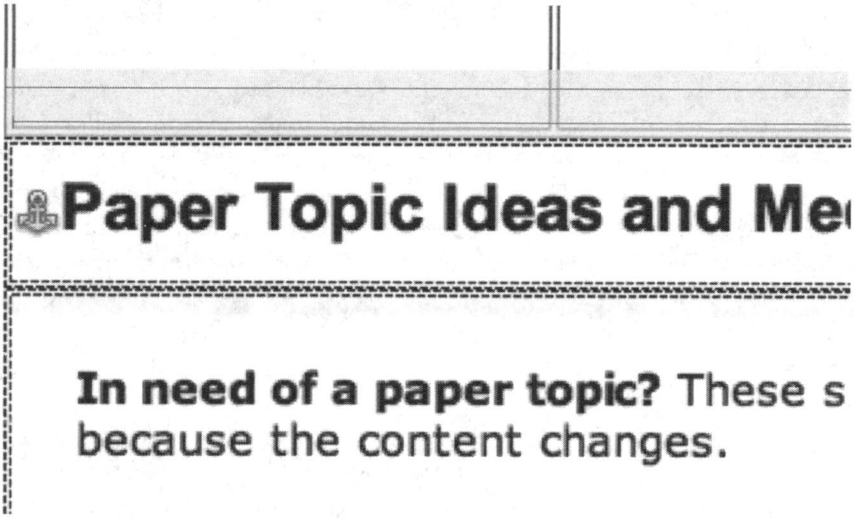

**⚓Paper Topic Ideas and Me**

**In need of a paper topic?** These s because the content changes.

FIGURE 3.6 *Anchor links are signified by an anchor icon: A top-of-the-page link to "paper topics" sends interactors deep into the page to this subsection outlining resources for paper topics*

**Inline links,** by contrast, bring content from somewhere else into the page being viewed. Images and graphics are the most common inline link content. In fact, virtually *all* images—photographic and graphical—appear courtesy of an inline link, which positions the photo on the page and makes it appear that the photo is physically part of the page. The image file is actually separate, located somewhere else, but downloads with the rest of the page to appear as one. **Anchors** are in-page or within-document navigational links, redirecting a visitor to another part of the same document or page. They are commonly used to create top-of-page navigation to sections below, often in text-intensive or lengthy webpages, in order to minimize the need to scroll.

### A Lesson From Bloggers

Research shows that bloggers use hyperlinks differently than do news websites. Mark Coddington, of the University of Texas, found that, while news sites link in ways this chapter describes, referring thematically to supplemental sources, bloggers tend to use links to make social connections. Bloggers link to the outside more than four-fifths of the time. And where news sites link to traditional, objective sources, bloggers commonly link to each other. Blogging journalists, Coddington found, "are to be situated between the two groups, appropriating some practices from each."

## LAYERS

The tools we have been discussing—headlines and subheads, lists, and hyperlinking— are among the choices writers and editors have when layering content for digital delivery.

Other options include adding video, photo slideshows, audio, information graphics, original sources and evidence, and spaces where the conversation can continue.

Layering is a response to the well-documented fact that interactors do not read. They just don't. They surf and scan, scroll and skip, hurtling through digital spaces searching for something they need or for something that grabs their attention. One early web usability study by Jakob Nielsen showed that perhaps more than three-fourths of web users merely scan any page they download, while only 16 percent reported reading word for word. And that was for the early web. These percentages have not since gone up. Acknowledging these patterns, Nielsen recommended several webpage characteristics to enhance "scan-ability," attributes that apply to most digital environments:

- highlighted key words;
- hyperlinks;
- typeface variations;
- variation in color;
- subheads;
- bulleted lists;
- paragraphs with one idea each;
- information presented in inverted pyramid style (with most important up top); and
- perhaps above all, brevity.

Combining these tools and techniques are story packages that link and array related content and that organize information in such a way that even a speeding surfer can quickly determine what to attend to and what not to. Readers can deep-dive into these packages or skim across the top, and often they can access the content in the order they want.

Let's begin a tour of layering examples with a rather pedestrian one, a scenario that could be replicated any number of ways, in any number of contexts. Let's say your team or club just won the championship. Let's make it the Chicago Cubs' first World Series in 108 years. You saw it live, but as a lifelong Cubbie fan, you want to luxuriate in the afterglow of the historic win by reading, watching, looking, and sharing. You visit the Cubs' website or mobile app, or those of your go-to sports news source, in order to read the immediate game write-ups. Layered just under these is a menu of video highlights. To the side are the box scores. In the "related content" section, there is a photo slide show of some of Game Seven's more memorable images, links to the post-game press conferences and interviews, and, of course, ways to buy World Series t-shirts, hats, and other tchotchkes. Layered at the bottom are what fans (and foes) are saying about the big game, comment that includes channels for, at minimum, Twitter and Facebook. An hour whizzes by, but it doesn't matter, because Cub Nation has waited for this moment since 1908; you can't get enough. And the expert layering and combinations of media are meeting that need in a multi-sensory, buffet-style presentation.

Looking more closely at this hypothetical, the content layers the content producers had at their disposal include:

- headlines, subheads, and sub-subheads;
- one-sentence teasers and lead-ins;
- brief summary paragraphs or abstracts;
- visuals, photos, and information graphics;
- audio and video clips;
- related stories, interviews, timelines, and statistical charts;
- archival content going back to 1908, including old radio broadcasts, photography, and records;
- maps;
- discussion, chat, and ways to share the content; and
- related links out to the best of the web and apps on the topic.

These sorts of expertly layered content packages share several important digital capacities:

- *Easy, intuitive navigation.* Distance between any two elements or even media is inconsequential.
- *Hypertextuality.* This is what the web was created to do, and it's, of course, related to navigation. Make good, judicious use of internal and outbound hyperlinking.
- *Multimedia.* Media have very different abilities to deliver and engage, so give interactors different ways of experiencing the story.
- *Portability.* The ubiquity of smartphones means these packages can be enjoyed in airport waiting areas, at home with a cup of coffee, or even on a treadmill at the gym.

Finally, writers should think of content in terms of discrete, short (or small) pieces or packets. Few interactors read long articles, whether on their computers or via their phones. Look for opportunities to break up the text into discrete, digestible pieces or chunks. Chunking is a concept that originated in cognitive psychology, and it means breaking up text and multimedia content into smaller chunks to help users process, understand, and remember it better. Paragraph size should vary depending upon the nature of the content, but paragraphs of even 100 words can seem pretty long in a display screen. To chunk multimedia content, keep related pieces close together and aligned, and help users visually distinguish between what's related and what isn't using color schemes, horizontal rules, and white space.

Of great help here is the inverted pyramid style, a staple of traditional news. Imagine a pyramid. Now turn it upside down so that the base is up top. In this model, the article's most important information goes there, with additional information added in order of importance, down to a vanishing point. For digital spaces, we might imagine moving *into* a three-dimensional pyramid. The pyramid's base faces the reader, meaning that all of the most important story pieces or entry points are highlighted right there on the first view. For the Cubs' win, perhaps a main narrative story, a photo slide show, and a series of video clips. As the reader moves deeper into the pyramid or, to borrow from Lewis Carroll, uses links to navigate through *rabbit holes*, the reader accesses related sidebar information. The reader travels forward into the pyramid, or sideways through rabbit holes. As surfers approach the point of the pyramid, the reader isn't necessarily finished, because now facing the reader are more and more pyramids. Headlines, headers, hyperlinks, layers, and chunks are ways of helping readers through these spaces, or forward through our pyramids. As digital writers, then, we are architects of spaces and of navigational schemes through those spaces. It is a high calling.

One way to envision the planning for these spaces is to think about a Prezi presentation (prezi.com). Rather than providing a linear presentation, Prezi's create sort of galaxies of information, with a main sun or center connected to orbiting satellites of related information sized and interconnected according to its relationship to that center. In our Cubs Series win example, a main Game Seven story might be the sun, while perhaps a photo slide show, video clips, a historical timeline, and parade information orbit around that centerpiece story.

## EXAMPLES OF EXPERT, COMPELLING LAYERING

Let's look in on a group of representative but very different approaches to bundling content. These are among the very best of digital storytelling efforts, all from journalism, but each with immediate instructive value to public relations practitioners, marketers, and advertisers.

### The 45-Minute Mystery of Freddie Gray's Death, *The Baltimore Sun* (data.baltimoresun.com/freddie-gray/)

In April 2015, Baltimore's Freddie Gray, 25, was arrested for what police said was an illegal switchblade. While being moved in a police van that same day, Gray slipped into a coma and never re-gained consciousness. He died a week later. It was one of the biggest stories of the year, and it helped set the tone for race and justice conversations that continued nationally throughout the summer and following months. *The Baltimore Sun* tells the story of the critical 45 minutes of that fateful day with a layered presentation organized around the chronology. By zeroing in on a handful of key moments, then layering the presentation with photography, satellite mapping, and video, the *Sun* gives its interactors an immersive re-living of Gray's last conscious moments.

**FIGURE 3.7**
*The launch page for the Sun's Freddie Gray "mystery"*

**FIGURE 3.8**
*One of the half-dozen "moments," giving interactors content choices*

**FIGURE 3.9**
*The video clip for 9:24 a.m., when paramedics are delivering Gray to the trauma center.*

9:24 a.m.

Police arrive at the Western District station and call paramedics to tend to an "unconscious" Freddie Gray.

**FIGURE 3.10** *The Freddie Gray package also links out to related Sun coverage, including this text story written as a companion piece to the layered presentation.*

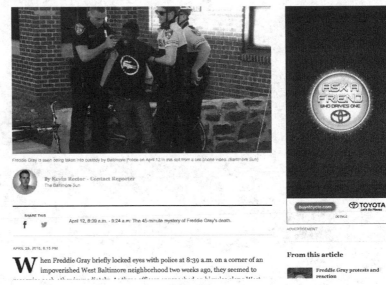

News / Maryland / Freddie Gray Case Trials

# The 45-minute mystery of Freddie Gray's death

Freddie Gray is seen being taken into custody by Baltimore Police on April 12 in this still from a cell phone video. (Baltimore Sun)

By Kevin Rector - Contact Reporter
The Baltimore Sun

SHARE THIS

April 12, 8:39 a.m. - 9:24 a.m: The 45-minute mystery of Freddie Gray's death.

APRIL 25, 2015, 6:15 PM

When Freddie Gray briefly locked eyes with police at 8:39 a.m. on a corner of an impoverished West Baltimore neighborhood two weeks ago, they seemed to

ADVERTISEMENT

From this article

Freddie Gray protests and reaction

## Serial Podcasts on the Trial of Adnan Syed (serialpodcast.org/season-one)

Serial's initial podcast series, from the creators of *This American Life*, broke ground in many ways, and, though it is primarily an audio presentation, the layering of content here includes blog posts, a trove of source documents and maps, and, of course, written narrative. Serial (serialpodcast.org/) became so popular so fast, Slate had to create a meta podcast about the Serial podcasts, which were timed perfectly with the resurgence of digital audio on smartphones. Aljazeera America's Treasured Island (projects. aljazeera.com/2014/tangier-island/), documenting life on Tangier Island, VA, is another example of expert layering that leverages audio. The recordings are layered on top of the text narrative *and* behind large, rich, eye-popping photography.

## Virtual Reality

Increasingly, we will see journalistic, marketing, and public relations applications of virtual reality, which went mainstream in 2015 with Facebook's commitment to and sizeable investment in developing VR experiences, hardware, and software. Digital

**FIGURE 3.11**
*The New York Times's VR launch page*

storytelling is rushing to leverage the immersive, experiential potential of VR, including stories and apps from journalists at:

- ABC—abcnews.go.com/
- The New York Times—nytimes.com/newsgraphics/2015/nytvr/
- Vice—with.in/watch/vice-news-vr-millions-march-nyc-12–13–14/
- Discovery—discoveryvr.com/

## Washington Post's Exodus (washingtonpost.com/graphics/world/exodus/black-route/)

Stunning photography keys this richly layered multimedia slideshow tracing the journey of one Syrian family fleeing their home for Europe. The layers here include a lengthy written narrative, screen-filling full-color photography, rich data (apps.washingtonpost.com/g/page/world/recent-conflicts-lead-to-record-numbers-of-refugees-and-displaced-people/1672/), and pull quotes.

## The Making of a Narco-terrorist, ProPublica (projects.propublica.org/graphics/narco)

Perhaps the most visually exotic of the samples presented here is an interactive "experience" that feels a bit like a card game and comic book all in one. Chronicled here are five criminals in different parts of the world, five Drug Enforcement Administration sting operations, and what the site describes as "five dubious links between drugs and

FIGURE 3.12
*Washington Post's Exodus (washingtonpost.com/graphics/world/exodus/black-route/)*

EVZONOI, Greece — They've made it 1,600 miles by boat, train, car and on foot. Now the light is fading as they finally reach the edge of Greece. "Let's move," Ahmed Jinaid beckons, his family trailing him up a hill in high grass. But then he stops.

He is standing beside an abandoned watchtower near the northern border, the one after which there's supposed to be no talking and, worse for a man with a weakness for Winstons, no smoking. The 42-year-old former deliveryman squints at his white Samsung Galaxy phone.

He is looking for directions.

"No, no, no," he mutters, blinking at the glowing screen. "What happened to the GPS?"

Ahmed is eight weeks out of Syria, part of a historic exodus of Arabs, Africans and Asians fleeing war and oppression. More than 102,000 migrants have risked the Mediterranean Sea to reach Europe this year, outpacing even 2014's record arrivals.

Many land in Italy, but a surging number of migrants are coming ashore in Greece. From there, they venture north through the Balkans to the rest of the European Union — a web of perilous trails stretching hundreds of miles. Aid workers have nicknamed it the Black Route. Ahmed had meticulously plotted the trek on his phone's GPS.

Part of the series **Exodus**
An occasional series examining the causes and impact of a global wave of migration driven by war, oppression and poverty.

On a steep hill ahead, the gaudy glow of red neon burns. That's Macedonia and the casino town they need to avoid. Gangs armed with guns and lead pipes roam the woods, beating and robbing migrants. There

☐ Schengen countries    |—— 300 miles ——|

**FIGURE 3.13**
*The Making of a Narco-terrorist, ProPublica (projects. propublica.org/ graphics/narco)*

**FIGURE 3.14**
*The Making of a Narco-terrorist, ProPublica (projects.pro publica.org/ graphics/narco)*

*By Ginger Thompson, ProPublica, Susie Cagle, special to ProPublica, and Lena Groeger, ProPublica*
*December 15, 2015*

Five criminals in far-flung parts of the world, five D.E.A. sting operations, five dubious links between drugs and terror. The characters are different but the story remains the same. Authorities said each case demonstrated alliances between terrorists and drug traffickers, but most of the alleged links fell apart in court. Here's how narco-terrorism cases are made. *Related Story »*

*Click on a headshot below to see how each case unfolded.*

BOUTERSE

**FIGURE 3.15**
*Missed Signs. Fatal Consequences, The Austin American Statesman (projects. statesman.com/ news/cps-missed-signs/)*

Austin American-Statesman
INVESTIGATES

Introduction — Missed signs
Part 1 — Gaps in protection
Part 2 — Stumbling blocks
Part 3 — Inside CPS
Interactive — Explore the data

# MISSED SIGNS. FATAL CONSEQUENCES.

*How Texas missed deadly patterns and key pieces of information that could have helped protect vulnerable children.*

In 2009, the Legislature ordered Child Protective Services to publicly record every abuse- and neglect-related death in the state in hopes of identifying patterns and discovering ways to prevent abuse deaths. But the Statesman has learned that CPS has not systematically analyzed those reports, meaning that in important ways, Texas' child protection workers effectively have been operating with blinders, missing deadly patterns and key pieces of information that could help protect kids.

terror." Each case dramatizes the alliances common among terrorists and drug traffickers. The campy, hand-made, all-original illustrations belie the serious journalism here that raises questions about sting operations carried out by the DEA and the agency's claims that drug smugglers are funding terror. Also instructive here is how these kinds of playful, interactive, immersive presentations could drive multimedia public relations or marketing efforts on any number of causes, topics, and issues.

## Missed Signs. Fatal Consequences, *The Austin American Statesman* (projects.statesman.com/news/cps-missed-signs/

Perhaps saving the best for last, learn from the dedicated journalists at Austin, TX's *Austin American Statesman* newspaper and site, which, in a massive three-part series, investigate the state of child protective services in Texas. It is a tour-de-force, layering investigative journalism of the highest order with source documents and data, photography, video, maps, charts, and multiple sidebars (or related stories). Also incorporated in this exhaustive narrative are comments and photos from the *Statesman*'s Facebook community, adding a crowdsourced element to the award-winning journalism. The navigation scheme is intuitive, allowing interactors to read and surf in any order they choose, but held together by the compelling narrative.

## WHAT RESEARCH TELLS US INTERACTORS DO

It's also important to know something about how your audience wants to use or interact with your content, habits that vary depending on the device, medium, or machine that your interactors are using. In a study by the Poynter Institute, researchers tracked web users' eye movements, particularly those of people who read newspapers online. Here is a sampling of what the Eyetrack researchers found, and you will see that several of the findings are counter-intuitive:

- Interactors' eyes most often fixate in the upper left quadrant of a webpage first, before hovering, then moving left to right. The "F" pattern of readership is well established in describing how and how much time and attention are dedicated to webpage content, generally, with attention concentrated along the top and down the left side, with some attention left to right at a second level of the page.
- Dominant headlines most often draw the eye upon entering the webpage, not photographs, especially when placed in the upper left quadrant of the page. In contrast to print, online photos are not ideal entry points. So, text rules on computer screens, at least generally, both in terms of when it is viewed and in how much time is spent interacting with it.
- Though headlines prove better entry points than do photos or graphics, surprisingly smaller headlines are more closely read than are the larger, which are merely scanned; the larger headlines can be perceived as graphical elements as opposed to text. The Poynter study shows that smaller type encourages focused viewing, while larger type promotes scanning.
- When a headline is bold and in the same size as the deckhead, both are read, as opposed to scanned or skipped. When the headline is larger, however, and the deckhead text is on a separate line, readers skip the deck.
- Navigation placed at the top of the homepage performed best, and by a wide margin, outperforming navigation on either side of the page or placed at the bottom.
- Shorter paragraphs are more highly read than long ones by a factor of two. One-column formats are more highly read than those with more than one column of text, which is a change from print newspaper readership. And summary descriptions, or abstracts, are well received. Boldface summary descriptions are read 95 percent of the time.
- By contrast, static advertisements typically are ignored. Those graphical ads that are attended to get only a half second to 1.5 seconds of the reader's

attention. Text ads, however, garner nearly seven seconds of attention, underlining text's primacy online.

- Mug shots (or head shots) are ignored. The average size of photos on news sites is 230 pixels wide and 230 deep, which, surprisingly, is not the golden rectangle with a 3:2 ratio for which print traditionally strives. These small, boxy photos online are attended to by 30 percent of visitors.
- The most read typefaces online include Arial, Courier, Georgia, and Verdana, none of which are a surprise. Verdana, for example, was developed for Microsoft by typeface master Matthew Carter, and sans serif fonts generally render better in pixelated environments.

Poynter's Eyetrack research has also looked at iPad use, revealing the very different ways that tablet users interact with content. Not surprisingly, "touch" is all important. According to the Eyetrack study's findings:

- iPad users are either closely involved with the screen while reading, keeping nearly constant contact by touching, tapping, pinching, and swiping to adjust their views, or they arrange a full screen of text before sitting back to read.
- Active users, which represented 61 percent of the study's sample population, are, not surprisingly, highly focused, reading a line or two of text before swiping to move the text much like a teleprompter.
- Many text stories are read completely; however, an average of about 1.5 minutes were spent on the first story selected by the study's participants.
- People not finishing a story read for an average of about 78 seconds, which suggests that at about that point in the text, we should insert some visual element to keep the reader in the story package.
- An average of 18 items are viewed before the first selection to read is made. The high number means some headlines or images are seen multiple times before a choice is made.
- Importantly, participants preferred holding the tablet in horizontal or landscape position, with 70 percent preferring it to the vertical or portrait position. This preference has to do with the screen dimension for watching video.
- iPad users tend to enter a screen through a dominant element, often a photograph, with faces in photographs and videos attracting a lot of attention.
- Importantly for navigation design, iPad users preferred using a browser to navigate between stories, even where navigation was designed into the publication. About 65 percent of the participants used a browser's back button rather than the publication's navigation design. Not surprisingly, then, people default to what they know.

## BOX 3.1

## Sources to Help Journalists Transition to the Digital Age

- Code with me, @codewithme, two-day workshops in major U.S. cities that promise to "help journalists overcome their fear of code."
- Lynda.com, www.lynda.com, for website coding tutorials.
- Mozilla Thimble, thimble.mozilla.org/en-US/, a static text editor that allows users to publish finished webpages from the site. (JSFiddle and CodePen are similar resources.) Mozilla offers several "Webmaker" tools, including a timeline-based video editing software called Popcorn Maker.
- Treehouse, teamtreehouse.com, for help with most major programming languages, with Android and iOS development, and for project-based tutorials.
- Codecademy, codecademy.com, for an interactive method of learning to program.

## CHAPTER ACTIVITIES

1. Develop and complete the content piece you detailed in Chapters 1 and 2. Develop and present the piece for online readership by using the techniques and tools we've discussed so far. Do not merely post a large block of text or cut-and-paste from Word. This assignment asks you to apply what you have been learning. Be sure to spend plenty of time editing, including fact-checking, spell checking, and editing for grammar, punctuation, and organization.

    *Length:* About 750 words.

2. Pick a site or app and examine it to learn as much as you can about its audience. Access its FAQs, perhaps its "About Us" page. Identify the site or app type (news, entertainment, reference, etc.); the kinds of content available there; the demographics of the people who visit the site or subscribe to the app (ages, education, etc.); the interests or needs catered to by the content; the kinds of feedback, comments, and user interaction the site encourages and receives. From this information, write up a user profile for this site or app.

3. Find three examples online of poor headlines and provide their solutions. In other words, fix the headlines. Be sure to include the source for each bad headline, including that source's URL, where applicable. Example:

Headline: Chubby Babies in Breast Cancer Link
Problem: Awkward. Possibly offensive ("chubby"). No verb.
Solution: Infant Size Linked to Cancer Risk
Source: CNN.com, January 17, 2017
cnn.com/2017/HEALTH/01/17/infant.cancer/index.html

4. Find at least one article online that you think could be improved by deploying lists, either unordered or ordered. Submit the "before" version and your edited "after" version of the article, or edited part of the article.

5. Re-write the headline for your Chapter 1 writing sample with this chapter informing your work. Write subheads and insert where appropriate. Add lists where appropriate. Begin thinking about graphical and multimedia content that might be developed to create a layered experience.

6. To practice writing to specification, write three different headlines for the following story fragment. Make the first headline eight words and the second six words. For the third headline, provide both a headline and a subhead: a headline of about six words and a subhead of about eight words. Separate the head and the subhead with a colon (for example, "Dodgers edge Braves: Dickey's 3-hitter wasted as Atlanta bats remain silent").

## The story fragment:

ACWORTH, Ga.—An Acworth man turned himself in to police Sunday night after robbing a Motel 6 here and later attempting to mug a second victim on North Main Street.

Howard E. Smithton, 54, a resident of the Gazebo Park apartments on Old Cowan Street in Acworth, entered the Motel 6, also on Cowan, at 8:50 p.m. Sunday night and demanded money.

The clerk on duty, who said he knew Smithton, withheld his name for fear of his safety. He said he refused to give Smithton any money. A struggle ensued. Smithton overpowered the clerk, forced him to open the cash register, and left with an undisclosed amount of cash, according to the clerk. Smithton then attempted a second burglary approximately one hour later on the 4800 block of North Main.

Smithton demanded that the victim, 59-year-old Bob Wilson, a member of Acworth's board of aldermen, give Smithton his wallet. Wilson said he refused and began beating Smithton over the head with a walking stick, which chased Smithton away.

Smithton later turned himself in at Acworth police headquarters on Industrial Drive at approximately 10:30 p.m. He is being held on a $10,000 bond at the Acworth City Jail, according to Michael Rose, Acworth's sheriff.

The money from the Motel 6 has been returned, Rose said.

7. For the story in the previous activity, write a tweet promoting readership and directing traffic. Also for this exercise, sketch out a public relations response on behalf of Motel 6, including a news release and at least some preliminary thoughts about how to tweak SEO to minimize the damage from this story.

8. Developing a rich media layered multimedia project would take at least a semester. For this exercise, take a hot issue or broad topic, such as "The Path to Brexit," and storyboard just such a project.

- What elements would you include?
- How would you facilitate intuitive navigation?
- What kinds of source documents and data would you want to incorporate?
- How would you utilize photography?
- What kinds of information graphics would you develop?
- How would you facilitate crowdsourcing? Audio? Video?
- What questions remain unanswered?

## Digital Resources

### Case Studies in this chapter:

- The 45-minute Mystery of Freddie Gray's Death, The Baltimore Sun (data.baltimoresun.com/freddie-gray/)
- Serial Podcasts on the Trial of Adnan Syed (serialpodcast.org/season-one)
- Aljazeera America's Treasured Island (projects.aljazeera.com/2014/tangier-island/)
- Washington Post's Exodus (washingtonpost.com/graphics/world/exodus/black-route/)
- The Making of a Narco-terrorist, ProPublica (projects.propublica.org/graphics/narco)
- Missed Signs. Fatal Consequences, The Austin American Statesman (projects.statesman.com/news/cps-missed-signs/)

### Google's AdWords Keyword Planner (adwords.google.com/KeywordPlanner)

### Google Trends (google.com/trends/)

### Keyword Discovery Database (KeywordDiscovery.com)

### Steve Krug's Usability Website (www.sensible.com)
Krug takes the individual user's perspective and is sensitive to small business and small publication owners.

### Mapping the Intersection of Two Cultures: Interactive Documentary and Digital Journalism (opendoclab.mit.edu/interactivejournalism/Mapping_the_Intersection_of_Two_Cultures_Interactive_Documentary_and_Digital_Journalism.pdf)

The findings of an eight-month research project mapping and assessing the dynamics of an ongoing convergence between interactive and participatory documentary practices and digital journalism.

**Nielsen Norman Group (nngroup.com/topic/writing-web/)**
This section of the usability company's site aggregates articles on maximizing readership.

**Virtual Reality Case Studies**

- ABC—abcnews.go.com/
- The New York Times—nytimes.com/newsgraphics/2015/nytvr/
- Vice—with.in/watch/vice-news-vr-millions-march-nyc-12–13–14/
- Discovery—discoveryvr.com/

**Wandering Rocks Blog (wanderingrocks.wordpress.com)**
**Web Style Guide, 3rd Edition (www.webstyleguide.com/)**
Now a bit old, but still rock solid and worth studying is this companion site to *Web Style Guide: Basic Design Principles for Creating Web Sites*, by Patrick J. Lynch and Sarah Horton.

**Wordle (wordle.net)**
**WordTracker app (app.wordtracker.com/)**

## BIBLIOGRAPHY

Brooks, Brian S. and Sissors, Jack Z., *The Art of Editing* (Boston, MA: Allyn & Bacon, 2000).

Coddington, Mark, "Building Frames Link by Link: The Linking Practices of Blogs and News Sites," *International Journal of Communication* 6 (2012): 2007–2026.

De Ridder, Isabelle, "Visible or Invisible Links: Does the Highlighting of Hyperlinks Affect Incidental Vocabulary Learning, Text Comprehension, and the Reading Process?" *Language, Learning & Technology* 6, no. 1 (January 2002): 123.

Garcia, Mario, *iPad Design* (New York, NY: F+W Media, 2012).

Garst, Robert E. and Bernstein, Theodore M., *Headlines and Deadlines: A Manual for Copy Editors* (New York, NY: Columbia University Press, 1982).

King, Jason, "The Great Fall of Chyna: How WWE's Greatest Female Wrestler Disappeared," *B/R Mag* (September 15 2016), available: http://thelab.bleacherreport.com/the-great-fall-of-chyna/.

Landow, George P., *Hypertext 2.0* (Baltimore, MD: Johns Hopkins University Press, 1997).

LaRocque, Paul, *Heads You Win!: An Easy Guide to Better Headline and Caption Writing* (Oak Park, CA: Marion Street Press, 2003).

Lynch, Patrick and Horton, Sarah, *Web Style Guide 2* (New Haven, CT: Yale University Press, 2001), available: www.webstyleguide.com.

McAlpine, Rachel, *Web Word Wizardry: A Guide to Writing for the Web and Intranet* (Berkeley, CA: Ten Speed Press, 2001).

Mayfield, Kendra, "Reality Check for Web Design," *Wired* (October 2 2002), available: www.wired.com/news/technology/0,1282,55190,00.html.

Morris, Errol, "Hear, All Ye People; Hearken, O Earth (Part One)," *The New York Times* (August 8 2012), available: http://opinionator.blogs.nytimes.com/2012/08/08/hear-all-ye-people-hearken-o-earth/.

Nielsen, Jakob, *Designing Web Usability* (Indianapolis, IN: New Riders, 2000).

Parker, Roger C., *Guide to Web Content and Design* (New York, NY: MIS Press, 1997).

Perez-Pena, Richard, "A Venerable Magazine Energizes Its Web Site," *The New York Times* (January 21 2008): C4.

Powell, Thomas, *Web Design: The Complete Reference* (Berkeley, CA: Osborne/McGraw-Hill, 2000).

Price, Jonathan and Price, Lisa, *Hot Text: Web Writing That Works* (Indianapolis, IN: New Riders, 2002).

Quinn, Sarah, "New Poynter Eyetrack Research Reveals How People Read News on Tablets," *Poynter Institute* (October 17 2012), available: www.poynter.org/how-tos/newsgathering-story telling/visual-voice/191875/new-poynter-eyetrack-research-reveals-how-people-read-news-on-tablets/.

Uricchio, William, *Mapping the Intersection of Two Cultures: Interactive Documentary and Digital Journalism* (Cambridge, MA: MIT Open Documentary Lab, 2015) available: http://opendoclab.mit.edu/interactivejournalism/Mapping_the_Intersection_of_Two_Cultures_Interactive_Documentary_and_Digital_Journalism.pdf.

Zinsser, William, *On Writing Well* (New York, NY: Harper & Row, 1976).

# Editing for Digital Media II

## Voice and Visual Style

*Not that the story need be long, but it will take a long while to make it short.*
—Henry David Thoreau

*You cannot save souls in an empty church.*
—David Ogilvy, advertising executive

*Man is the great pattern-maker and pattern perceiver. No matter how primitive his situation, no matter how tormented, he cannot live in a world of chaos.*
—Edmund Carpenter, media theorist

## INTRODUCTION

This chapter explores how a distinctive writing voice can be discovered and determined, a voice authentic to the writer and appropriate for his or her audiences. Style is also discussed, and in two very different contexts—writing style and visual style. Also presented are the principles for planning and designing webpages and apps, principles that are applicable to most digital environments. These principles are demonstrated in a few case studies. Finally, site and app usability is explained, including why even a little usability testing can be of great value.

## WRITING STYLE

Digital spaces put unprecedented burdens on writers and editors because the exercise or activity of "reading" these spaces is so different from reading traditional print. Early research on web reading conducted by Jakob Nielsen indicated, for example, that web users read about 25 percent more slowly on their computer screens than they do physical ink on tactile paper. They also "read" comparatively less, implying that writing for digital spaces must be concise and direct, qualities that have always been rewarded in journalism, public relations, and related fields. Nielsen controversially recommended a word count for online writing about half of the standard word count for the same piece were it written for print. Rarely are interactors aimlessly wandering the web or the App Store for simply beautiful prose; they are choosing information that satisfies a need, that helps them in some way, and that makes this utility and help immediately perceptible.

## Dialing Into Your Voice

An important aspect of a writing style is voice, or the personality that is expressed in your writing. For some, this voice comes naturally. For others, it takes work. For all, voice must be appropriate for the content, the medium, and the audience. The media formats themselves provide some cues as to what kinds of voices are appropriate. For example, one of the great promises of social media is their capacity to convey personality and to reward an authentically human voice. With its 140-character limit, Twitter, the second-most utilized social media platform by public relations practitioners to Facebook, is ideally suited for quick rejoinders; for short, pithy commentary; and for referring people to sites and pages. Some writers have personalities for which this communication channel is a perfect fit, making the delivery of this personality in the writing of the tweets a relatively easy exercise.

Donald Trump's use of Twitter to win the presidency is now legendary in part because the format is ideally suited to showcase his freewheeling nature, his penchant for digs and rejoinders, and his perceived willingness to speak his mind in real time. His aggressive and unconventional use of Twitter drove the agendas for most news outlets covering the campaign, even and especially when he violated political and social norms by being offensive and uncivil. In short, Twitter is perfect for the sound bites politicians and their handlers so desperately need. To make this point a very different way, imagine Trump as a prolific blogger. It is difficult to do, making the point that for many digital writers, and for more substantial messages, the more text-intensive format of blogs might be a better match.

Because social media are designed primarily to facilitate conversation, and because conversation typically requires authentically human voices, the capacity of social media to express this humanity presents big organizations with an opportunity to put a human face on what otherwise can be perceived as an unthinking, unfeeling bureaucracy. Common on these social media platforms and in these digital environments are more casual or informal styles of writing, styles encouraged by the platforms themselves. It is this informality that can be a great advantage, as Trump's embrace and use of Twitter put on such dramatic, show-stopping display.

Vanderbilt University Medical Center provides a very different example when it uses Twitter to reach out to its patients and their families. You will find on its feed responses to patient-posed questions from individuals within the medical center, real human beings who have been authorized to address specific problems and who have information on how to solve them. Informal banter, a sense of humor and fun, and, most importantly, a human voice mark these conversations in refreshing contrast to the ways most hospitals choose to communicate.

The decision of who to tweet on behalf of the hospital was an important one. Vanderbilt Medical Center tapped someone with experience with Twitter, someone who has already developed a natural voice for the format. Judging by the tweets, this person is obviously authorized to tweet about more than just Vanderbilt-related matters. This is smart, because anyone who tweets about one and only one thing will inevitably become boring and repetitious. This official tweeter has been liberated to share her passions and interests, within limits, of course, and she judiciously integrates this personal information with information more immediate to the purpose of the tweet.

And Vanderbilt doesn't rely solely on Twitter; the feed is only one part of a larger communication strategy that considers several target audiences in medium-specific ways. You don't see content from other channels and formats dumped into Vandy's Twitter feed. You don't see Twitter used simply as another form of RSS or email push—one-way communication meant only to promote "the brand." This is important, because Twitter followers are tech-savvy; they will intuit when they are getting re-purposed pablum. The goal, then, is to empower real people to say and tweet (or Facebook or blog) authentically human things in situationally appropriate ways.

## Using Typeface as a Guide

To step back and think about the bigger picture, consider just how you determine, decide, or discover your voice and, more generally, your digital persona. How do you do this in a larger organizational context, where others of the organization's many communication imperatives might be in competition? First, recognize that while you can be informal, casual, and more human in social media environments, your writing must still be professional and consistent with the overall ethos of the organization. Second, it might help to think about voice metaphorically by looking at descriptions of various typefaces. Why typefaces? Because typography lacks its own vocabulary or vernacular, individual typefaces are often and even typically described as if they were human beings, or at least as if they have human characteristics. "I like that typeface because it's honest and straightforward, contemporary without being radical. It inspires trust." "What about this typeface here?" "No, it's. . . too frilly. Pretentious." So, choosing (or at least experimenting with) voice might be as simple as choosing (or trying out) a typeface. Consistently communicating in the chosen voice is, of course, another matter. But knowing your voice's hallmarks and characteristics can be an important first step.

To demonstrate this time-saving exercise, let's look at a few typeface families and what we can apply from their descriptions to establishing a writerly voice. The first case study: Gotham (see Figure 4.1). You saw it on President Barack Obama's official campaign website in 2012 as that campaign's primary display typeface. Gotham was first developed for *GQ Magazine*, and it appears on the official Ground Zero memorial in Lower Manhattan.

Here is a description of Gotham as written by its developer, the Hoefler & Frere-Jones type factory in New York (Gotham) City (emphasis added):

> Gotham is that rarest of designs, the new typeface that somehow feels **familiar.** From the lettering that inspired it, Gotham inherited an **honest** tone that's **assertive** but **never imposing, friendly but never folksy, confident but never aloof.** The inclusion of so many original ingredients—a lowercase, italics, and a comprehensive range of weights—enhances these forms' **plainspokenness** with a **welcome sophistication,** and brings a broad range of expressive voices to the Gotham family.

These bolded words describe a voice that would likely be effective for many organizations, companies, and news organizations. As an aggregate description, these words hopefully describe the voice you read and hear in this textbook.

FIGURE 4.1

DONATE     ORGANIZING *for* ACTION

OBAMACARE:
SIGNED. SEALED.
DELIVERING...

For a very different voice, take a look at the description of the typeface Tungsten, which also comes from Hoefler & Frere-Jones:

> Tungsten is a **compact** and **sporty** sans serif that's **disarming** instead of pushy—**not just loud, but persuasive** . . . one that employed **confidence** and **subtlety** instead of just raw testosterone. . . **more Steve McQueen than Steven Seagal** . . . **whiskey highball, not a martini** . . . a tight family of **high-impact** fonts **that doesn't sacrifice wit, versatility, or style.**

Tungsten's descriptors present a very different voice and persona, one that might work well on Twitter or in a single-author blog. The writing found on the BMW USA website could be described with this same paragraph, and that's not surprising given that brand's "personality" as it has been crafted over time.

Here are a few more typefaces, with their descriptions, from Hoefler & Frere-Jones:

- **Forza: succinct** geometries make for an **expressive** type family that's **ardent, disciplined, shrewd, and commanding.** In twelve styles, from the crisp Thin to the powerhouse Black.
- **Vitesse:** engineered for **responsive** handling and a **sporty** ride, Vitesse is a 21st-century slab serif that's **agile, steady, confident, and suave.** Six weights from Thin to Black, each with a matching italic.
- **Whitney:** signage fonts favor **clarity,** editorial ones demand space **efficiency.** Our Whitney family tackles both challenges—and now features extensions into the Greek and Cyrillic alphabets, covering more than 200 languages worldwide.
- **Sentinel:** for everyone who wishes Clarendons had italics, and everyone whose favorite slab serif is shy a few weights: Sentinel is a **fresh** take on a **lovely** and useful **historical** style, a **thoughtful** and complete family that's serviceable for both text and display.
- **Verlag:** from out of the six typefaces originally created for the Guggenheim Museum comes Verlag, a family of 30 sans serifs that brings a **welcome eloquence** to the **can-do sensibility** of pre-war Modernism.

## The FAQ List

Still another exercise helpful for dialing into voice is to develop a frequently asked questions (FAQs) page or list for your organization, company, or entity. To appreciate two very different voices, take a look at some FAQ lists found on the web, one an example of a "just the facts, ma'am" approach, from Google, and another from Rosie O'Donnell that expresses her own brand of saucy insouciance.

## Example 1: Gmail (Excerpted)

1. What makes Gmail different?

   Yes, Gmail is another email service. But it's different in lots of ways, starting with a philosophy: that communications can be made simpler, more efficient, and more fun. When building Gmail, we looked at the frustrations people were having with email, and started with our product from scratch. The result is something that's faster, cleaner, and more intuitive. For example, Gmail automatically groups an email and its replies into a conversation, so you can easily follow the back and forth of an email exchange. It's just like you were chatting. And now, you can chat in Gmail too.

   There are no pop-ups or banner ads in Gmail, and very little spam. With Google search, it's easier for you to find the things that matter to you. And Gmail even has some personality. But don't take our word for it, try it yourself. Think of it as a fresh start.

2. How do I sign up?

   You can get a Gmail account if you're invited by someone who already has one. Or, you can sign up for an account using your mobile phone.

## Example 2: Rosie O'Donnell (Excerpted From rosie.com)

is this the frequently asked questions page?

yep

are you sure?

positive

how do you make the movies?

on a mac

use iphoto slideshow

or imovie

it's ez—u can do it 2

why can't I see the movies?

try this

Mac: www.apple.com/quicktime/download/mac.html

Windows: www.apple.com/quicktime/download/win.html

why and when are comments off?

no rhyme or reason

just my mood

why don't you use punctuation?

just lazy i guess

Your objective in developing a FAQ list is to think for your audience(s), even as that audience, and be able to anticipate their questions and needs. This exercise asks you to speak to these questions in a voice appropriate both for those audiences and for your organization. It is the process that is most important here, not the product. Don't worry too much about design or layout or aesthetics. Focus instead on voice. Should you adopt an authoritative, institutional voice, or a more interpersonal, informal voice? Or something altogether different? Recalling the typeface example, think about the adjectives you would want your interactors to use to describe your voice, or the overall personality of your content and presentation. Here are a few choices: authoritative, friendly, quirky, respectful, upbeat, matter-of-fact, edgy, irreverent, conversational, informative, provocative, trendy.

A third mental exercise for thinking about voice is to essentially role-play. First, as you did with the FAQ exercise, generate a short list of adjectives that describe the voice through which you wish to communicate, and to help you do this, imagine what clothes you might wear to match this voice. This thought exercise asks you to think about level of formality (or informality), tone or attitude (sincere, snarky, ironic, empathetic), and distinctiveness. Next, create a list of the attributes or positive connotations of this desired voice and consider whether this list matches your interactors' expectations. Lastly, role-play by writing a few samples in this desired voice, trying it on much as you would a new suit. To help, here are a few examples from public relations materials generated for a large healthcare provider.

## Example 1: Professional Voice

Attributes: Direct, informative, fact-based, authoritative, journalistic, respectful
  Role to play: Chief executive

> Nearly 75 percent of our employees are voluntary members of the BlueTeam, an organization that helps grow our healthcare business and better serve our community. This section of the BlueTeam website connects members to more information about the organization's activities and with ways to immediately get involved.

## Example 2: Fun and Friendly

Attributes: Witty, quirky (but not snarky), funny, mildly provocative
  Role: Co-worker, colleague, or friend

> Ice cream, flash mobs, and rock bands may not be the first things that come to mind when you think about fundraising, but they are what the BlueTeam is all about. And

you've got to see it to believe it. Come out to Ridge Ferry Park this Saturday to see the BlueTeam in action, and please consider joining us in reaching out to the community. We guarantee you'll have fun, and you can keep the volunteer t-shirt as a memento of a great day spent with new friends.

## Example 3: Direct

Attributes: Simple, matter-of-fact, personable, concise, easy-to-understand
Role: Coach or teacher

We need your help. If you'd like to be a part of something that serves our community and raises money to provide healthcare to those who most need it, please contact me about joining the BlueTeam. It's a volunteer organization that's put a priority on making sure at-risk residents in our community get the healthcare they need, regardless of whether they have insurance or not. We've touched a lot of lives since we formed in 1983, and we'd love to have you as part of the team. Email me, Lisa Simpson, at lsimpson@BlueTeam.org, or call or text me at 706–369–6844. I can help you get up to speed and contributing in no time.

## A Voice Editor?

Voice is so important to "deal of the day" website Groupon that the company has a voice editor, someone responsible for ensuring that all of the posts, offers, and copy are consistent in the voice they express. The company's fast rise had as much to do with how its writers communicate as the site's daily deals. Even a casual interaction with the site will reveal the value Groupon has placed on good, crisp, clean writing in a voice that is human and authentic. Writers deliberately avoid the overt pitch or the ham-fisted ad sell. And they *are* writers, not advertising associates who happen to write or computer nerds who are forced to write as part of their job duties.

Let's take a look at one of Groupon's daily deals, virtually at random—a visit to Pine River Stables. After the initial write-up for Pine River was complete, it went to fact-checking. That's right—Groupon hires editors who check the fact claims in all of their deals. Next, the copy went to the Groupon's voice editor, who makes sure there is consistency in how Groupon communicates across all of its content. It's his job to ensure consistency of voice and that the tone of any one deal is appropriate to the product or service. So Groupon's content creation is a multi-step process.

It is really significant that Groupon does not want to be thought of as a marketer or as an ad agency, recognizing that when shopping and comparing, visitors are prioritizing utility and integrity of the information. Listen to one of Groupon's executives: "People have grown numb to the elements of advertising that pander to their fears and hopes, that insult their intelligence with safe, bland approaches at creativity," he told the *New York Times*. "We're mixing business with art and creating our own voice. About 30 percent of our subscriber base makes over $100,000 a year. They don't need $20 off at a restaurant." Subscribers are responding to Groupon's voice and attitude, which contribute to even a sense of community and affinity. Groupon wants its users to perceive it as an impartial guide to a city or a neighborhood, somewhat in the manner of the local paper's weekend section, and to be thought of as an amenity like a public park or symphony orchestra.

Of course, none of this is an accident. The company has had at its zenith more than 400 writers and editors, or a larger editorial department than the *Chicago Tribune*. The company's quiz and writing test used in the hiring process reveals much of what the company is looking for in staffing this huge editorial team:

Which is the most interesting way to describe a 4,700-pound chandelier?

A.  Blinged out
**B.  *More brilliant than a studious Christmas tree***
C.  A death trap
D.  Really big and shiny

Select the most enticing descriptor for devil's food cupcake.

A.  delicious
B.  sure to go straight to your hips
C.  ooey-gooey
**D.  *velvety***

Choose the most innovative simile.

A.  as pretty as a picture
**B.  *as crafty as a pair of scissors***
C.  as hard as a rock
D.  As strong as an army

What are three synonyms for "customer" that you might use when describing a boating tour?

A lot of web humor is snarky, or based on perceived or imagined superiority, but Groupon avoids any hint of laughing at the well-deserved misfortune of idiots. There is no shock value, no patronizing, but instead plenty of pleasant surprises. Perhaps most importantly of all, the writing has energy; passive voice is simply not allowed at Groupon.

## Taking the Right Tone

Another principle for voice that Groupon models is avoiding sounding like a marketing pitch. Research shows that interactors are turned off by language easily identified as advertising or marketing. These interactors tend to rank sites that use what could be called "marketing-ese" as less credible than sites that do not, which implies that a more objective, balanced tone will be more effective even when the goal is to sell, or market, or persuade. Digital writers have to earn a reader's trust, which can be lost or blocked by exaggerated claims, boastful language, or obvious sales pitches. Marketing slogans and unsupported claims, particularly in content presented as neutral information, are perceived as tacky and unprofessional.

Digital content is accessed and read globally, in all time zones, placing a premium on subject-verb-object sentences that are simple, straightforward, and free of jargon. Watch for technical language and specialized terms, noting where you should provide explanation. Acronyms, colloquial expressions, culturally bound metaphors, and gobbledygook terms will slow down your readers, as will legal-sounding verbiage, slang, and idioms. Rein in phrasal verbs, or those that consist of two or more words, such as pick up, pick away at, let on, and go on about. Translate your copy into several foreign languages and back to English to pick up on the threats to comprehension. This exercise will point to the dangers of ambiguous pronouns, particularly gender-based pronouns. Not all languages handle these in the same ways.

Use a readability checker to find out how complex your writing is and the reading age someone needs to be to understand it. Readability checkers include the Flesch-Kincaid reading ease score, the Gunning Fog score, and the SMOG index (Simple Measure of Gobbledygook). These indices and readability formulas count the variables that have the biggest impact on readers being able to comprehend, including sentence length, number of syllables per word, and number of passive sentences. Most daily newspapers and websites, for example, strive for a sixth-grade education level to hit the broadest possible swath of the reading public. This textbook chapter came out at approximately tenth grade, or the level of London's *The Financial Times* newspaper. All three readability indices are available for free at The Writer (thewriter.com/what-we-think/readability-checker/).

## VISUAL STYLE

We turn now to visual style, or the visual aesthetics of a site or app achieved by strategically using and placing images, colors, shapes, type, and other elements. A successful visual design enhances the non-visual content by engaging users, making navigation and context manifest, building trust, and communicating voice. Regardless of your individual visual choices, you will need to design and display easily discerned, intuitive navigation. Navigation isn't simply a feature of your website or app; it *is* your website or app. Interactors should always have a clear sense of where they are and exactly how where they are relates to the rest of the environment.

For these reasons, writers and editors of digital content need to at least be comfortable and conversant with the literature in visual communication, visual design, and user experience (UX). Content producers should be involved at all levels of web and app design and development to ensure service to message and service to audience. Specifically, editors should be involved to make sure that the site or app:

- Presents clear navigation aids throughout the environment. Visitors should be able to easily return to the homepage or start screen from anywhere else.
- Presents a consistent navigational scheme. Each webpage should communicate through its navigational links how it relates to the site as a whole, and all the site's pages should do this in a uniform way.
- Gives visitors direct access. Provide interactors with what they want in the fewest possible steps. Artist Frank Stella famously said, "What you see is what you see." For digital, what interactors see is what they will use, click, touch, and scroll.
- Directs but does not dictate. Make suggestions and be clear, but allow interactors to access information in the order and to the degree they wish.
- Keeps it simple, salient, (and scannable) (KISS). Navigation should be immediately familiar and logical.

The repetition and consistency advocated in this list will help to orient interactors and reassure them, however imperceptibly, by enabling them to predict the locations of the information they seek. When laying out and mapping your content, when choosing and using graphics and typefaces, and when building your navigational scheme, strive for simplicity and consistency. As with your writerly voice, all of the visual content should be perceived as if it all came out of the same mind. Using the same basic library of elements, from typeface to photography, contributes to this predictability and familiarity. At MiniUSA.com, for example, most pages render a large photo, a paragraph of text, and then it's on to the next page or scroll-down. This layout produces a quickened reading rhythm and a visual style that is relatively quiet and uncluttered, even peaceful. Repetition doesn't have to be boring, as MiniUSA. com shows, and it can give a site a consistent graphic identity that reinforces a distinct sense of "place."

As an analogy, think of your favorite print magazine and note the ways in which the selection and placement of text and images, their sizes and shapes, their abundance or scarcity, determine the rhythm or pace of that information for the reader. The typography and text size, the use of color, how much visual and textual information is on the page—all of this sets a mood and establishes a rhythm. Readers of *Cosmopolitan*, for example, can quickly breeze through the issue, pausing for a few seconds on the larger images, but moving quickly because they are invited or asked to read very little. *New Yorker* readers, however, linger with longer articles and features and relatively few graphics or photos.

## A Case Study: MiniUSA.com

The MiniUSA site (miniusa.com) for the Mini Cooper automobile line just mentioned demonstrates many of the principles we've been discussing. (Unfortunately, MiniUSA would not permit screen grabs to be re-published in any form.) Visit any one page in the site and that page's relationship to the rest of the site is readily discernible thanks to two lines or layers of ubiquitous navigation. The presentation, which details a fairly complex topic (motor cars), is quite easily scanned and navigated. Visual elements simplify navigation and index the content. Perhaps the site's greatest strength is how seamlessly it reconfigures information depending on what is clicked. And the fairly simple, stacked design ensures that mobile and web users see basically the same things.

Keeping the site simple without sacrificing sophistication is its judicious use of graphical content. The few images that are used are sized and positioned for maximum impact. They direct the visitor's attention by interacting with the text and by prioritizing information. Web designers Patrick Lynch and Sarah Horton warn against what they call "clown pants," or too much graphic embellishment and clutter. It's an exquisite metaphor. Imagine the sort of first impression you make walking into a job interview wearing clown pants, oversized red shoes, and a big red nose. You'd certainly make an impression, but not the right one. Similarly, websites and apps that overuse or misuse graphics, features, and special effects can also make a bad first impression by trying too hard to stand out. The MiniUSA site is understated, from its undersized logo to minimalist text to shaded navigational text. In short, *less is more*.

The Gestalt of the MiniUSA site, or effect of the whole as opposed to the simple addition of its component parts, is consistent with the product it is selling. This is significant. The sophistication, unity, and usability of the website support the overall message of the brand, which is also meant to communicate sophistication and style, consistency across its product line, and ease (and fun) of use. The visual style of the site and app, the writing voice of the text, and the personality of the brand all are in harmony. Thus, from the MiniUSA case study, here are three general principles to guide your visual style:

- Make content easy to find. (What you see is what you see.)
- Make it easy to read.
- Make it visually appealing.

## Another Case Study: BBC News

Another, very different website, one devoted to news, also demonstrates these basic principles but in drastically different ways. BBC News (bbc.co.uk) demonstrates effective visual style by arraying its content in layers and by developing an easily perceived, consistent scheme for its navigation, even using a primary color scheme to make sure visitors know where they are. Macro-site navigation is positioned at the top. When a section tab (News, Sports, Weather, etc.) is clicked or touched, the tab enlarges and the color scheme of the page or screen changes to match the tab. In addition, a third line documents the path from the home page or start screen to the individual article or element. An interactor never has to wonder where in the site or app she is, or how to move around to other sections and stories. The site's layers are, therefore, easily discerned:

- top layer: BBC News home;
- second layer: sections of the site;
- third layer: subsections of the selected news section; and
- fourth layer: the selected story.

Once on an interior webpage for a specific article, the interactor can readily see related content on the right side, with macro navigation placed at the top and bottom of the page. Most of the real estate, in fact, is navigational. It is worth noting that BBC articles contain very few hyperlinks; the site prefers instead to group linked content in its subsections or menus. The site begins articles in boldface, for the first paragraph and for its headlines and subheads, in order to slow readers down. Virtually every story also has a video or photo element, adding another important layer of information and another way to experience

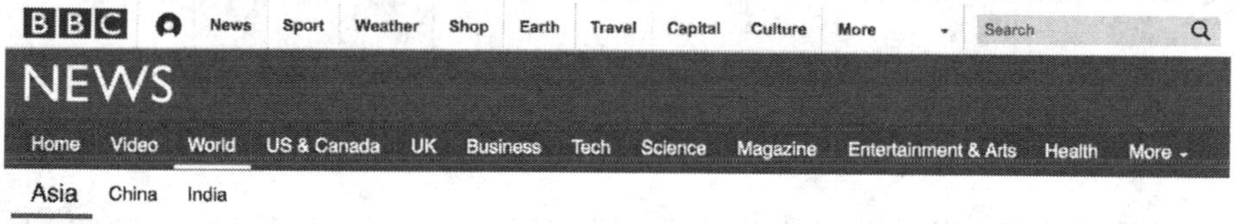

FIGURE 4.2
*BBC.co.uk's top-line navigation*

FIGURE 4.3 *Layered navigation at BBC.co.uk*

**More on this story**

▶ **Protest brings tribes together**
1 September

**What is Standing Rock and why are 1.4m 'checking in' there?**
2 November

**Riot police move in on North Dakota pipeline protesters**
28 October

▣ **Life in the Native American oil protest camps**
2 September

## US & Canada >

**Obama warns of 'crude nationalism'**
🕐 15 November    US & Canada

**US demands electric cars make noise**
🕐 15 November    Technology

the story and to grab attention. These elements are arrayed in clear layers, typically one on top of the text, and then breaking up the article every few paragraphs through to the end. This allows a reader to make decisions about what to read or view and in what sequence, while suggesting a 1–2–3 linear path through the information.

In terms of layout, the BBC News website is a model of simplicity. Using a main center gutter means the content will be easily viewed regardless of monitor or screen size, and it means that content will flow easily into the BBC's mobile app. The BBC's centered layout facilitates the kind of scrolling that mobile apps encourage, avoiding horizontal scrolling or movement that usability studies show interactors do not like. Though advertising does appear, the ads don't scar the page as they do on most newspaper websites, and each is clearly distinguished as commercial content.

## PLANNING THE PAGES

The minimalist elegance of the MiniUSA homepage, the straightforward utility of the BBC News website—these are not accidents. What isn't visible is the planning that went into these sites' development. A site map is the equivalent of having a blueprint before any mortar is mixed. Developing a site map demands that designers think through how pages, sections, and elements are going to be configured and, therefore, what kind of navigational scheme will be needed. The site map in Figure 4.4 shows the sections and subpages of a travel site, visually representing the relationships among and between the elements. From this mapping you can tell what should link to what. After mapping out a site, start storyboarding individual pages (see Figure 4.5). The term "storyboard" comes from a practice in filmmaking in which story conceivers graphically map out the content of the movie—the story—on a series of placards or posters (see Figure 4.6).

These storyboards can be crude visual representations of what will populate individual webpages. They are inexpensive and easy to make, and they take relatively little time to generate, so there is really no reason not to storyboard. The time spent at this stage can save quite a bit of time and headache further into development. Wading into web authoring with a general idea but no storyboards will lead to pages or even entire sites that ultimately prove unworkable or are not scalable. Rookie page designers end up designing themselves into a corner, whereas storyboarding allows them to spot problems and issues relating to unity before they are baked into the site design.

Storyboarding places and positions design elements and content on paper, even if it is merely positioning the major pieces. To the degree possible, both the elements and

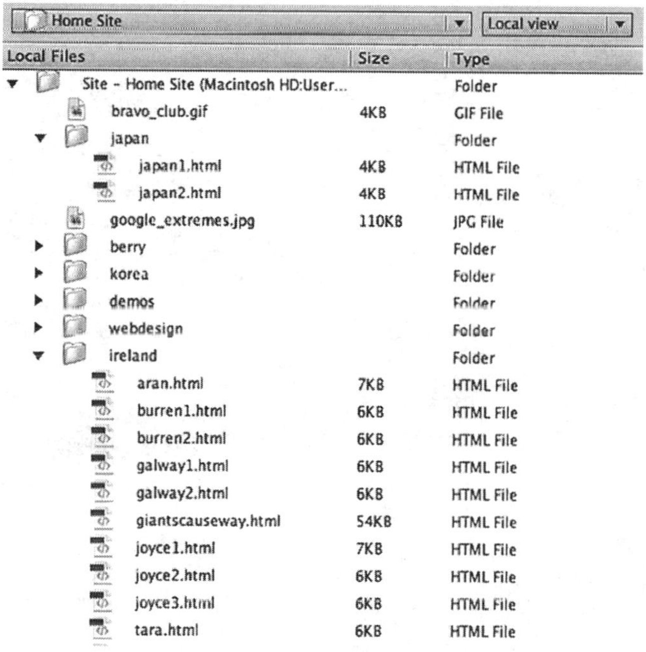

FIGURE 4.4

| Home Site | | Local view |
|---|---|---|
| **Local Files** | **Size** | **Type** |
| ▼ 📁 Site – Home Site (Macintosh HD:User... | | Folder |
| 🖼 bravo_club.gif | 4KB | GIF File |
| ▼ 📁 japan | | Folder |
| 📄 japan1.html | 4KB | HTML File |
| 📄 japan2.html | 4KB | HTML File |
| 🖼 google_extremes.jpg | 110KB | JPG File |
| ▶ 📁 berry | | Folder |
| ▶ 📁 korea | | Folder |
| ▶ 📁 demos | | Folder |
| ▶ 📁 webdesign | | Folder |
| ▼ 📁 ireland | | Folder |
| 📄 aran.html | 7KB | HTML File |
| 📄 burren1.html | 6KB | HTML File |
| 📄 burren2.html | 6KB | HTML File |
| 📄 galway1.html | 6KB | HTML File |
| 📄 galway2.html | 6KB | HTML File |
| 📄 giantscauseway.html | 54KB | HTML File |
| 📄 joyce1.html | 7KB | HTML File |
| 📄 joyce2.html | 6KB | HTML File |
| 📄 joyce3.html | 6KB | HTML File |
| 📄 tara.html | 6KB | HTML File |

**FIGURE 4.5**

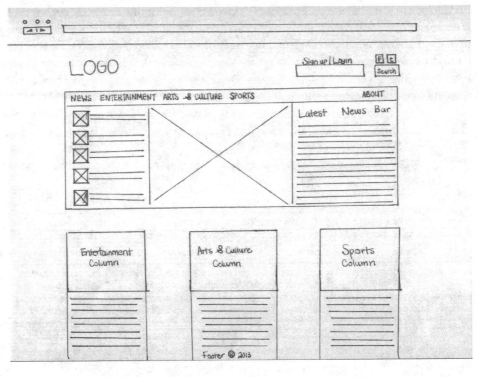

**FIGURE 4.6**

the content should be described, including typeface choices, rough sizes of content elements, and color. Interactors will first see only basic shapes, dominant colors, and big masses of text, discerning foreground first, then midground and background content. Only after this orientation will they see specific elements and text, deciding at that point on what to focus attention. A storyboard helps the designer see what readers will see, and in the same order. To these ends, storyboards should provide:

- a basic hierarchy for headlines and subheads;
- cues for consistency in color and typography; and
- a logical map or path for the reader's eye.

In developing storyboards, a good rule of thumb for internal pages is for content to account for between 50 and 80 percent of a page's design space, leaving no less than 20 percent of the space for navigation. This guideline does not apply to homepages, however, where introducing the navigational scheme might require more space. To prioritize the content, Jakob Nielsen's usability studies suggest a useful method: Evaluate all of the design elements on the page by eliminating them one at a time, if only hypothetically. If the design works better or even the same without the element, leave that element out. *Less is more.*

For websites, but especially for mobile apps where every pixel matters, the key is load time. Navigation needs to be simple, or even non-existent—simply a straight scroll down. Sections on apps are optional. When mapping the app's content, you want to ensure an easy-in/easy-out experience, so think through what people will have to click or touch. Respect their time. Oh, and seamlessly integrate your content with social media and with other apps, because mobile and social media are joined at the hip. Because most apps are essentially firehoses blowing content into the smartphone, the mapping is relatively simple. More important is how the content is organized on the production side, before it enters the hose and then flows into the user's phone.

For the web, your interactors are using any number of laptops, monitor sizes, and computer types, so take a responsive, "lowest common denominator" approach. Assume a low baseline and use resolution-independent pages, which allow designs to adapt to the screen size. Using percentage-based sizing in frames and tables rather than fixed, pixel-based sizes, for example, can be an effective way to accomplish a flexible design format. And responsive web development promises that your content will configure according to the device being used on the user side. Good designers test and re-test their pages on a variety of machines, devices, and browsers to see what works and how.

After you have finished storyboarding for the web, evaluate your plans to make sure each of the following is included on every page:

- **What:** a title, such as the text that appears on the browser's top bar and the text that appears when users add the site to their "favorites" lists. This heading should make absolutely clear what the page is about or includes.

- **Who:** somewhere on each page should be its author's identity and institutional affiliation.
- **When:** when the page was created or last revised.
- **Where:** clear, uniform navigation.

## Visual Rhythm

Visual rhythm is established through the placement and repetition of shapes, colors, typefaces, textures, and spatial relationships, as well as by the sheer number of elements on any one screen or webpage. If quick and lively is the rhythm you seek, you might use lots of small, closely placed shapes. If, however, solemn and dignified is a more appropriate rhythm, you will likely use larger, more solitary shapes. Both MiniUSA and the BBC achieve a very moderate pacing of information, doing so with relatively large content blocks and plenty of white space, which creates visual rest.

To appreciate how different the rhythm of presentation can vary, imagine stopping at a newsstand at the airport and thumbing through a few magazines: *Wired, Cosmopolitan, Transworld Skateboarding, Southern Bride, PC Gamer, Rolling Stone, The Economist*. If you were to think about the layouts and visual presentations in terms of pacing of information, how would you compare these publications? How "fast" or "slow" is any one of these titles? How much information is placed on the pages? What libraries of elements does the publication use? What kinds of layouts are common? What is consistent throughout the publication? The skateboarding magazine crowds its pages with graphical content of wildly varying shapes, sizes, and colors. The rhythm is super fast, upbeat, perhaps even frenetic. *The Economist*, by contrast, is mostly text, with minimal photography decorating the pages. The tone is sober, the pace deliberate.

Choosing or determining visual rhythm is as simple as plotting content out on a grid. Grid-based design and layouts ensure that *all* of the space is considered, including white space and margin areas. Text, photos, illustrations, and logos all can be placed on a grid, which is an analogue of the pixel-based environments for which you are planning and designing. There are a lot of grids from which to choose (see Figure 4.7). Determining which to use could be as simple as finding a website or app with the basic rhythm you want to create, then plotting what you see on that site or app onto a grid. Remove the content, and that grid can serve as the starting point for one of your own.

For a homepage, Figure 4.8 provides an example of plotting basic content layout on a grid.

More than ever before, digital content is something we carry in our pockets and handbags. Thus, there has been a shift in digital design to mobile-first approaches, or designs that think first about how content will flow into smartphones. This approach calls on layouts to be centered, modular, and stackable, allowing a series of largely

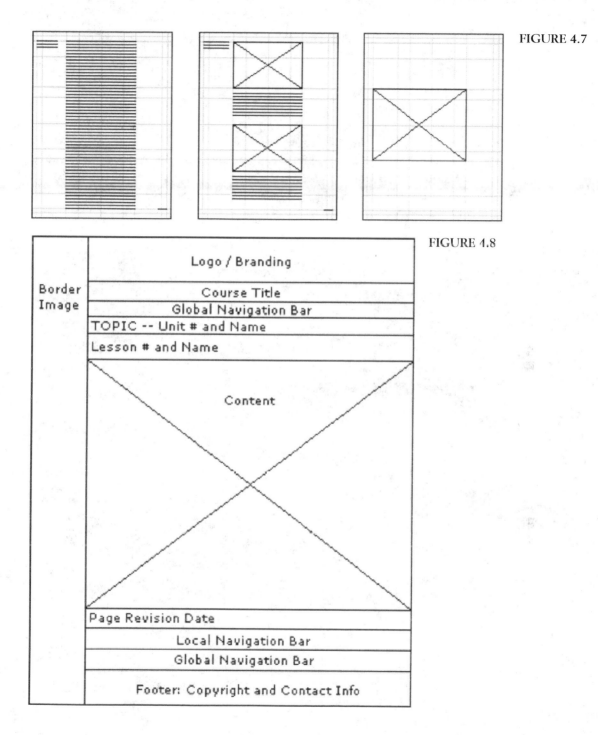

FIGURE 4.7

FIGURE 4.8

squares and rectangles to stack on top of one another down a center gutter or smart-phone scroll. Enabling content to configure in smartphones, desktops and laptops, and e-readers and tablets is "responsive design," an approach that relies on media queries to target specific devices and viewport sizes. A site or server communicates with a user's device to determine how to deliver the content.

Mobile-first requires writing CSS code for mobile devices, then using media queries to selectively serve up additional styling as the viewport size increases. Mobile-first approaches have simplified design and layout, because the grids for these center gutter alignments are so much more basic compared to those for exclusively desktop and the web. The difficulty now is in writing the code to translate these more basic layouts into working sites across browsers, machines, devices, and screens.

**FIGURE 4.9**
*A navigational section on the City of New York's mobile-first website, www1.nyc.gov/*

**FIGURE 4.10**
*Smartphone-ready content at nyc.gov*

One of the simpler layout patterns for any medium is the "Z" path that guides the human eye through most text documents from the upper left to the right, then down diagonally to the left, then a sweep along the bottom to the big finish at right. Most print advertisements depend on this ingrained pattern of reading and viewing. Starting this path is a focal point, an obvious point of entry. Most print ads clearly use the Z path that Western readers' brains instinctively follow. We begin in the upper left of an ad, sweep right, then down diagonally to the left hand corner or quadrant, then left to right, where the brand or logo usually awaits. Print ads also typically use the inverted pyramid style, delivering the main message with a dominant visual and headline.

## COLLABORATIVE TOOLS

Web and app development are not solo events. You will work in teams; you will collaborate. To do some of the activities described in this chapter, a collaboration or software can mitigate the barriers of space and time that can separate individual team members. A few examples of these tools, most of which live or reside in the cloud, are:

- Trello (trello.com): This project management software uses message boards, shared lists, and Trello "cards" to log assignments, add names of team members who need to know about a task, and enter due dates. Each of the cards can contain embedded photos, documents, tweets—anything that's relevant to the task. Other project collaboration software like Trello include Evernote, Asana, and Wrike. Google Hangouts also provides same of the same functionality.
- Diigo (addons.mozilla.org/en-US/firefox/addon/diigo-web-highlighter-and-stic/): Team members can make notes on webpages and let others see them with this Firefox plug-in. Add a Diigo toolbar to your browser, then sign up for a free account at Diigo.com. After that, use the "Highlight and Comment" function in the toolbar to annotate a webpage. When you are done and want to let someone else see what you've marked, use the "Get Annotated Link" option under the "Send" button to get a URL that you can send to others.
- PDF Download (addons.mozilla.org/en-US/firefox/addon/pdf-download/): Also a Firefox plug-in, this one allows you to save any webpage as a PDF.
- Screengrab (addons.mozilla.org/en-US/firefox/addon/screengrab/): This Firefox plug-in lets you save a webpage, or a portion of one, as an image.
- FireShot (addons.mozilla.org/en-US/firefox/addon/fireshot/): A Firefox plug-in that allows you to take a screenshot of a web page, then annotate it with a set of easy-to-use tools, and save it as an image. This plug-in is useful for illustrating changes you want to make.

- Slideshare (slideshare.net/): This tool works like YouTube for slideshows. Sign up for a free account and upload a slideshow file. You will then be able to send others a link so they can see the slideshow without having to worry about bulky email attachments. You can also embed the uploaded slideshow on a page on your website.
- Google Docs (google.com/intl/en/docs/about): A free web-based application in which documents and spreadsheets can be created, edited, and stored online. Files can be accessed from any computer with an Internet connection and a browser, and Google Docs is compatible with most presentation software and word processor applications.
- Dropbox (dropbox.com): A file hosting service that offers cloud storage, file synchronization, personal cloud, and client software.

FIGURE 4.11 *Trello's project collaboration software*

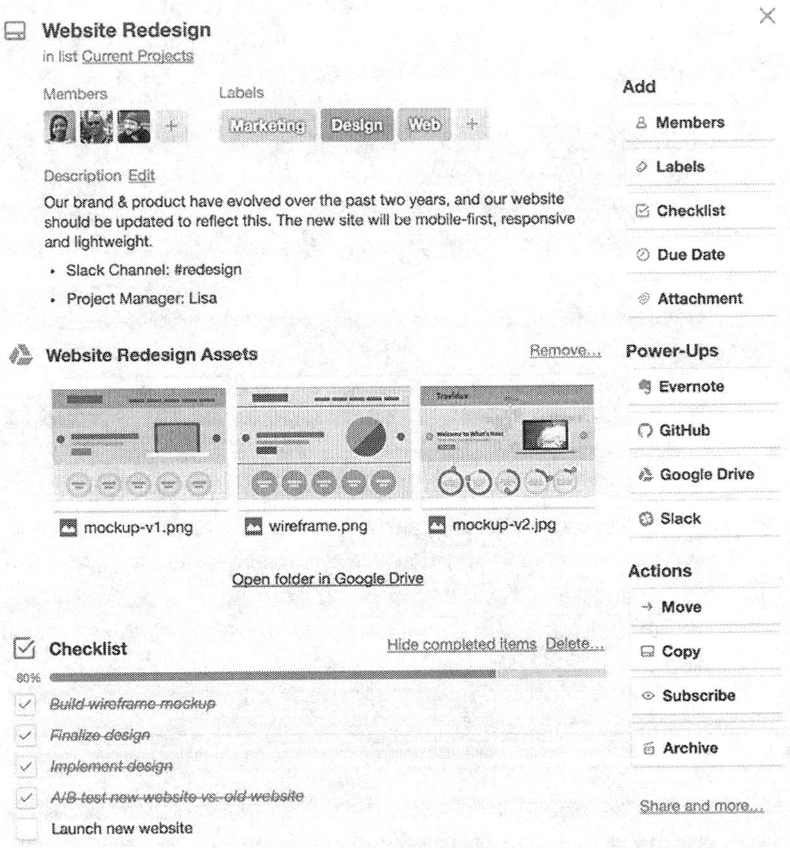

114

## USABILITY

You identified your core mission or purpose and stuck to it. You were careful planning, mapping, and storyboarding your content. You determined your voice. Now, it's time to think about making sure everything works. Do the graphics appear in the right places and render in correct ways? Do all of the hyperlinks work? Are there formatting or layout issues? Usability expert Steve Krug advises that even a little usability research is better than none, so asking even one other person to take a look at your pages or app and read your content can generate valuable feedback to inform updates and changes.

A real-world example: When undergraduate students of a web design class at Berry College in Mount Berry, GA, were asked to develop a site for the local Habitat for Humanity chapter, the class first met with the executive director to discuss his goals for the organization's site. To guide that discussion, the class prepared a list of questions:

1. What do you definitely want the site (or app) to do?
2. What do you definitely want the site *not* to do?
3. When are you hoping to have a working site up and active? What deadline do you suggest?
4. Who will host the site (or maintain the app)? How will we publish the site to the web?
5. What graphics or art do you have already? What art do you want to use (logos, photos, charts)? What art do you know you do not want to use, or cannot use?
6. What content do you have or are you planning to get?
7. Of these elements, what will be frequently and/or routinely updated?
8. Which parts of the site will be temporary, such as an event of the month, and what will be permanent (or at least long lived)?
9. What are your expectations for this site? What are your expectations for our involvement in developing the site, both now and longer term?
10. How complex does the site need to be? What functionality do you want it to have (e.g., enabling supporters to donate online, to volunteer online, etc.)?
11. What tone, mood, or attitude should the site communicate? What tone, mood, or attitude should be avoided?
12. Do you have examples of sites you like, sites similar in approach or philosophy to what you want?
13. What are your plans for usability testing?
14. Who is going to maintain and update the site?

Habitat wanted site visitors to be able to "get it" without having to ask, "Where do I start?" or "Can I click on that?" Good website usability design means that visitors will not have to ask:

- Where am I?
- Where should I begin?
- Where did they put _____?
- What's most important here?
- Why did they call it that?

Interactors do not always choose the BEST path on the page to take them where they want to go. It is up to you to make the pathways to their destinations immediately clear. With these priorities in mind, the Habitat site design team's goals included:

- creating a clear visual hierarchy on each page;
- taking advantage of conventions;
- breaking up pages into clearly defined areas;
- making it obvious what is and what is not clickable on each page; and
- minimizing noise and distractions.

In addition, the development team sought to make sure that the elements users see on the page, including search boxes, links, and nav (navigation) buttons, accurately convey their importance and utility. The more important the content, the more prominently it was placed.

Krug points out that navigation is not just a feature of a website, it *is* the website. The top priority, then, is clear, predictable, uniform, ubiquitous navigation. There are two types of users: hunters and gatherers. The search-dominant hunters ask, "Where's the search box?" The information gatherers instead ask, "Where are the links?" Layout and design should help both types of users get from one place to another and orient them within at all times. They should signal what is available, and they should transparently reveal the content. Think of the kinds of maps you typically find in shopping malls or subway terminals, those that clearly show "YOU ARE HERE." Implicitly, these maps also communicate how big a place is and they situate you in relationship to everything else within that place or space.

A good model of a clear navigation scheme can be found at MLB.com, the website for Major League Baseball. Finding a box score for the latest Yankees game, for example, is intuitive and simple, and the path to do it is clearly displayed: Home >> Scores >> Yankees >> Box. The reader knows precisely where he or she is in the site in relation to the rest of the site and is able to return to any previous part of the site with just one click.

So, at a glance, a homepage should be able to quickly and clearly:

- establish identity and mission;
- show site hierarchy;
- show where to start;

- show what's there;
- indicate shortcuts to main, most desired pages and sections;
- convey the big picture; and
- avoid clutter.

Several institutions and organizations have conducted comprehensive usability studies that inform other, more local usability evaluations. The National Cancer Institute (NCI), for example, published its *Usability Guidelines* (usability.gov), a site describing what the institute has learned about its own usability, which is quite a bit, and that covers topics such as:

- What Is Usability?
- Why Is It Important?
- How Much Does It Cost?
- Can Usability Be Measured?

The NCI offers research-based guidelines for page layout, navigation, links, text appearance, graphic design, accessibility, and search, and it provides a toolbox of templates and examples.

FIGURE 4.12

# CHAPTER ACTIVITIES

1. Imagine that you have been commissioned to choose or create a typeface for a 2017 update and adaptation of the Jane Austen novel, *Emma*. Alexander McCall Smith re-wrote the classic Austen novel as part of a larger effort to revise and refresh Austen's many classics. It's your job to choose the typeface for the new book's cover. Your choice should communicate both classicism *and* modernity. Include with your choice a few paragraphs explaining and justifying your selection. Why did you choose *that* typeface rather than another? Present the title "Emma" in the typeface you choose, so we can see it, as well as an A-to-Z, 0–9 snapshot of your typeface choice. This is an exercise that uses typeface to dial into voice and even tone.

2. You are running for mayor of your city. Choose a typeface for your political campaign signage, bumper stickers, website, and app. The typeface needs to reflect the essence of what you represent and, if elected, what values you will adhere to as mayor of your community. Thus, it needs to communicate, if only implicitly, your core values and probably connote energy, relevance, and vitality, as well. Include your campaign tagline in the typeface you choose, and include a couple of paragraphs about why that's THE typeface for you as candidate. This also will help you to dial into your distinctive voice.

3. Choose a website you visit regularly, one where you read a lot of the content. Imagine that you have been hired as the site's new editor-in-chief. Make specific recommendations to improve the presentation of content on the site, integrating and referencing the chapter as much as possible.

   - Is the voice effective?
   - Is the tone appropriate?
   - What elements or features promote use of the site?
   - How are graphics and visuals incorporated, and do they encourage or discourage use?
   - How do they do this?
   - How much thought was given to navigation throughout the site?
   - Are the elements—graphical, navigational, and metaphorical—consistently applied throughout the site?
   - Is the tone or rhythm of the site consistent throughout?
   - Do these dimensions match the audience(s) for the site?

Here is a categorical checklist of site dimensions to critique:

   - navigation;
   - page layouts (balance/contrast/unity);
   - consistency;
   - tone and voice;
   - writing quality;
   - site organization.

Length of your critique: approximately 750–1,000 words.

4. This next assignment is also presented as an activity in this chapter. Create an interactive FAQ help page for some entity (publication, company, or organization), preferably one with which you have some connection. Your frequently asked questions section should anticipate common problems and questions that users, customers, or clients might have about that publication, organization, or company.

    The primary objective in this assignment is to think for your audience(s) and anticipate their questions and needs. It is the process that is most important, not the final product. So, don't spend too much time on the design or layout or aesthetics of the list. As the chapter described, this assignment is also useful in determining or deciding the appropriate voice for the entity, or for you writing for that entity. Before working on your list, go online and read some FAQ lists for organizations similar to that for which you are writing.

5. Using a grid-based layout, deconstruct a favorite website or app by laying out on the grid its major elements. One way to learn good design is to reverse-engineer examples of good designs.

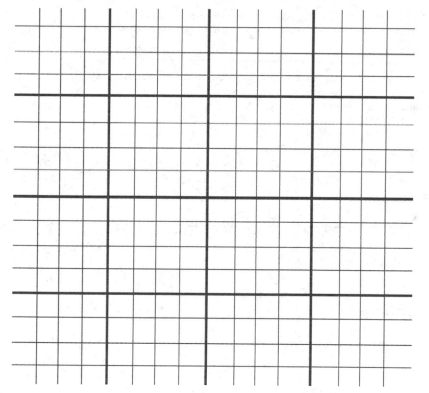

FIGURE 4.13 *A layout grid*

You don't have to deconstruct an entire site or app, just a representative page or two, including perhaps a sectional front page. In choosing a mobile app, a search of "best-selling mobile apps" would reveal some good possibilities. Apple charts top-selling apps across multiple categories at www.apple.com/itunes/charts/.

## Digital Resources

**BBC News (bbc.com/news/)**

**MiniUSA (miniusa.com)**

**The National Cancer Institute (NCI) Usability Guidelines (usability.gov)**

**The Writer (thewriter.com/what-we-think/readability-checker/)**
For readability indices.

**Collaborative Tools:**

- **Diigo (addons.mozilla.org/en-US/firefox/addon/diigo-web-highlighter-and-stic/)**
- **Dropbox (dropbox.com)**
- **FireShot (addons.mozilla.org/en-US/firefox/addon/fireshot/)**
- **Google Docs (google.com/intl/en/docs/about)**
- **PDF Download (addons.mozilla.org/en-US/firefox/addon/pdf-download/)**
- **Screengrab (addons.mozilla.org/en-US/firefox/addon/screengrab/)**
- **Slideshare (slideshare.net/)**
- **Trello (trello.com)**

## BIBLIOGRAPHY

Barr, Chris, *The Yahoo! Style Guide* (New York, NY: St. Martin's Griffin, 2010).

Dowling, Carolyn, *Writing and Learning with Computers* (Camberwell, Australia: Acer Press, 1999).

Fagerjord, Anders, "Rhetorical Convergence: Studying Web Media," in *Digital Media Revisited*, Gunnar Liestol, Andrew Morrison, and Terje Rasmussen (eds.) (Cambridge, MA: MIT Press, 2003): 293–326.

Glick, Jeff, "When, How to Tell Stories with Text, Multimedia," *Poynter Institute* (2004), available: http://poynterextra.org/eyetrack2004/jeffglick.htm2.

Krug, Steve, *Don't Make Me Think* (Upper Saddle River, NJ: New Riders Press, 2000).

Lynch, Patrick and Horton, Sarah, *Web Style Guide 2* (New Haven, CT: Yale University Press, 2001).

McAlpine, Rachel, *Web Word Wizardry: A Guide to Writing for the Web and Intranet* (Berkeley, CA: Ten Speed Press, 2001).

Morkes, John and Nielsen, Jakob, "Concise, SCANNABLE, and Objective: How to Write for the Web," (1997), available: www.useit.com/papers/webwriting/writing.html.

Nielsen, Jakob, *Designing Web Usability* (Indianapolis, IN: New Riders, 2000).

Nielsen, Jakob, "How Users Read on the Web," (1997), available: www.useit.com/alertbox/9710a. html.

Parker, Roger C., *Guide to Web Content and Design* (New York, NY: MIS Press, 1997).

Powell, Thomas A., *Web Design: The Complete Reference* (New York, NY: McGraw Hill, 2000).

Streitfeld, David, "Funny or Die: Groupon's Fate Hinges on Words," *The New York Times* (May 28 2011), available: www.nytimes.com/2011/05/29/business/29groupon.html.

Tedesco, Anthony, "Adapt Your Writing to the Web," *The Writer* 114, no. 5 (May 2001): 16.

Wallace, Nathan, "Web Writing for Many Interest Levels," (1999), available: www.e-gineer.com/articles/web-writing-for-many-interest-levels.html.

# Establishing and Communicating Credibility in Digital Spaces

*A lie can travel half way around the world while the truth is putting on its shoes.*

—Charles Spurgeon

*Whoever is careless with the truth in small matters cannot be trusted with important matters.*

—Albert Einstein

*Love all, trust a few, do wrong to none.*
—William Shakespeare, *All's Well That Ends Well*

## INTRODUCTION

Communication professionals want to be perceived by their digital audiences as trustworthy. This chapter looks at how credibility is established and communicated in digital spaces, both subjectively and objectively, and how these activities differ from those for traditional media. At the heart of these differences is the fact that interactors do not merely read or view; as the term implies, they interact with the content, because digital media, in sharp contrast with print and broadcast media, rely on spatial relationships. Most digital spaces, and certainly the good ones, facilitate and encourage interaction and movement. Behind the scenes, it is hypertext, JavaScript, CSS, and myriad other coding languages that enable non-hierarchical, non-linear presentations, such that interacting in these digital spaces is far more like entering a sort of matrix and moving around within it than it is like reading a book or watching TV.

## THE MORE THINGS CHANGE, THE MORE THINGS . . .

Though digital media have wrought fundamental changes throughout the communication and media industries, some things have remained constant. We learned how to structure information in older media, primarily books, so it shouldn't surprise us that newer media forms borrow heavily from those that came before. The fact that writing appears on a computer screen or smartphone rather than a bound book does not diminish, then, the values of clarity, concision, accuracy, and completeness. Good writing is valued in digital forms just as it has been in other, older media. It may seem like there is more poor writing because there is so much information being posted, published, and shared, when anyone with a data plan can tweet out to hundreds, even thousands of followers. But Sturgeon's law holds: 90 percent of everything is still crap, including writing, whether it's published in a book, posted to a Facebook wall, or tweeted. What has been produced for all media across time largely has been mediocre or worse. Rudyard Kipling saw this in 1890, writing in *The Light That Failed*, "Four-fifths of everybody's work must be bad." Because of the Internet and the ubiquity of mobile connectivity, there is exponentially so much more information, so of course there is more mediocrity, more gunk, spam, junk, and crap. Quality still counts, and it is still most rare.

Also unchanged by newer media forms are many of the important roles of the writer:

- **Communicator of a message:** How much "trending" content fails to communicate anything of value? How much "click-bait" is there only to titillate before evaporating into the Internet ether forever? The skilled digital writer conveys a message in provocative, clever, amusing, interesting, or profound ways regardless of the medium. This writer succeeds by making wise rhetorical choices and employing medium-specific tools and techniques.
- **Organizer of information:** With so much information, never have the roles of organizer, guide, and curator been more important. Decisions must be made about what is most important and, in leaving information out, what is not important enough. Good digital writers help readers to prioritize and create order out of what often seems like overwhelming tides of information rolling up on our shores, all of it competing for our attention.
- **Interpreter:** The message has to be right for the medium, and the medium has to be right for the message. Digital writers tailor messages to leverage

a medium's strengths and mitigate its weaknesses, realizing that there are particular kinds of freight each medium is especially suited to carry. Try debating politics using only church bells, smoke signals, or even tweets. It can't meaningfully be done. Imagine a 25,000-word blog post on, say, the contributions to art and culture by any one of the many Kardashians?

## THINKING IN TERMS OF SPACE

The matrix-like spatial environments that digital media allow contrast dramatically with the fairly predictable paths of readership for print media. Think about the words we use to describe information and how to get to it online, words such as *hypertext*, *hyperlinks*, and *cyberspace*. These are spatial terms that connote movement. On the web, we *visit* a site and *navigate* in and through it. To get where we want to go, we Google or key in an address, a *Universal Resource Locator* (URL). These are ideas and terms that do not apply to flat, two-dimensional printed pages. With smartphones, the shift is just as fundamental, such that these mobile devices have become nearly a part of us. When a person receives a text, tweet, "like," or news blast, his or her leg or butt actually vibrates—a physical sensation to a digital "event." In terms of human-to-media relationships, this is unprecedented. The news has never been so intimate. Digital natives often sleep with their phones mere inches from their heads, afraid as they are to miss even one text or phone call.

Thus, we should consider ourselves architects of spaces and places, as authors and guides for interactors navigating through these networked, socially mediated spaces. The luxury, or perhaps simplicity, of working with linear, sequential documents is a thing of the printed past. In meaningfully engineering these networked spaces and editing within them, we are asked to anticipate the needs and wants of interactors and the many paths they may want to pursue. This places a premium on providing consistent, clear navigation throughout their journey, navigation that minimizes if not eliminates disorientation. It also rewards those who create "experiences." Millennials, in contrast to their parents, aren't interested in accumulating "stuff"—material goods—as much as they are seeking experiences and the digital esteem those experiences elicit in their social networks.

To dramatize the challenge that spatial orientation requires, imagine having a job interview in Chicago, somewhere, say, in the John Hancock Center downtown. Your cab deposits you at the massive building's front doors. After walking into the spacious lobby, you wonder how to find your way to the interview. You ask the security detail at the front desk, or you consult a posted directory. With the floor and office designation now in hand, you head for the bank of elevators. Because the path you took was predictable, well marked, and basically linear, you will have a pretty good sense of how to get back to the lobby and back out onto Michigan Avenue once the interview has concluded.

Now imagine receiving a *Matrix* movie-like phone call that teleports you from wherever you are sitting at this moment, immediately and directly, to that same office suite in one of Chicago's tallest skyscrapers. This type of instant transportation would likely disorient you, and you might find it difficult to figure out just where you had ended up. Even identifying that it is Chicago would be a challenge, despite the floor-to-ceiling skyline-view windows. This analogy is meant to dramatize the ways that interactors flit about on the web, using search findings to navigate deep within a website, ignoring or simply unaware of or uninterested in that site's homepage. This direct flight is facilitated by, among other things, tweeted (and re-tweeted) hyperlinks, search findings, Facebook "likes," and QR codes. Lost with this ease of movement is knowledge of how the site's other pages and content interconnect, as the floors and offices of a skyscraper might, and the comfort or ease of mind that comes with that holistic knowledge and context. So it is up to us as engineers of digital spaces to provide and readily communicate the navigation and something of the contextual relationships of these spaces to minimize disorientation and discomfort.

For the web and for mobile, this means that each page, even each article or content block, must stand on its own as a self-contained entity or island that does not require readers to navigate to it by following any sort of prescribed path. At the same time, good navigation communicates that in fact the page is just one part of a networked world of similar or related content, a world that facilitates and even encourages teleporting to lots of other interesting spaces and places. One of the downsides of these shifts is that articles compete against each other almost irrespective of their source or origin or brand, allowing derivative, recycled content and even the utterly false and fictional to compete against traditionally trusted news sources on an article-by-article basis. The result, not surprisingly, has been a sort of informational chaos or circus, one in which the metaphorically "shiny" content gets the immediate, albeit evanescent attention.

Digital media have also changed interactors' notions of timeliness; they demand immediacy. With their easy access to information, Millennials have grown up living each natural disaster, shooting, and terror attack in real time. Gone are traditional conceptions of workflow and production cycles, and in their place is a 24/7 orientation to updating and refreshing content slipped into a never-ending stream. Because information can be disseminated instantly, it *is* published and shared instantly, and to audiences that now expect such immediacy, even at the expense of accuracy and context. Loading fast; providing a clean, easy-to-scan interface; and making every pixel count are the demands on app designers. And gone as a reliable or useful metric is how much time an interactor spends per visit, page view, or session.

## READABILITY AND "SCAN-ABILITY"

Research shows that attention spans have diminished and that people interacting with digital media aren't, in fact, *reading* as that activity has been traditionally understood. Interactors on the web sit with hand on mouse scanning text on a monitor that is an uncomfortable distance away, inspiring Dale Dougherty's "three-second rule": a website has approximately three seconds to download properly, present itself, and engage the interactor. A similarly punishing rule might apply to apps, and perhaps especially so because smartphone users often are on the move, waiting in line at the movie theater, or simply accustomed to checking their devices hundreds of times per day. A study by Deloitte found that Americans check their smartphones an *average* of 74 times per day. These users demand an easy-in, easy-out experience. Try the rule for yourself: Count off three seconds while waiting for, say, CNN.com to load all of its media. One... two... three... Time's up. And while the desktop has diminished in importance, it is still dominant in the workplace. And CRT (cathode ray tube) computer monitor screens make reading physiologically uncomfortable, especially compared to the tactilely pleasant experience of reading ink on paper. So interactors *scan* rather than read word for word for word. And scanners need cues and clues, signposts and highlights. They need expertly written headlines, deckheads, subheads, hyperlinks, lists, and variation in typeface.

The implications for digital writers should be obvious: Get to the point and respect your interactors' time. Brevity is valued in and by all media, but it has to be a top priority for digital spaces. Rachel McAlpine, author of *Web Word Wizardry: A Guide to Writing for the Web and Intranet*, advised that to successfully write for the web, "You need to switch from 'think paper' mode to 'think Web' mode," because web users are "monsters of impatience." The mouse button and the sheer abundance of apps put your content one click or scroll away from oblivion. Our writing must immediately engage. With the ubiquity of social media, that engagement must be integrated with social, mobile media.

Consider a few more of the definitional differences between digital and analog media. Unlike ink on paper, the 0s and 1s of computer code are ephemeral and manipulable. Digital media, therefore, can accommodate both the shopper (or surfer) and the hunter. And though electronic ink, tablets, and e-readers have remarkably improved the digital reading experience, it is still uncommon for people to curl up next to the fire with their computers or laptops to luxuriate in the prose of, say, Sir Arthur Conan Doyle and *The Complete Adventures of Sherlock Holmes*. The typical interactor, whether on the web or on her smartphone, typically has an immediate need for specific information. With the exception of perhaps reference books, only digital media facilitate such specificity and search. Thus the boom in micropublishing, niche publishing, and narrowcasting—content for small, targeted audiences. The spectacular growth in blogging, apps, music, and video channels attests to these game-changing phenomena. It also implies that whatever we are creating, it needs to integrate seamlessly with social media. Mobile media and social media are joined at the hip, or at least they should be. According to Pew, fully seven-in-ten of those ages 18–29 either prefer or only use mobile for getting their digital news, compared with 53 percent of those 30–49, 29 percent of those 50–64, and just 16 percent of those 65 and over. According to this same comprehensive survey, about two-thirds (63 percent) of Americans say family and friends are an important way they get news, whether online or offline; 10 percent see them as the most important, and that percentage is rising.

## CREDIBILITY

All three of the important roles of the writer described earlier (communicator, organizer, and interpreter) rely upon the writer's and the digital space's credibility. The ways in which credibility is established, maintained, and measured in digital spaces are different than those for traditional media. And as our consumption habits change, so do the ways we evaluate information. Relative to determining source credibility in traditional media, doing so with digital media has only become more problematic. Misinformation, unverified reports, and pure gossip and rumor are much more prevalent in this socially mediated age. A majority of Millennials don't believe *any* news is accurate. Thus, credibility can be a valuable differentiator.

While credibility as a subject of study dates back to the ancient Greeks, systematic empirical research began as recently as the 1930s and 1940s. People became interested during wartime in how best to persuade, in particular how to develop propaganda for the new medium of radio. More recently, scholars have been interested in learning about the relationship between perceptions of diminishing credibility among newspapers and what has been a long-term decline in newspaper readership.

Since the 1930s, there has been no widely agreed upon definition of credibility, as journalism researcher Philip Meyer pointed out. Meyer surveyed credibility research in mass communication and developed an index for the two key dimensions of credibility that he identified in the literature: "believability" and "community affiliation." Believability is based on the notion that news media present accurate, unbiased, and complete accounts of news and events. Community affiliation encompasses a news organization's efforts to unify and lead the community it serves, efforts that require some degree of harmony in outlook or perspective. Meyer's two dimensions are important in suggesting that the public can disapprove of the way in which a media outlet or source covers a story but still believe what it says.

The rise of the Internet in the late 1990s and early 2000s fueled interest in research on credibility in and for online media. Surprisingly, many if not most of these newer studies suggest that those who do look online for their information deem what they find as more credible than that found in traditional print media. Increasing numbers of Americans access digital spaces and places for their information, and studies examining web credibility show that the more people go online, the more credible they evaluate the information they find there. In fact, the amount of time a person spends online might be the single best predictor of that person's perceptions of credibility for an online medium. The more users rely on blogs, for example, the higher their assessments of credibility, in spite of the fact that bias (or perspective or point of view) is recognized and even seen as a virtue by blog readers. Blog readers are "seeking out information to support their views and are likely to consider information they receive from blogs as highly credible," researchers Thomas J. Johnson and Barbara K. Kaye found.

## BIAS

Johnson's and Kaye's finding is worth further consideration. Research has shown that the credibility of blogs has much to do with bias—that is, the inclusion of the writer's perspective in the writing. The term has been pejoratively defined as "intentional prejudice," or even as discrimination. More to the point here is a definition that assumes the bias is implicit, perhaps even subconscious—a bias a person didn't invite or ask to have. Removing this bias, both real and perceived, has been a priority for most legitimate traditional news media, which cite journalistic objectivity as an essential goal. As one blogging journalist put it, "Veteran journalists know that the objectivity ethos is the 'big lie' of their profession. . . journalists are beholden to various points to view" (Zachary, 2006). Geneva Overholser, professor at the University of Missouri School of Journalism, told the authors of *blog!* that the year 2005 would be remembered as the year "when it finally became unmistakably clear that 'objectivity' has outlived its usefulness as an ethical touchstone of journalism" (cited in Kline and Burstein, 2005, p. 9). Acknowledging bias, but not necessarily rooting it out, then, is an important new dimension to credibility of information in a digital age.

## IDENTIFICATION

Identification is a foundational communication concept that helps us to understand how blogs, Twitter feeds, YouTube channels, and other single-author digital media communicate trust and engender loyalty among their interactors. While theorists since Aristotle have focused on the role of persuasion in public discourse, Kenneth Burke called into question traditional notions of persuasion by introducing a theory grounded in identification. "You persuade a man insofar as you talk his language by speech, gesture, tonality, order, image, attitude, idea, identifying your way with his," Burke explained (cited in Foss et al., 1986, p. 158). Humans are individuals, according to Burke, but when their interests are joined, or one perceives or is persuaded to believe that they are joined, then identification occurs. This explanation is consistent at the individual level with Meyer's notion of community affiliation. Burke wrote that one is "both joined and separate, at once a distinct substance and consubstantial with another," with consubstantiality rooted in the notion of a perceived "sameness" (Foss et al., p. 158). Burke, therefore, provides insight into the apparent resurgence of authenticity and genuineness as significant factors in establishing and communicating credibility in digital media.

Blogs, Facebook, Twitter, Reddit, Instagram, Pinterest, and Snapchat, to name just a few, are proving to be powerful tools in building audience, even community, by offering more expression by individual voices, with all their flaws and because of their personality. The "everyday person" voice of many blogs, for example, encourages identification in ways the dispassionate, clinical, filtered voices of traditional media cannot. These voices provide a sense of presence with the reader in a way that traditional media's detachment, which is, in part, the result of allegiance to professional norms such as objectivity, actually prevents. This is doubly important with interactive media because for these media the roles of sender and receiver are blurred, even interchangeable, making distinctions between the two less meaningful. Importantly for digital writers, this blurring and blending is being welcomed by online and mobile audiences.

## TRANSPARENCY

Digital writers should aim to adopt more of the practices and techniques of good bloggers, who have showed how valuable committing to and communicating transparency can be. Blog readers have time and time again responded to authors' willingness to disclose their personal politics and biases, their readiness to acknowledge error and to incorporate or consider new information, and the sharing of and pointing to original source materials used to write the blog posts.

As early as 2005, *The New York Times* seemed to awaken to the need for greater transparency in its attempts to transition to digital media from print. Then-*Times* executive editor Bill Keller acknowledged that his newspaper could no longer argue "reflexively that our work speaks for itself. . . We need to be more assertive about explaining ourselves—our decisions, our methods, our values, how we operate" (*The New York Times*, July 4, 2005, C1, C4). Echoing Keller's sentiments several weeks later, Richard Sambrook, director of the BBC World Service and Global News Division, said, "We don't own the news anymore. This is a fundamental realignment of the relationship between large media companies and the public."

Of course, allowing journalists, public relations practitioners, or marketers to acknowledge and even base comments on their biases, as well as to point to and otherwise reveal source materials, is to relinquish control, and institutions are reticent to yield control. In response to this reticence, New York University journalism professor Jay Rosen argued that the new values and priorities should allow individual digital writers, even in large organizations, to themselves be involved in creating trust, to be at the point of the transaction of trust with the reader, rather than merely relying on the institutional trust of the publication, firm, or brand. In doing so, these individual digital writers can add to the organization's reputational capital rather than merely spending or ruining it, addressing at the individual level the key problem of eroding credibility.

## ACCOUNTABILITY

Accountability requires that individuals, companies, and organizations explain themselves. It asks these organizations to be clearer with readers about how they operate and why. In journalism, for example, a backlash against objectivity, and a general misunderstanding of even what it is, has pushed editors and publishers on the defensive. Mainstream journalism has struggled to embrace newer media forms in part because it has insisted on objectivity and, in the process, is guilty of killing the human voice. Blogs, Rosen argued, marked the return of "real human voices" and "real human conversations" (Rosen, 2005). Facebook, Twitter, and a host of social media platforms offer further evidence of the primacy in digital spaces of these conversations and of the interpersonal dimension to a lot of what is being communicated online and on smartphones. A big question for news organizations, public relations firms, and marketers, among others, then, is how to adhere to professional standards, such as ethical newsgathering and balance, in the overall presentation of perspectives, but at the same time communicate in "real human voices." For a public to hold an organization accountable, that public must first know to what standards the organization is holding itself.

## IMPROVING CREDIBILITY

Credibility studies suggest several elements that can give interactors confidence and engender trust in a digital source and its author(s). Briefly, these include:

- easy-to-use, intuitive navigation;
- user-friendly design;
- high-quality graphics;
- good writing;
- full contact information;

- expertise in the subject area; and
- links outside to other relevant sources and sites.

One of the goals of Stanford University's Persuasive Technology Lab (credibility.stanford.edu/) is to understand those design elements that have an impact upon credibility. The lab's web credibility project found that a broad range of design decisions ranging from visual elements to information architecture to the use of advertising can powerfully influence whether visitors are likely to find a website credible. Like human communicators, websites benefit (or suffer) based upon their appearance. Among the project's many findings are these highlights:

- First impressions are important. People tend to determine the credibility of a website based upon how professional they think the site looks.
- An organization's name appearing in the URL increases credibility.
- Designers should make sure there is a clear distinction between information and advertising. Sources for the information presented should be identified and the authors' credentials presented.
- Navigation should be intuitive.
- Everything should work, including links, downloads, graphics, and multimedia, and they should work immediately.
- The company a site keeps matters. Links to, or affiliations with, other organizations, whether online or off, can have an impact on credibility.

The Persuasive Technology Lab itemized a multitude of factors that affect credibility, factors presented here in rank order of importance or potential impact. These factors can each be placed into one of the general guidelines just mentioned.

A credible site:

1. has proven useful to you before;
2. is by or for an organization that is well respected;
3. provides a quick response to your questions;
4. lists the organization's physical address;
5. has been updated since your last visit;
6. gives a contact phone number;
7. appears professionally designed;
8. gives a contact email address;
9. is arranged in a way that makes sense to you; and
10. provides comprehensive information that is attributed to a specific source.

For information-rich sites, credibility is based, in part, on:

- the authors' credentials;
- transparency about citations and references; and
- the sites and sources to which the articles link.

The Lab's findings also recommend that sites:

- state their privacy policies;
- feature design appropriate to their subject matter;
- provide search;
- link to outside materials and sources;
- rank highly in search engine results; and
- recognize who has visited before.

Generally, there are two website categories that typically have consistently low credibility, according to the Lab's research: websites with commercial purposes and those that give the impression that they have been produced by amateurs. People assign much

Dr. Francis Collins is Director of the National Institutes of Health. Dr. Arati Prabhakar is Director of the Defense Advanced Research Projects Agency.

Follow new developments relating to the BRAIN Initiative and other advances in science and technology at the White House Office of Science and Technology Policy Blog and @whitehouseostp on Twitter.

**FIGURE 5.1**
*Author credentials as listed at Whitehouse.gov.*

**FIGURE 5.2** *eBay's site recognizes return visitors*

Hi, Brian! ▼  |  Daily Deals  |  ebay  Shop by category ▼

less credibility to a site they know is trying to sell them something. More than one ad on a page, no matter whether or not the site is primarily commercial, can greatly decrease credibility, which is a huge problem for news sites blanketed with display advertising. If a site is going to have ads, those ads should be for reputable products or organizations. The more reputable the ad, the more credibility it communicates. Technical errors and less-than-frequent updates are typical problems for amateur sites, as are non-professional appearances and less adequate or complete contact information.

Diminishing credibility for a site, in rank order from greatest to least, according to the Persuasive Technology Lab's research, are:

1. making it difficult to distinguish ads from content;
2. rarely updating with new content;
3. automating pop-up ads;
4. making it difficult to navigate;
5. linking to sites not perceived as credible;
6. leaving dead links;
7. making typographical errors;
8. using a domain name that does not match the company's name;
9. hosting by a third party; and
10. having a commercial purpose.

For mobile media, credibility is also related to load times and ease of use. For websites migrating to mobile, the challenge is not unlike moving from a five-bedroom house into a studio apartment. What do you do? Get rid of a whole bunch of stuff, because for an app to be seen as credible, it must load fast and make clear what people have to do to interact with it. Navigation needs to be simple, if it exists at all, and it needs to help interactors manage the firehose of content blowing past them. While on the content generation side of the app, we metaphorically pour content into different buckets; on the consumer side, it will be simply a flow into their phones. So, help them get in quickly and easily, manage that flow, and integrate their experience with what they want to do with their social media. (The website Quirktools.com has a diagnostic tool that shows you how your site is or will be seen on various devices, including smartphones, tablets, and smart televisions.)

## TOOLS AND TECHNOLOGY: THE MEDIUM IS THE MESSAGE

Neil Postman, author of *Amusing Ourselves to Death*, observed that a technology, any technology, is "to a medium as the brain is to the mind. Like a brain, a technology is a physical apparatus. Like the mind, a medium is a use to which a physical apparatus is put. . . Only those who know nothing of the history of technology believe that technology is entirely neutral" (1985, p. 84). In other words, the form in which an idea is expressed, the medium used to deliver or communicate it, affects what the idea can even be.

To think about what Postman was describing and to build toward a better understanding of the capacities of digital media, let's consider the medium of television. TV operates with its own rhetoric, one that is predicated on a few essential qualities. Because screens are typically small—and with smartphones, video screens are even smaller—TV programming has to emphasize characters rather than the sweeping, epic dramas for which cinema is known. For the big stories—think *Iron Man*, *Star Wars*, or *Independence Day*—we turn to motion pictures, which are shown in multi-speaker rooms with wall-sized screens, often in 3D, 4D, or IMAX. Because TV delivers moving images, its rhetoric is about experiencing something emotionally (pathos) and experiencing it right now. TV knows only one verb tense—the present. Even a documentary on the History Channel on World War II gives the viewer a present tense experience of the war. TV's rhetoric is incapable of helping us process a great deal of information or to think rationally about complex topics. For this reason, TV must entertain. Even that WWII documentary must, above all else, amuse and entertain. Because TV is turned to for entertainment, it must ask very little of its audience. Even multi-part TV series allow viewers to drop in, in the middle of the series, and quickly figure out what is going on. Because many can view a program simultaneously in different geographic locations—and, when crises strike, they often do—TV specializes in enabling a sort of societal communion or ritualized viewing. Think of the coverage on 9/11 or perhaps the last episode of *Walking Dead* or *Game of Thrones*. In important ways, the rhetoric of the medium becomes part of the message itself.

What does any of this have to do with us as digital writers and editors? We should think carefully about why we are deploying moving images, and whether video is the right medium for our content. What part of the story is the rhetoric of video best suited to deliver? The widely acclaimed "Snow Fall" package from *The New York Times*, for example, uses video clips of some of the skiing tragedy's survivors to put the interactor and the survivor in the same room, in the present tense. Such immediacy is powerful, and it enables an emotional connection between interactor and subject. Snow Fall's Flash-driven animation, on the other hand, is used to explain visually and in motion the power and punch of avalanches, while the multimedia package's dazzling photography gives interactors poignant images to gaze at and to contemplate.

Even during the last few years, improvements in capacities for streaming and showing video have vastly improved. Download times have decreased while resolution and fidelity have gone up. The currency of the realm is still brevity, however, and attention spans are punishingly short; videos of only a few minutes are the norm. YouTube, for example, discourages videos longer than ten minutes. And there are other media choices:

**Flash presentations** can combine text and pictures, video and audio, interactive buttons, and animated charts and graphs. Flash employs vector graphics, which means Flash does not require a lot of bandwidth—much less than video. Flash is also widely misused, often employed merely to generate eye candy. Flash animation is best suited for explaining and breaking down complex processes and chains of events, and for creating "how to" demonstrations. The publisher of Flash, Adobe, wisely uses Flash to demonstrate how to, among other activities, make a Flash movie. These "how to" Flash tutorials take something fairly complex and sequential, break it down, and make the discrete steps visible and repeatable. However, Flash requires a browser plug-in, and it doesn't play on most smartphones. While browser software often automatically updates interactors' browsers for the latest plug-ins, not all browsers are always up to date, and any time interactors are required to take action, like updating or downloading software, the potential audience shrinks. Not everyone is willing or even able to take that action.

**Still images** best tell some stories or parts of stories because they enable a lingering gaze and an emotional connection with the subject. Still images can rely on iconic messages implicit even in their composition, like the Madonna-and-child form seen in Dorothea Lange's "Migrant Woman" photograph taken in 1936. In other words, photography is intrinsically related to memory. Only still images are described, metaphorically, as "burning" something into our minds, searing our memories. Most of our memories, after all, are mental images, because images, like memory, freeze time and preserve one slice of it for recall, observation, and reflection. To create and publish slideshows, with or without sound, there are an abundance of free and low-cost software programs, including Soundslides, Apple's iPhoto, Flickr, and Google Photos.

Our media choices are important. Establishing and communicating credibility are important, even to the life of an interactor's own community. The civically engaged are more likely than the less engaged to use and value news, Pew found. Those who report having a strong connection to their communities consistently display stronger local news habits across a range of measures: news interest, news intake, and news attitudes. Americans who rate their local communities as excellent have more positive views of their news media than those who rate their communities less highly, and vice versa.

---

**BOX 5.1**

## Computer Code: The Building Blocks of Webpages

Computer programming codes like HTML and CSS are the principal languages of the web. Although few web writers and editors are asked to build websites from scratch, they should be aware of how web-authoring code works and how it makes digital content manifest in a browser window. It's important to know, for example, that text on a computer screen isn't really text at all. Computer code assembles the tiny building blocks of pixels to form the letters we see on our screen. Photos and graphics are also never part of a webpage, regardless of how they appear in the browser. The webpage and its constituent graphical parts are always separate files, coalescing in a download to appear as a singular entity. Webpages are coded or built to make it seem as if their images are knitted into their fabric.

The languages most often used to create interactive or hypertextual content are HTML; HTML's progeny, XHTML; XML (extensible markup language); and CSS (cascading style sheets). XML is used especially for data-rich content and to enhance HTML by using attribute tags to categorize information. For example, an XML tag can tell other computers and search engines whether a certain piece of text is a phone number, a job application, an order form, an invoice, or whatever the coder writes into the language. Special search engines can then index documents in XML with great accuracy, regardless of the operating system or computer being used. Flash and ActionScript, JavaScript, Ajax, and Spry, as well as Fireworks, all enable webpages to be dynamic and interactive. Web writers and editors do not necessarily need to become proficient in these web programming languages, nor do they necessarily need to know how to develop an app. But it certainly helps to be able to hand-code pages and to understand the capacities and limitations of these coding languages. Fortunately, most sites now use authoring software programs, webpage templates, and content management systems to speed the process and better ensure consistency, taking a huge load off of digital writers and editors to become and remain conversant in what is a dizzying range of languages.

Most journalism websites use content management systems (CMSs), which are complex systems designed to automate most web publishing. These CMSs handle all sorts of digital content, from text files to audio, photo, and video, and they allow anyone within an organization to see all of the files and component parts. Also important to news organizations are application programming interfaces (APIs), which are programming tools that allow one site or program to interact with or otherwise accommodate other sites or programs. Facebook famously opened up its environment to third-party applications, while Apple allows anyone to develop and offer an application for and via its iPhone. Similarly, APIs allow third-party development and collaboration on or for news organizations, which are seeking to leverage the popularity of such sites as YouTube, Facebook, and Reddit, to name just three examples. APIs give developers controlled access to the various websites and platforms.

To put those new to web design at ease, what follows are some basics about the primary coding languages, HTML and CSS. To see how this code generates what you see through your browser, you can go to almost any webpage, right-click (PC) or control-click (Mac), choose "view page source" (or its equivalent, depending on which browser you are using), and view the code. HTML uses tags, such as <body>, while CSS uses brackets and semantic style directions:

```
{
background-color: #000000
}
```

This simple CSS command stipulates a page's background color as black, using the hexadecimal (or six-character alphanumeric code) for the color black (000000). CSS also supports semantic instructions:

```
{
background-color: black
}
```

For web-based media environments, including blogs, extranets, and intranets, learning at least the basics of HTML can aid design and streamline content development. HTML source codes are what make webpages behave or, when the code is faulty, what cause the pages to misbehave. In the code are instructions to browsers, including what to show and how to show it.

In short, HTML does just what its name implies: It marks up language to allow browsers and those using browsers to interact with that language. This markup allows hyperlinks or references in the code to other sites, web-pages, or other places within the same website or page (called anchors). This markup allows images to appear on or in the page.

To introduce HTML, here is a look at a few very basic tags (the commands appearing inside angle brackets < > that are used to build most webpages). After showing the tags, we will break down what they are and how they work:

```
<html>
<head>
<title>A primer on HTML source code</title>
<meta name = "description" content = "learning about
HTML">
</head>
<body bgcolor = "FFFFFF">
<h1><font: Georgia, Arial, sans serif>The basics of HTML
</h1><p>
</p>
</font>
</body>
</html>
```

Eight tags were used in the small sample above; two of them are essential. The <html> tag tells browsers that they can in fact read the code, doing so by signifying that the page is in HTML format. The </html> turns the HTML off, or closes the document. The <body> tag tells the browser what to display in the browser window. Most tags come in pairs: one to turn a feature or behavior on and one to turn it off again, much like light switches. The tag , for example, turns on boldface type. Adding a forward slash turns the behavior off again: . Failure to add the "off" tag would render whatever followed also in boldface. The tag </body>, then, ends the section viewable through the web browser.

The <head> tag indicates header information, such as the title of the webpage, the information that appears in the browser at the very top; it does not signify a headline. The `<h1>` tag turns on a heading, which is or can be like a headline, and specifies the size. The `</h1>`, then, would turn it off. The `<body bgcolor>` tag specifies a background color for the page, which in this case is white (`#FFFFFF`). Each of the web's 256 basic colors is assigned a hexadecimal code, or six letter-number combination. For example, black is `#000000` and brown is `#CC6600`.

Any tag with a "/" in it is called an "off" tag. An example: `<p>` starts a paragraph, while `</p>` turns the same feature off, ending the paragraph. The font is specified with a `<font>` tag, then turned off with `</font>`. Arial font would begin `<font face = "Arial">`. When the font changes, Arial would be turned off, `</font face = "Arial">` and the new font turned on.

Metatags apply to the entire site. The term also comes from the fact that metatags provide data about data. Their content does not direct the browser and is not, therefore, displayed in a browser. These tags direct search engines as to how to sort the site, its pages, and content by providing key words, descriptions, and the like. They also cue other programmers by providing authorship information, copyright information, and general design notes, among other messages. A common metatag sequence might look like this one, from the *Online Journalism Review* (www.ojr.org):

```
<meta name = "description" content = "News, commentary and
help for online publishers and bloggers, from the USC An-
nenberg School for Communication.">
```

Here are a few more common tags used in XHTML:

Paragraph Break: `<p>` `</p>`

Line Break: `<br />` (this XHTML tag comprises both the opening and closing tags; by adding the forward slash, the tag also "closes" or turns off the line break command)

```
Horizontal Rule: <hr> </hr>
<strong> something written in boldface </strong>
<em> something appearing in italics </em>
<a href = " www.cubanxgiants.com "> something hy-
perlinked to the CubanXGiants webpage </a>
```

Unordered list:

```
<ul>
<li> laptops
<li> desktop PCs
</ul>
```

Ordered list:

```
<ol>
<li> dolphins
<li> panthers
<li> jaguars
</ol>
```

Inserting anchors, which are used for internal page navigation, is easy. Anchors are internal hyperlinks, or links that take a reader to another part of the same webpage or to a specific section in another page of the same website. Here is what an anchored page would look like in code, inside a page of frequently asked questions (FAQs):

```
<a href = "#question1">Where do I find out more about
Crohn's?</a>
<a href = "#question2">Where does the support group
meet?</a>
```

Below, where the answers to the questions are presented, an anchor would be inserted just before each answer, a piece of code that is not visible in the browser. The anchor, which is signified by using the number sign (#) is merely a marker that enables the hyperlink—"question1"—to work, or to have a place to link. The two anchors for the two questions above would look something like this:

```
<a NAME = "question1"></a>Crohn's disease is a condition
that afflicts . . .
<a NAME = "question2"></a>The group meets in Rex
Hospital . . .
```

The <a NAME> refers to the name you gave the anchor in the hyperlink at the top of the page.

Perhaps the biggest difference between HTML and XHTML is that in the latter, all tags require a closing or off tag. In HTML, a command such as <p> to create a new paragraph does not absolutely require a closing tag—</p>—though HTML does recognize the closing tag. This is intuitive. Creating a paragraph creates an extra line break, which is a single action that would not seem to require an "off" command or closing tag. XHTML is stricter, and one manifestation of this lower tolerance is the requirement that all tags, all actions, have opening and closing tags.

Another manifestation is the prohibition in XHTML on capital letters. That same paragraph tag in HTML could be either <p> or <P>. Not so in XHTML. Finally, XHTML varies by requiring quotation marks (single or double) for all attribute values. For example, in HTML, a tag reading <td rowspan = 3>, indicating a table with three rows, would be acceptable. In XHTML, the specification requires quotation marks: <td rowspan = "3">.

CSS is an incredibly powerful coding language that is used for two primary purposes: coding individual webpages with a more semantic or intuitive syntax than is used in HTML/XHTML, and creating "parent" style sheets that can be applied to an infinite number of "children," or pages that refer to the style sheets for their attributes. In other words, CSS can be used merely to indicate (or declare) something simple, like the typeface on a webpage:

```
{
font-family: Verdana, Arial, Helvetica
}
```

Or CSS can be used to generate entire style sheets that determine attributes for any page referring to that style sheet. A change made to the one style sheet, which is uploaded to the web along with all its children, will ripple out into all of those pages referring to the style sheet. For large sites, CSS saves an enormous amount of time, contributes to consistency, and prevents error. These are just some of the reasons why, for many web developers, CSS replaced HTML wherever possible.

HTML5, so named because it was the fifth revision of the HTML standard, has enabled an approach to desktop web and mobile web design that adjusts depending on the size of the device and screen of the user. Called "responsive design," this approach combines HTML5 and CSS to allow content to be refitted to almost any screen size automatically, with the use of a single CSS style sheet. Ever smaller screen sizes have presented monumental challenges to web designers, and they have made single column, stacked web design the norm, because this design works on most phones. It is responsive design that makes it possible to accommodate smartphone screens, while at the same time delivering the content to big desktop monitors. A mobile-first approach stipulates that webpages be lean and modular, so that content can stack. By using media queries or element queries, which allow websites and browsers to "speak" to each other, web designers can have their sites ask a user's device the size of the screen being used. The answer can then trigger any number of versions of content. For example, if a media or element query reveals that a user is accessing a site from a Mac desktop, he or she might get a large high-resolution image. If the query determines that the user is accessing via a phone, the site will load only a small, lower-res image, reconfiguring the content based on the size of the screen.

The challenges to responsive design are fairly significant. It requires far more time and effort than does traditional web design. And more testing has to be done to see what users get depending on the device they are using. In addition, advertising forms have to be kept very lean, lightweight, and simple. Rich visualization and large interstitial ads are largely not supported. Finally, screen sizes smaller than desktops but larger than smartphones, such as those on tablets and e-readers, also need to be accommodated.

The goal in this box was merely to provide a taste of HTML and CSS, or just enough so that web writers and editors would not be intimidated by these authoring languages and the terms they use. The web design or HTML section of any local bookstore will have a dizzying depth and breadth of literature available on the topic. It is enough for now to learn what HTML tags are and how they operate in an HTTP (hypertext transfer protocol) environment such as the web. Many will prefer to hand-code because of the precision this control offers; others would rather save time in page-building by using web-authoring software packages, leaving more time for other tasks. There are hundreds of websites designed to help you learn and use these coding languages.

The coding discussed in this chapter has largely to do with what is called front-end code, or the languages that build and design pages and sites. The primary front-end code languages are JavaScript, HTML, and CSS. On the server side, back-end coding languages are used to help send data to web applications, like those that populate news websites with news articles or weather sites with up-to-date weather conditions and forecasts. This code is meant to make it easier to manipulate data, render templates, and filter and sort data.

# CHAPTER ACTIVITIES

1. Visit the PewResearchCenter's subsite for journalism and the news (journalism.org/). Use the vast research resources here to craft an executive memo describing how your news organization or public relations firm—real or imagined—will respond to what is a credibility crisis for digital information sources. Fake news, gossip, and hacking are spreading confusion. How will your organization establish, communicate, and maintain credibility to your interactors and publics? Anchor your strategy in the research. Length: About 1,000 words.

2. Further format your writing sample you created in Chapter 1 and refined in Chapter 2 with some basic HTML coding. Blogging software can be very helpful in this exercise, particularly because most offer an HTML or Code view, which will show you all of the code generated to create the web presentation. Use this chapter to inform your formatting. You will need to know or experiment with some HTML, or have some familiarity with a web authoring software package like Dreamweaver or Mozilla, both of which offer CSS support. Both Blogger.com and WordPress also accept HTML coding, provided you first select the "Edit HTML" or "Code" view, rather than "Compose" or "Visual." If you use the shortcut buttons in your blog software, be sure to inspect or view the code to learn something of how the formatting is added. In addition, the W3Schools webpage, w3schools.com/tags, provides tutorials and allows you to experiment with coding, including tags.

3. Your news team is preparing a multimedia series on race relations in your local community. As a thought piece, brainstorm which media you will use to tell different parts of the story. Outline what you will do with, for example, video, information graphics, text, still photos, Flash animation, and locator maps. Include a section on how you will integrate this content with social media—how you will maximize its share-ability or virality. Length: About 1,000 words.

## Digital Resources

**New York Times's Snow Fall multimedia package (nytimes.com/projects/2012/snow-fall/#/?part=tunnel-creek)**

**Nielson Norman Group (www.nngroup.com/)**
Jakob Nielsen's site for usability studies and a wealth of intelligence on design.

**PewResearchCenter (journalism.org/)**

**Stanford University Persuasive Technology Lab (credibility.stanford.edu/)**

**University of California Berkeley's School of Journalism (journalism.berkeley.edu/multimedia/tutorials)**
A series of multimedia tutorials.

**YouTube's Creator Hub (youtube.com/yt/creators)**
A repository of resources for doing video, growing audience, and creating a YouTube channel.

**Additional Web Resources**
For learning basic HTML/XHTML, including publishing to the Web:

- Dave's Site (davesite.com/webstation/html);
- HTML Goodies (htmlgoodies.com);
- HTML Guides/References from NASA (heasarc.gsfc.nasa.gov/docs/heasarc/Style_Guide/html.html);
- Lynda.com tutorials (lynda.com);
- Peachpit Press (peachpit.com/topics/topic.aspx?st=61442); and
- W3Schools for tutorials and coding help (w3schools.com/tags).

# BIBLIOGRAPHY

Ambrester, Roy, "Identification Within: Kenneth Burke's View of the Unconscious," *Philosophy and Rhetoric* 7 (1974): 205–216.

American Society of Newspaper Editors, *Newspaper Credibility: Building Reader Trust* (Washington, DC: ASNE Credibility Committee and Minnesota Opinion Research, April 1985).

American Society of Newspaper Editors, *Newspaper Credibility: 206 Practical Approaches to Heighten Reader Trust* (Washington, DC: ASNE Credibility Committee, April 1986).

American Society of Newspaper Editors, *Journalism Values Handbook* (Washington, DC: ASNE Ethics and Values Committee and The Harwood Group, 1995).

American Society of Newspaper Editors, *Timeless Values: Staying True to Journalistic Principles in the Age of New Media* (Washington, DC: ASNE New Media and Values Committee and The Harwood Group, April 1995).

American Society of Newspaper Editors, *Journalism Values Institute: Insights on the Values* (Washington, DC: ASNE Ethics and Values Committee and The Harwood Group, 1996).

American Society of Newspaper Editors, *Examining Our Credibility* (Washington, DC: ASNE and Urban Associates, 1999).

American Society of Newspaper Editors, *The Newspaper Credibility Handbook* (Washington, DC: ASNE Journalism Credibility Project, 2001).

Barthel, Michael, Holcomb, Jesse, Mahone, Jessica, and Mitchell, Amy, "Civic Engagement Strongly Tied to Local News Habits," *PewResearchCenter* (November 3 2016), available: www.journalism.org/2016/11/03/civic-engagement-strongly-tied-to-local-news-habits/.

Baxter, Gerald D. and Taylor, Pat M., "Burke's Theory of Consubstantiality and Whitehead's Concept of Concrescence," *Communication Monographs* 45 (1978): 173–180.

Benoit, William A., "Comparing the Clinton and Dole Advertising Campaigns: Identification and Division in 1996 Presidential Television Spots," *Communication Research Reports* 17, no. 1 (2009): 39–48.

Branch, John, "Snow Fall: The Avalanche at Tunnel Creek," *The New York Times* (December 19 2012), available: www.nytimes.com/projects/2012/snow-fall/.

Brooks, Brian and Sissors, Jack, *The Art of Editing* (Boston, MA: Allyn & Bacon, 2001).

Bullis, Connie and Bach, Betsy W., "Are Mentor Relationships Helping Organizations? An Exploration of Developing Mentee—Mentor Organizational Identifications Using Turning Point Analysis," *Communication Quarterly* 37 (1989): 199–213.

Carpenter, Ronald H., "A Stylistic Basis of Burkeian Identification," *Today's Speech* 20 (1972): 19–24.

Cheney, George, "The Rhetoric of Identification and the Study of Organizational Communication," *Quarterly Journal of Speech* 69 (1983): 143–158.

Cheney, George and Tompkins, Phillip, "Coming to Terms with Organizational Identification and Commitment," *Central States Speech Journal* 38 (1987): 1–15.

Cohen, Jonathan, "Defining Identification: A Theoretical Look at the Identification of Audiences With Media Characters," *Mass Communication & Society* 4, no. 3 (2001): 245–264.

Crable, Bryan, "Rhetoric, Anxiety, and Character Armor: Burke's Interactional Rhetoric of Identity 1," *Western Journal of Communication* 70, no. 1 (January 2006): 1–22.

Craig, Richard, *Online Journalism* (Toronto, ON: Thomson, 2005).

Day, Dennis, "Persuasion and the Concept of Identification," *Quarterly Journal of Speech* 46 (1960): 270–273.

Dougherty, Dale, "Don't Forget to Write," *Webreview.com*, available: http://web.archive.org/web/20010414062442/www.webreview.com/1997/10_10/strategists/10_10_97_6.shtml.

Dowling, Carolyn, *Writing and Learning with Computers* (Camberwell, Australia: Acer Press, 1999).

Eadicicco, Lisa, "Americans Check Their Phones 8 Billion Times a Day," *Time* (December 15 2015), available: http://time.com/4147614/smartphone-usage-us-2015/.

Flanigin, Andrew J. and Metzger, Miriam J., "Perceptions of Internet Information Credibility," *Journalism & Mass Communication Quarterly* 77, no. 3 (2000): 515–539.

Foss, Sonja K., Foss, Karen A., and Trapp, Robert, *Contemporary Perspectives on Rhetoric* (Prospect Heights, IL: Waveland Press, 1986).

Greer, Jennifer, "Evaluating the Credibility of Online Information: A Test of Source and Advertising Influence," *Mass Communication & Society* 6 (2003): 11–28.

Greer, Jennifer and Mensing, Donica, "U.S. News Web Sites Better, But Small Papers Still Lag," *Newspaper Research Journal* 25, no. 2 (Spring 2004): 98–112.

Hovland, Carl I., Janis, Irving L., and Kelley, Harold H., *Communication and Persuasion: Psychological Studies of Opinion Change* (New Haven, CT: Yale University Press, 1953).

Jarmul, Katharine, "Tips & Tools for Journalists Who Want to Learn Programming Skills," *Poynter Institute* (2011), available: www.poynter.org/how-tos/digital-strategies/153925/tips-tools-for-journalists-who-want-to-learn-programming-skills/.

Johnson, Thomas J. and Kaye, Barbara K., "Cruising is Believing? Comparing Internet and Traditional Sources on Media Credibility Measures," *Journalism & Mass Communication Quarterly* 75 (1998): 325–340.

Johnson, Thomas J. and Kaye, Barbara K., "Using is Believing: The Influence of Reliance on the Credibility of Online Political Information Among Politically Interested Internet Users," *Journalism & Mass Communication Quarterly* 77 (2000): 865–879.

Johnson, Thomas J. and Kaye, Barbara K., "Webelievability: A Path Model Examining How Convenience and Reliance Predict Online Credibility," *Journalism & Mass Communication Quarterly* 79 (2002): 619–642.

Johnson, Thomas J. and Kaye, Barbara K., "Wag the Blog: How Reliance on Traditional Media and the Internet Influence Credibility Perceptions of Weblogs Among Blog Users," *Journalism & Mass Communication Quarterly* 81, no. 3 (2004): 622–642.

Journalism.org, "The State of the News Media," *Journalism.org* (2006).

Kirk, John, "Kenneth Burke and Identification," *Quarterly Journal of Speech* 47, no. 4 (December 1961): 414–415

Kline, David and Burstein, Dan, *Blog! How the Newest Media Revolution Is Changing Politics, Business and Culture* (New York, NY: CDS Books, 2005).

Kovach, Bill and Rosenstiel, Tom, *Elements of Journalism* (New York, NY: Three Rivers Press, 2007).

McAlpine, Rachel, *Web Word Wizardry: A Guide to Writing for the Web and Intranet* (Berkeley, CA: Ten Speed Press, 2001). McAlpine also has a companion website that is very good: Quality Web Content, available: www.webpagecontent.com.

McCroskey, James C., "Scales for the Measurement of Ethos," *Speech Monographs* 33 (1966): 65–72.

McCroskey, James C., "A Survey of Experimental Research on the Effects of Evidence in Persuasive Communication," *Speech Monographs* 55 (1969): 169–176.

Meyer, John C., "Humor as a Double-Edged Sword: Four Functions of Humor in Communication," *Communication Theory* 10, no. 3 (August 2000): 310–331.

Meyer, Philip, "Defining and Measuring Credibility of Newspapers: Developing an Index," *Journalism Quarterly* 65 (1988): 567–574, 588.

Mitchell, Amy, Gottfried, Jeffrey, Barthel, Michael, and Shearer, Elisa, "Pathways to News," *PewResearchCenter* (July 7 2016), available: www.journalism.org/2016/07/07/pathways-to-news/.

Morkes, John and Nielsen, Jakob, "Concise, SCANNABLE, and Objective: How to Write for the Web," (1997), available: www.useit.com/papers/webwriting/writing.html.

Nielsen, Jakob, "How Users Read on the Web," available: www.useit.com/alertbox/9710a.html.

Parker, Roger C., *Guide to Web Content and Design* (New York, NY: MIS Press, 1997).

Postman, Neil, *Amusing Ourselves to Death: Public Discourse in the Age of Show Business* (New York, NY: Penguin, 1985).

Tedesco, Anthony, "Adapt Your Writing to the Web," *The Writer* 114, no. 5 (May 2001): 16.

Tompkins, Phillip K., Fisher, Jeanne, Infante, Dominic, and Tompkins, Elaine, "Kenneth Burke and the Inherent Characteristics of Formal Organizations: A Field Study," *Speech Monographs* (1975): 135–142.

Wright, Mark, "Burkeian and Freudian Theories of Identification," *Communication Quarterly* 42, no. 3 (Summer 1994): 301–310.

Zachary, G. Pascal, "A Journalism Manifesto," *AlterNet* (February 9, 2006), available: www.alternet.org/story/31775.

# Knowing and (Ethically) Serving Your Audience

*Your audience gives you everything you need. They tell you. There is no director who can direct you like an audience.*

—Fanny Brice, entertainer

*Personality is the glitter that sends your little gleam across the footlights and the orchestra pit into that big black space where the audience is.*

—Mae West

*Consistency is contrary to nature, contrary to life. The only completely consistent people are dead.*

—Aldous Huxley

**CHAPTER OBJECTIVES**

After studying this chapter, you will be able to:

- understand audience needs and preferences;
- attract interactors and keep them coming back;
- develop and use style guides for clarity, consistency, and efficiency; and
- develop and apply a code of ethics in service to your audience.

## INTRODUCTION

Artistic expression can be for its own sake, but in communication fields and industries, expression is in service to an audience and to a message. To serve an audience well, we have to know that audience well. We need intelligence on an audience's information needs, habits, sensitivities, and objectives. This chapter provides a roadmap for finding and charting this information. Also covered is how to begin developing a style guide, also in service to audience. Useful, user-friendly, accessible style guides help maintain consistency across all of our content in terms of both voice and personality.

## KNOCK, KNOCK...

Before we even write a word of content, we need the answers to at least three fundamental questions. Who is our audience? What do they need? What is our core goal or purpose or mission? Whatever we determine that purpose to be, we then need to deliver, and in a way specific to the audience we are serving. For public relations practitioners, the term for audience is publics, and serving these publics is in a larger context of serving a particular client or cause. In marketing and advertising, audience might be better termed a target demographic. Regardless, the more contact we have with our audience/publics/target demographic, the more relevant our content will be. And as intuitive as this sounds, it's often unheeded advice. An awful lot of web and app development occurs instead in a vacuum.

**FIGURE 6.1**

*This quiz-taker's result places him according to his usage choices in eastern Florida*

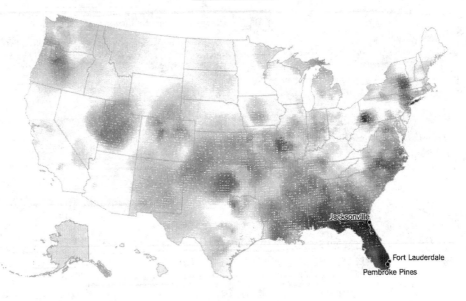

### Your Map

See the pattern of your dialect in the map below. Three of the most similar cities are shown.

Least similar    Most similar    Show least similar    SHARE YOUR MAP:

These maps show your most distinctive answer for each of these cities.

As a starting point, think about where on an information spectrum, from information-rich at one extreme to sensory-oriented on the other, your content is or should be. YouTube, for example, lives at the sensory extreme by emphasizing the visual and, with almost exclusively short videos, creating impressions and evoking emotions. Similarly, Instagram, Pinterest, and Snapchat are mostly sensory, allowing users to share or trade photos. On the other end of the spectrum, we might put corporate intranets, reference sites such as the Library of Congress, and sites by and for institutions of higher education. In the middle are those sites that provide some information but also seek to provide an experience of some kind, like most news sites. Knowing where your project fits on this spectrum can inform the kinds of content that should be developed and the ways in which that content should be presented.

On the sensory end of the spectrum is an interactive feature from *The New York Times* called the personal dialect map (www.nytimes.com/interactive/2013/12/20/sunday-review/dialect-quiz-map.html). The feature, which is the single most popular piece of content the *Times* has created in terms of page views, draws from a database of 350,000 surveys to create a personalized dialect map based on a visitor's responses to a 25-question quiz. Before adding the feature, *Times* content developers knew they wanted something to provide an experience, something entertaining that could deliver

**FIGURE 6.2**
*Source: www. cdc.gov/ncbddd/ cp/causes.html*

near-instant gratification. Knowing the purpose and the audience informed the development of the feature. And to drive traffic, the newspaper sent alerts about the new feature via Facebook, its various blogs, and Twitter.

On the other end of the information-sensory spectrum might be a webpage designed by the Centers for Disease Control and Prevention to help parents diagnose cerebral palsy. Not surprising given the subject, this page is very high on information and very low on entertainment or emotion. A sober tone, the logical organization of information, and a clear demonstration of credibility and authority meet audience expectations for a site offering this type of information.

## MAXIMIZING CONTENT FITNESS

Next, consider your audience in terms of the *kinds* of information they are looking for, or how the information you provide might fit into the larger puzzle that your audience is trying to piece together over time. Information science researchers call this "fitness," which research has found to be far more important than, say, technology or visual sophistication. Researchers Kuan-Tsae Huang, Yang W. Lee, and Richard Y. Wang found that when people visit a website, they base their judgments of the quality of information more on how well that information matches what they are seeking and less on how sophisticated the site is in terms of its technological bells and whistles. The research suggests four dimensions of information quality (see Figure 6.3).

The IQ dimensions identified and organized in the study provide a useful checklist for evaluating the fitness of content for the audience you are trying to serve. Are they

FIGURE 6.3

| Information quality (IQ) category | IQ DIMENSION |
|---|---|
| **Intrinsic IQ,** or information that has quality for the user in its own right | • accuracy<br>• objectivity<br>• believability<br>• reputation |
| **Contextual IQ,** or information that must be considered within the context of the user's tasks | • relevancy<br>• value-added<br>• timeliness<br>• completeness<br>• amount |
| **Representational IQ,** or user issues surrounding systems that provide information, such as databases | • interpretability<br>• ease of understanding<br>• concise representation<br>• consistent representation |
| **Accessibility IQ,** or user issues surrounding the provision of information | • access<br>• security |

visiting your site to buy something? If that's the case, access and security, or Accessibility IQ dimensions, will rank highly. Are they looking to you for information on cerebral palsy? Intrinsic IQ dimensions are going to rank at the top. A news site will need to score well on nearly all of the dimensions in the chart.

Specific reasons to access your content might include to read, to learn, to be entertained, to get service or support, to get advice, or to buy. How will you meet these needs? What will your interactors find most valuable about your site or app? What will they find least valuable? What could you add to better meet those needs and to create a better experience with your content? Why would they choose your site or app? Are they going to recommend you to their friends? Why?

## ... WHO'S THERE?

Your next challenge is to identify and understand the people you hope to attract to your content. Think in terms of a funnel, wide at the top and increasingly narrow as you get closer to the end. So, first think in terms of categories: occupational types, demographics, gender, culture, and age ranges, for example. This will require research, but don't be intimidated. Even a few simple interactor profiles will go a long way to making sure your content and its presentation match up with your audience's expectations. Consider the CDC's page on cerebral palsy. With a primary audience of very concerned parents, writers for this page knew the content needed enough detail and substance to truly inform, but not so much that the information overwhelms. They also knew that abstraction was not an option. Similarly, readers in professional fields, such as business, science, or technology, likely will expect a wealth of empirical data, perhaps supporting charts and graphs, as well.

Does your audience need "how to" information? You'll likely develop sequential content or demonstrations that walk a reader through a process step by step. Does your audience need to collaborate? What social networking tools and communication environments will you offer? Are they looking for pleasure or efficiency, advice or participation in something meaningful? At any stage of this research process, consider doing even an informal survey of potential interactors. It takes only minutes to set one up at any of the free survey tools on the web, such as surveymonkey.com, a survey that can then be shared via social media.

At a very basic level, you'll want to know:

- Where your audience lives. Are they local, national, or international?
- What kinds of sites, publications, and apps your audience uses already.
- Where your interactors go to satisfy their information needs.
- Their ages, occupations, gender, income levels, education levels, races, and ethnicities.

- Their challenges accessing information.
- Cultural factors that might influence what you do and do not do.

Cast a wide net when determining where your interactors go to get what they need. Think of specific sites and apps, but also newspapers and magazines, radio and television programming, newsletters and competitors, and social media sources. You can learn both what to do and what not to do from evaluating these other sources. What conventions can your designs borrow from these other types of information sources? Familiarity will make your content more appealing, and you will spend less time in design and development.

How often do you anticipate interactions with your audience? Hourly, daily, weekly, monthly? The frequency will determine how often your content should be updated or go out. How will you drive traffic to the site? Is your audience already active on Facebook? Twitter? Instagram, LinkedIn, or Google+? You will have to go where they are already and join their conversations to attract visitors to your content. Join the groups and platforms they already use. Read everything you can about your audience. Spend time with and among the members of your audience in social networking contexts.

## INFORMATION ARCHITECTURE

The next question is how to present your information. This planning and organization of information is referred to as information architecture, a process complex enough that there are entire academic departments dedicated to its study. At its most basic level, the aim of information architecture is to determine a hierarchy for a site by grouping related information. These groupings should be presented according to some hierarchy of importance, which can then determine page layouts and site tree development. A site tree is a graphical representation of how a site's parts relate or link to one another. Once the hierarchy has been determined, map it out graphically on paper for the beginnings of a site tree (see Figure 6.4).

There are many possible models for site architecture, some linear or sequential, and some non-linear. Again, it might be helpful to think in terms of a spectrum, with a 1–2–3 sequence or linear model at one end and a highly interconnected web model at the other. Slideshows, for example, are sequential. Sites that walk users through a procedure, skill, or practice are, as well. They have a predictable structure and are, therefore, fairly simple to plan.

On the other extreme is a site like Wikipedia, which has no discrete beginning and no determinate end. Pages interconnect and cross-reference, providing a deep, rich web of information accessible in an almost infinite number of different sequences. Wikipedia is flexible and scalable, changing all the time. Wikipedia is, therefore, a very complex

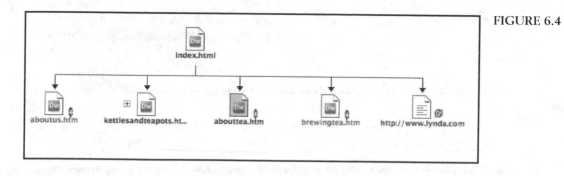

FIGURE 6.4

site, but its architecture permits and facilitates this interconnectedness and its ability to continually expand.

Some sites and many intranets combine these models. In the aggregate, most corporate intranets are webs of interconnected, hyperlinked information. But you're likely to find a section or two for training, sections that follow a sequential progression. *The New York Times* site has a clear beginning—the front page or homepage, but a reader may wish to access a wide variety of different kinds of articles in any number of sequences. The *Times* site, therefore, is organized into sections and areas of interest rather than by sequential order.

## STYLE GUIDES AND STYLEBOOKS

Editors are known to obsess over proper adherence to a particular style, making the house stylebook the organization's editorial "bible." Why is style that big of a deal? Well, consider this usage example taken from *Eats, Shoots & Leaves*, a one-time bestseller in the United Kingdom on the subject of punctuation. (That's right—a bestseller on punctuation.) As the book's title also colorfully illustrates, this example shows that even a jot or a tittle (a dot or a dash) can alter the meaning of a sentence.

> "A woman, without her man, is nothing."
> "A woman: without her, man is nothing."

The only difference in the two, besides their entire meaning, is one colon and one comma. Here's another, from the description of Christ's crucifixion in the New Testament, specifically the Gospel of Luke:

> "Then he said, 'Jesus, remember me when you come into your kingdom.'
> Jesus answered him, 'Truly I tell you, today you will be with me in paradise.' "

Because the original Greek lacked contemporary punctuation options, where the commas go in this dialogue were, at best, educated guesses. Thus, this exchange of words might actually have gone down like this:

> "Then he said, 'Jesus, remember me when you come into your kingdom.'
> Jesus answered him, 'Truly I tell you today, you will be with me in paradise.' "

One comma placement, therefore, can make all the difference. For your in-house style, are you going to use the Associated Press comma scheme of "A, B and C"? Or, are you going to embrace what is called the Oxford comma and instead stipulate "A, B, and C"? Despite the raging controversy on this question (http://mentalfloss.com/article/33637/best-shots-fired-oxford-comma-wars), the important point here isn't which style to use, but rather to make that decision so that your team is consistent in its usage, in service to your audience.

Stylebooks list rules, recommendations, guidelines, and examples on topics as far-ranging as abbreviation and acronyms, capitalization, numerals, grammar, and terms and jargon. Some of the rules might at first seem arbitrary, but the intent is to ensure clarity and consistency. Over time, the in-house stylebook will catalog the accumulated wisdom and experience of editors and writers encountering new usage questions and determining their answers. The implicit message to your interactors is that you and your fellow content producers are conscientious, careful, and reliable. And by offering established norms and solutions, a stylebook saves time and contributes to speed and efficiency. In anticipating and answering questions, stylebooks sweat the small stuff so that writers and editors can spend their time on bigger problems. For instance, writers don't have to wonder whether to write "NASA" or "National Aeronautics and Space Administration" (or "National Aeronautics & Space Administration," for that matter) on first reference. Their stylebook will tell them. Thus, the organization doesn't end up constantly second-guessing itself on usage questions.

The goals of style guides and stylebooks are those of good writing: clarity, concision, and consistency. And these attributes are needed wherever type appears. Style guides should, therefore, stipulate recommendations on style for headlines, deckheads, subheads, and photo cutlines. These stipulations might include typeface designations, including one for headlines and another for body copy and perhaps still another for cutlines. If your organization is active in social media, your style guide should specify guidelines for these communications, as well. The purpose here isn't to restrict content creators, but rather to give them structure, models, and norms that will contribute to consistency of voice.

The Associated Press Stylebook (www.apstylebook.com) is the industry standard for journalism and public relations. Another standard style, *The Chicago Manual of Style*, emerged more than a century ago when one proofreader began writing down on a single sheet of paper a few basic style rules. This list became a booklet, then in 1906 the first edition of *The Chicago Manual of Style* was published. The 16th edition (www.chicagomanualofstyle.org/home.html) checked in at a whopping 1,026 pages. One reason this style is so strong, besides its detailed instructions, is the manual's balance between establishing rules and allowing the writer or publisher flexibility out of "respect for the author's individuality, purpose, and style, tempered though it is with a deeply felt responsibility to prune from work whatever stylistic infelicities, inconsistencies, and ambiguities might have gained stealthy entrance" (*The Chicago Manual of Style*, 2010, Preface, p. viii).

*Wired Style*, by Constance Hale and Jessie Scanlon, was one of the first style guides native to the Internet, and it communicates and embodies an attitude specific to the Wired family of media. (Oddly, for an Internet style guide, *Wired Style* isn't available anywhere online.) *Wired Style* began on a single sheet of paper. Copy editors simply documented style questions as they cropped up, along with the answers to those questions as they were negotiated on the fly by the publishing company's editorial staff. That single page evolved into a lengthy computer file, which ultimately produced Hale's and Scanlon's book.

Like all style guides, the one in use at *Wired* evolved from year to year. The book had two print runs, in 1996 and 1999, but hasn't been produced since. When it was revised, Wired staff wrestled with terms and words, and when a new term, buzzword, or acronym emerged, they debated its style and proper usage. Somehow out of all the email messages and debates, agreement emerged. As examples, here are two terms and their style explained from *Wired*'s usage book:

### FDDI

Pronounced "fiddy" and standing in for "fiber distributed data interface," this fiberbased network architecture offers a faster and more dependable alternative to Ethernet or Token Ring. (It transmits at 100 Mbits per second over LANs and MANs.) Of course, with gigabit Ethernet on the horizon, the future of FDDI looks bleak.

### FILE NAME

Two words, like "screen name" and "domain name." In the early DOS days, computers wouldn't allow spaces in names and forced users to make file names one word. But "file name" was never closed up—in DOS or in English.

For a comparison, here are a few entries from the *Associated Press Stylebook*, from the "A" section at the front of the volume. These entries make far fewer assumptions about the guide's readers than does *Wired*'s, which is a reflection of the wide adoption of AP's stylebook across industry:

- **academic degrees**—Put an apostrophe in bachelor's degree and master's degree. This is to show possession. The degree belongs to the bachelor or master (that's you). Even when shortened to bachelor's and master's (no "degree" afterward), you keep the apostrophe.
- **addresses**—Abbreviate the words street, avenue and boulevard (think S-A-B), but only if they appear after a numbered address. Also abbreviate compass directions, but only if they appear with a numbered address. So, you'd write 50 S. Court St., but if you leave off the house number, you'd write South Court Street. Got it? Never abbreviate drive, highway, place, or any of the other words that might follow an actual street name such as Court, Union, Ventura, Lombard, Pennsylvania or whatever. Let's use this system for Utah addresses: 1160 E. 100 South St.

## Developing Your Own Stylebook

Larger news and public relations organizations typically develop their own house styles. *The Economist* (www.economist.com/styleguide/introduction), for instance, and *The Guardian* (www.theguardian.com/guardian-observer-style-guide-a) each have their own guides to harmonize their many disparate writers and voices. For most organizations, it makes sense to adopt an existing style guide as a foundation, then add to and amend that guide specific to your organization's needs, usage questions, and audience sensitivities. This textbook relies on the *AP Stylebook* for text and Lynch's and Horton's *Web Style Guide* for its visual style. Collect case studies and examples over time from which to write individual stylebook entries.

No style guide is ever truly finished, all-inclusive, or complete; all are works in progress. The *AP Stylebook* is updated with a new print edition annually, and it is updated more frequently for subscribers online. The University of North Carolina School of Media & Journalism created an addendum to the *AP Stylebook* to govern usage specific to UNC. Here is that addendum's entry on academic degrees, an important and recurring subject for reporters and editors covering the university:

**Academic Degrees:** In general, reserve the title Dr. for M.D.s and other medical degrees. Use Ph.D., LL.D. and other degrees to establish a person's credentials. The preferred form is to use a title or phrase. (John Bruno, assistant professor of marine ecology and conservation.) Do not precede a name with a courtesy title for an academic degree and follow it with the abbreviation for the degree. Wrong: Dr. Jane Smith, M.D. Use an apostrophe with bachelor's and master's degrees, but not in Bachelor of Science or Master of Arts. Avoid academic degree abbreviations; use the reference in a phrase (Gayle Smith, who has a doctorate in medicine). Examples of degrees awarded at North Carolina include:

- bachelor of arts (B.A.) (a bachelor's);
- bachelor of science (B.S.);
- doctor of education (Ed.D.);
- doctor of law (J.D.) (a doctorate);
- doctor of medicine (M.D.);
- doctor of pharmacy (Pharm.D.);
- doctor of philosophy (Ph.D.);
- doctor of public health (Dr. P.H.);
- master of arts (M.A.) (a master's);
- master of business administration (M.B.A.);
- master of public health (M.P.H.); and
- master of science (M.S.).

Similarly, the *News & Record* newspaper (www.greensboro.com) in Greensboro, NC, augments the *AP Stylebook* with its own wiki-hosted stylebook at http://nrcopydesk. wikifoundry.com/. In addition to entries on Greensboro-specific topics, such as O. Henry and the Atlantic Coast Conference, the copy desk wiki lists names, titles, and contact information for local government officials, and it lists alphabetically local companies and organizations, such as the Winn-Dixie grocery chain and the North Carolina Zoo. Also helpful is a listing of trademarked names, including, from the "L" section:

**Liquid Plumr** drain opener;
**Lite** light beer by Miller;
**Little League** baseball sports services;
**Little Tikes** preschool toys;
**Loafer** shoes;
**Lotus 1–2–3** computer software;
**Lucite** acrylic resin, paints; and
**Lycra** spandex fibers.

If your organization, company, or site decides to develop its own style guide, there are several sections you will want to consider, including:

- vocabulary;
- abbreviations and acronyms;
- italics, bolds, quotation marks, and parentheses;
- hyphens and dashes;
- punctuation;
- capitalization;
- headlines and subheads, including colors and font types and sizes;
- hyperlinking protocols (active, visited, etc.);
- ordered and unordered lists;
- graphic design issues;
- photo captions;
- numbers;
- spacing; and
- logos, slogans, taglines.

A site with medical information is going to be very different than one providing help in real estate. Terminology; graphics, photography, and diagrams; tables and charts; and level of formality in writing also will vary. And your own style guide will evolve over time. Implicit, then, is that language and usage are always changing.

## Specific Usage Categories

Like *Wired Style*, your stylebook should address usage questions common to webpages and specific to digital communication. For example, you might stipulate something like the following

When presenting file names, use only lowercase letters. Examples:
florence.wmv
asparagus_recipe.docx
siena.jpg OR siena.jpeg
verona.pptx

On first reference, put technical terms in italics:
"Viewing this movie requires a *Flash plug-in*."
Except when beginning a sentence, follow proprietary company name conventions. Examples:

amazon
bebo
ebay
General Motors

When presenting URLs, use only lowercase letters: http://cubanxgiants.com.

## Numerals and Numbers

One of the largest sections of your stylebook will be that devoted to presenting numbers and numerals. For example, for dates, will you go with the "month, day, year" sequence that is convention in the United States (November 18, 2017) or the "day, month, year" order more common in Europe (18 November 2017)? As the Associated Press stipulates, will you spell out numbers less than 10 and switch to numerals in references of more than nine? Any good stylebook will cover these basic scenarios. When presenting currency amounts, AP Style stipulates the following, to cite only a few examples:

- $4.2 billion
- $100
- 30,000 British pounds

Here are several other categories for numbers and numerals as presented by AP Style, and in them you can see a consistency of approach:
Use numerals for

## Academic course numbers:

- Calculus 2
- English 101

## Addresses:

- 1600 Pennsylvania Avenue

Spell out numbered streets nine and under. For example,

- The address is 5 Sixth St.
- Go to the restaurant at 1500 32nd St.

### Ages:

- A 6-year-old boy
- An 8-year-old car
- A 4-year-old house

Use hyphens for ages expressed as adjectives before a noun or as substitutes for a noun. For example,

- The 5-year-old boy

—but—

- The boy is 5 years old.

Also,

- The boy, 5, has a sister, 10.
- The race is for 3-year-olds.
- The woman is in her 30s.
- She is a 30-something.

—but—

- Thirty-something to start a sentence.

You get the idea. Your section on numerals, then, will cover ages, dates, times, fractions and decimals, units of measure, money and currency, percentages and ratios, phone numbers, and perhaps stock quotes, sports scores, and temperature readings, depending on the kinds of content your organization regularly produces.

## ETHICS

Just as a stylebook can routinize the many small decisions that writers and editors have to make about usage in a workday, a code of ethics can routinize some pretty big decisions, such as how to balance competing interests and priorities, establish and communicate integrity, and, ultimately, win the trust of their audience(s). Lawyers who violate their profession's code of ethics can be disbarred. Physicians also can be prohibited from practicing medicine. But digital communicators? Bloggers? Tweeters? Shame is usually the only punishment. Creating, maintaining, and applying a code of ethics are voluntary activities, therefore, and freedom of expression demands that this be the case. However, professional integrity implies fealty to standards generally agreed to be best practices for your particular field. Most journalists, for example, follow the Society of Professional Journalists' (SPJ's) Code of Ethics, a list of standards that translates well to the digital environments. In fact, some bloggers have developed ethical codes based on SPJ's version, which is excerpted here:

The SPJ code calls journalists to:

- Seek Truth and Report It
  Journalists should be honest, fair and courageous in gathering, reporting and interpreting information.
- Minimize Harm
  Ethical journalists treat sources, subjects and colleagues as human beings deserving of respect.
- Act Independently
  Journalists should be free of obligation to any interest other than the public's right to know.
- Be Accountable
- Journalists are accountable to their readers, listeners, viewers and each other.

—Society of Professional Journalists' Code of Ethics
(www.spj.org/ethicscode.asp)

For another, very different example, take a look at blogging pioneer Rebecca Blood's attempt at codifying good hygiene for bloggers, excerpted from her book *The Weblog Handbook*:

1. Publish as fact only that which you believe to be true. If a statement is merely speculation, it should be so stated.
2. If material exists online, link to it when you reference it. Readers can judge for themselves and a founding principle of blogging is exercising freedom of expression and the marketplace of ideas. Online readers "deserve, as much as possible, access to all of the facts," Blood writes.
3. Publicly correct any misinformation. Typically entries are not rewritten or corrected, but later entries should correct inaccurate information in those earlier posts. Inaccurate and erroneous information on other blogs should also be corrected in the spirit of the greater blogging community's responsibility to one another and to its readers.
4. Write each entry as if it could not be changed; add to, but do not re-write or delete, any entry. "Post deliberately," Blood advises.

5. Disclose any conflict of interest.
6. Note questionable or unbiased sources.

Blood's code, published in the very early stages of blogging's history, and the Society of Professional Journalists' Code of Ethics share some significant characteristics. Both espouse:

- publishing the truth;
- supporting arguments with credible sources;
- being accountable;
- spending time writing as though changes could not be made; and
- disclosing conflicts of interests, articulated by the SPJ as acting independently.

## Putting It Into Practice

Once you've developed a code to guide decision-making, you are halfway there. The remaining piece of the puzzle is to establish a process. Many confuse ethical imperatives with moral values, thinking that making an ethical decision is as simple as "doing the right thing." This is naïve and, in times of crisis, unreliable. Ethical decision-making should be a multi-step collaborative, systematic process, which makes it a skill that can be learned.

Borrowing heavily from Bill Mitchell's "Ethics Tool," developed when Mitchell was with the Poynter Institute, here's how to do it. This breakdown can be applied in either journalistic or public relations organizations:

## Step One: Define the Goal

What do you need to decide, and when do you need to decide it?

## Step Two: Start With the Facts

What do you know for sure? What can you independently verify and corroborate? What has happened so far? What pieces of the puzzle are still missing? What do you not yet know? What are your assumptions? How might you be wrong? What are the facts from the point of view of those who might be harmed by our decision? Do you know enough to make this decision now? What else do you need to know?

## Step Three: Know Your Purpose

What does your audience need? What are your obligations in terms of the information you should provide that audience?

## Step Four: Consider the Ethical Principles at Stake. These Might, and for Journalistic Operations Likely Will, Include:

- reporting the truth;
- serving the public interest;
- protecting independence;
- informing the public;
- minimizing harm;
- modeling for citizens, both process and result;
- giving citizens the information they need to govern themselves;
- holding government accountable;
- shining a light into dark places;
- keeping promises;
- acting justly;
- not deceiving; and
- helping those in need.

Consider your mission. What are your over-arching goals and imperatives? Your code of ethics should articulate and perhaps even rank these imperatives. (Ethical principles can be developed by reading the work of Immanuel Kant, W. D. Ross, Aristotle, Thomas Aquinas, and Bernard Gert.)

## Step Five: Identify the Principles That Are in Tension With One Another

Put a check mark beside those you identified in Step Four that are in conflict. Usually— almost always—an ethical crisis pits at least two of these values against each other. It is this tension that likely gives rise to the ethical dilemma in the first place. Weed out those principles that are not applicable so you can focus on those few that are most relevant.

## Step Six: Identify the Stakeholders

Who are they?

- sources;
- subjects;
- clients;
- families of subjects or sources;
- institutions;
- your organization;

- other organizations;
- person or people making the decision; and
- others.

This is not an all-inclusive list, just one to provoke or inspire thinking. Next, think about which of the stakeholders are most affected, and which of the stakeholders are most vulnerable.

## Step Seven: Identify Your Options

Put all of your options on the table before discerning which, if any, are viable, remembering that rarely is there only one right answer. What alternative courses of action are possible?

## Step Eight: Evaluate Those Options

Look at the principles you listed as most relevant in this case in Step Five. Discuss the impact of each option on the most relevant principles at stake. The stakeholders don't decide for you what you should do, but imagining their preferences can be useful, and it focuses you on minimizing harm.

## Step Nine: Make a Choice

All things considered, what's the best option? What can be done to reduce the harm to a principle that is being sublimated by your choice of what to do? For example, if you chose to inform people of something that jeopardizes another person's privacy, how can you reduce the impact on those whose privacy is being compromised? How can you minimize harm to vulnerable stakeholders?

## Step Ten: Test Your Thinking

This is the last chance to question your decision, the last opportunity for devil's advocacy. Don't hold anything back. This is also the time to articulate your justification. Imagine being interviewed by, say, CBS's *60 Minutes*. How will you explain to a television audience the decision your news organization made? Or, write a news story explaining your news organization's reasoning, whether you plan to publish it or not.

In your justification, fill in some of these blanks:

- We have decided to _____
- We reached the decision after weighing _____

- We also considered _____
- We think this decision best upholds the principle of _____
- We believe our obligation to _____ is outweighed in this case by or because _____
- To reduce damage or harm to _____, we will _____

You will want to explain and justify your decision-making process. Explain how you determined what to do, and what the tradeoffs were. Transparency builds trust. Thinking through how you would explain the decision ensures that you've been deliberate in making your decision. We serve an audience; we are accountable to that public. What we decide, therefore, should be publicly justifiable.

The secret sauce is to have this process established *before* crisis hits and, thus, anticipate and even get some practice weighing the values that compete in ethical dilemmas. These crises seem to hit right before deadline or when it's time to call it a day and go home.

While it is fine to listen to your gut, don't let that gut reaction fool you into thinking that you know the answer before working through the issues. Trust the process and follow all of the steps. Seek diverse points of view. You need several people with different perspectives, including at least one from a devil's advocate or contrarian point of view, in order to consider all of the options and their consequences. The line between good gut decision-making and fickle instinct is a fine one, if it exists at all. It is also fine to consider the interests of your own organization. After all, your credibility is at stake. But self-serving concerns can't drive the decision, and they can't count more than the interests of the audience you serve or the people who might be hurt by your decision.

This section on ethics might be the most important, most valuable section of this textbook. The 2016 presidential election in the United States gave rise to an alarming spread of fake news online, so much false information that out-going president, Barack Obama, spoke out against it in one of his last major addresses: "Because in an age where there's so much active misinformation and it's packaged very well and it looks the same when you see it on a Facebook page or you turn on your television—if everything seems to be the same and no distinctions are made, then we don't know what to protect," he told an audience in Berlin. "If we are not serious about facts and what's true and what's not, and particularly in an age of social media when so many people are getting their information in sound bites and off their phones, if we can't discriminate between serious arguments and propaganda, then we have problems." Obama was so impassioned on the subject of fake news, he uncharacteristically lost track of the question he had been asked.

Sen. Daniel Patrick Moynihan famously said, "Everyone is entitled to his own opinion, but not his own facts." Yet, bogus news stories appearing online and on social media had by most accounts a more significant impact on the presidential campaign season in its late stages than coverage by authoritative, mainstream news organizations such as *The New York Times* and the *Washington Post*. The seeming preference for fake news by so many led more than a few commentators to describe the U.S. electorate, with the election of Trump, as having entered a "post-fact era." The preponderance of fake news is a problem of quality *and* quantity, one so serious that Facebook was forced after the election to look at how the site deals with fake news and misinformation. Professional propagandists, fringe elements, and conspiracy theorists, who once lurked in the Internet's shadows, now are the center of the public discourse. The priority on ethical decision-making with respect to information gathering and publishing has perhaps never been higher. So, with the provisos articulated here, let's work through a hypothetical scenario in digital journalism to get experience with the process:

A new president of Egypt has just been named, Suleyman bin Daoud, a Shiite who had been an outspoken critic of President Hosni Mubarak and had lived in exile before the revolution of 2011. Shortly after taking office, bin Daoud is kidnapped, along with five American journalists, by a rival Sunni faction. Several hours later, the kidnappers say they have hanged the new president to protest the deposing of Mubarak. The kidnappers don't bother with cell phone video; they provide professional-looking video that shows the prime minister dropping through the platform. The video shows his head snapping off and his body, and head, falling to the floor.

The kidnappers have posted the video on their website, and American officials have independently confirmed that it shows what it says it does: the decapitation of the newly elected Egyptian leader. But American officials are asking American news organizations not to link to the video because, they claim, doing so will help the kidnappers achieve their ends. No American news site has linked to the terrorists' site yet, but your organization is eager to do so. You meet as an editorial team to discuss how to cover these events. Your key questions: Will you include a link to the hanging video and, therefore, the kidnappers' website, or not? Controversy is sure to follow whatever decision you make, thus the second question: How will you explain our decision? Whether you include the link or not, what else will you be sure to include and exclude from your coverage, including the requests from American officials? Use the step-by-step process to come up with both your decisions and their explanations.

## CHAPTER ACTIVITIES

**1** Identify a publication, company, or organization for or about which you will create online content. This entity can be real or imagined, corporate or non-profit, local or national or international: *Outside Magazine*, *The New York Times*, *Coin Collector's Digest*, Coca-Cola,

Habitat for Humanity, International Association of Business Communicators, the Miami Dolphins. The entity you choose should be a publication or organization with which you have or want to have some connection or affiliation, one with which you are already familiar. It can be the one for which you already work or want to work in the future.

Prepare a two-page summary of the audience needs for the publication or organization for which you will be writing and editing content. Do some research. Your summary should include:

- **Audience profile.** Who will be reading the content?
- **Purpose of publication.** Is it for entertainment, for news, for something else?
- **Frequency of publication.** Is it a monthly magazine? A mobile site updated on the hour?
- **The competition.** What are the sites and publications competing for the same audience?
- **Style issues.** Will you maintain the current style guide of the publication or organization, or is there need for a new one?
- **Information challenges.** What does the audience need to know, or what information does the organization need to broadcast? Do any special obstacles stand in the way of communicating that information quickly and clearly?
- **Your response to the information challenges.** How will you overcome any barriers and get your content out there?

If you have access to database providers such as Hoover's, Lexis Nexis, or Bloomberg, run some searches on competitors who serve the same audiences as those you seek. Learn what you can from what these competitors have experienced and are doing.

2 Detail the online content you will create for your organization or publication. What you write and develop is up to you, so you have the flexibility to do what makes sense and to write what can best serve you where you are now—in school, on the job, or on the job hunt. Possibilities for this assignment include:

- a news story or series of news stories;
- a feature story;
- criticism, such as a restaurant review, play or movie review, book review;
- an interactive press release; and
- a how-to feature.

These are just a few of the possibilities. Keep your publication's audience first and foremost in your mind. Identify the topic or angle of your proposed piece, making sure the topic is relevant and timely. This is a story or piece you will actually write, develop, and produce. You will gather the information, do the reporting, conduct the interviews, see the play—whatever is necessary to produce the copy.

**3** Develop a half-dozen style entries for how your organization will present numerals in various contexts. Choose from entries covering ages, dates, times, fractions and decimals, units of measure, money and currency, percentages and ratios, phone numbers, stock quotes, and sports scores. The Cubs beat the Indians 8–7 to win the Series? Or eight to seven? Or 8-to-7? It's your call.

**4** Divide up into groups and have each group begin drafting a code of ethics for your hypothetical organization. Think about the kinds of ethical questions and dilemmas that might come up and provide an ethical road map for navigating competing values or interests, such as timeliness and accuracy.

**5** If your group hypothesized being a journalistic organization, use the ethical code drafted above to discuss and come up with decisions about what to do in these difficult journalistic scenarios:

A. You discover that police have seized toxic chemicals from a group of young Syrian refugees living in town and are questioning them on suspicion of planning to drop the chemicals into the local water supply. The group's lawyer pleads with you to write nothing, saying that the matter will be cleared up and that publicity would exacerbate anti-refugee, anti-immigrant prejudices and make it impossible for them to remain in the community. Do you write about it? Write a justification for your decision based on your code of ethics.

B. You find that police have a new suspect in a high-profile local murder case and are interrogating him. An anonymous source inside law enforcement gives you a copy of the suspect's police file. The suspect's wife contacts you to beg you not to go public with the information in the file, saying the coverage would traumatize their three children and prevent her husband from receiving a fair trial as guaranteed by the Sixth Amendment to the U.S. Constitution. Do you break the story? Write a justification for your decision based on your code of ethics.

C. You learn that a local high school girls' lacrosse coach has been repeatedly accused of sexual misconduct and previously left two schools under similar accusations. The school system superintendent seems willing to simply allow the coach to move again before the next school year. You contact the coach, who says he is in fact leaving the area and pleads with you not to pursue the story. He seems to imply that if the story broke, he might kill himself to avoid the shame. What do you do? Write a justification for your decision based on your code of ethics.

## Digital Resources

**American Copy Editors Society (copydesk.org)**
Resources at the site include reference materials, quizzes, and help in discussion.

**Associated Press Stylebook (apstylebook.com/)**
*Chicago Manual of Style* Online (chicagomanualofstyle.org/home.html)

**Dictionary.com—Style Guides (dictionary.com/Dir/Arts/Writers_Resources/Style_Guides/)**
Online listing of style guides and manuals, including a handful of guides specifically for digital usage.

**Guide to Grammar and Style (andromeda.rutgers.edu/~jlynch/writing/)**
Online guide to grammar, style, and usage by Jack Lynch, professor of English at Rutgers University.

**InfoDesign (informationdesign.org/)**
Articles about information design.

**Oxford Dictionaries (oxforddictionaries.com/us)**
The online version is frequently updated, providing a rich source when determining style on newer terms and slang, such as "twerk" and "srsly."

**The Slot: A Spot for Copy Editors (theslot.com)**
Site of Bill Walsh, long-time copy editor and author of several books on editing.

**Society for News Design (snd.org)**
This society is for designers in journalism, and the site offers resources selected for the group.

**W3's Style Guide for Online Hypertext (w3.org/Provider/Style/)**
This document was written in the early days of the web, defining such terms as "webmaster," the "www.name.com" convention, and a few basic points which are just as valid today. Readers should note that the site has not been updated to discuss recent developments in HTML, and it is out of date in many places.

# BIBLIOGRAPHY

*Associated Press Stylebook*, 2016 edition (Washington, DC: Associated Press, 2016).

Blood, Rebecca, *The Weblog Handbook* (Cambridge, MA: Perseus Publishing, 2002).

*The Chicago Manual of Style*, 16th edition (Chicago, IL: University of Chicago Press, 2010).

Hale, Constance and Scanlon, Jessie, *Wired Style: Principles of English Usage in the Digital Age* (New York, NY: Broadway Books, 2002).

Hammerich, Irene and Harrison, Claire, *Developing Online Content: The Principles of Writing and Editing for the Web* (New York, NY: John Wiley & Sons, 2002).

Hilligloss, Susan and Howard, Tharon, *Visual Communication: A Writer's Guide* (New York, NY: Longman, 2002).

Huang, Kuan-Tsae, Lee, Yang W., and Wang, Richard Y., *Quality Information and Knowledge* (Upper Saddle River, NJ: Prentice Hall, 1999).

Kessler, Glenn, "Fact Checking in the aftermath of a historic election," *Washington Post* (November 10 2016), available: www.washingtonpost.com/news/fact-checker/wp/2016/11/10/fact-checking-in-the-aftermath-of-an-historic-election/.

Krug, Steve, *Don't Make Me Think: A Common Sense Approach to Web Usability* (Indianapolis, IN: Macmillan, 2000).

McCulloch, Gretchen, "*Wired Style*: A Linguist Explains Vintage Internet Slang," available: http://the-toast.net/2015/08/26/wired-style-a-linguist-explains-vintage-internet-slang.

McCulloch, Gretchen, *The Toast* (August 26 2015), available: http://the-toast.net/2015/08/26/wired-style-a-linguist-explains-vintage-internet-slang/.

McKay, Peter, "Just the (fake) facts, ma'am," *Pittsburgh Post-Gazette* (November 19 2016), available: www.post-gazette.com/life/lifestyle/2016/11/19/Peter-McKay-Just-the-fake-facts-ma-am/stories/201611190026.

Mozur, Paul and Scott, Mark, "Fake News in U.S. Election? Elsewhere, That's Nothing New," *The New York Times* (November 17 2016), available: www.nytimes.com/2016/11/18/technology/fake-news-on-facebook-in-foreign-elections-thats-not-new.html?.

Truss, Lynne, *Eats, Shoots & Leaves* (New York, NY: Gotham Books, 2004).

# Blogito Ergo Sum

*Whether explaining or complaining, joking or serious, the human voice is unmistakably genuine. It can't be faked.*
—Doc Searls, *The Cluetrain Manifesto*

*Blogging is to writing what extreme sports are to athletics: more free-form, more accident-prone, less formal, more alive. It is, in many ways, writing out loud.*
—Andrew Sullivan, prolific blogger and former editor of *The New Republic*

*If we can't discriminate between serious arguments and propaganda, then we have problems.*
—Barack Obama

## INTRODUCTION

The Supreme Court ruled in the landmark case *Branzburg v. Hayes* (1972) that the First Amendment's protections applied as much to "the lonely pamphleteer" as to the "large metropolitan publisher." Today, "the lonely pamphleteer" is anyone with a blog, a Twitter feed, or a Facebook page, which is both a boon and a bane to democracy. Anyone can publish, which is inherently egalitarian. Unfortunately, not all who do publish have any sort of loyalty to truth or the public good, as the last U.S. presidential election cycle put on stark, even terrifying display. At the forefront of digital media's re-ordering of the media landscape have been blogs and blogging. Bloggers daily influence changes in public opinion, how brands and products are perceived, and how political campaigns are won and lost. The blogosphere is a key piece of digital real estate and a longer form for writing than most social media offer. Blogging should be thought of, therefore, in a larger digital media context, one that includes and incorporates social media and social networks. This chapter covers the basics of this writing and publishing form, including live blogging and journalistic blogs. (Blogging for public relations is further covered in Chapter 9.)

## FOLKS BLOGGIN'

A "blog," from the longer term, "weblog," is simply a website powered by software that makes it easy to publish to the web, typically posting content as entries in reverse chronological order. The most recent posts typically appear on top. Other common attributes of blogs include archives, permalinks (or hyperlinks to specific posts and the comments published in response to those posts), time-and-date stamps, tags (or key word identification), and blogrolls (hyperlinked lists of other, recommended blogs). Blog posts typically connect their readers with source materials mentioned or used by the writer, a cross-referencing that provides layers of information and, by both displaying and providing access to source material, can contribute to credibility. When a blogger comments on a speech, for example, he or she likely will link to a transcript or audio recording of the speech, making it transparent to the reader where fact leaves off and opinion begins.

The shapes and forms blogging can take make broad categorizations of blogs a fool's errand. Types range from personal diaries to major news websites to collections of rants. At its simplest, the term "blog" means nothing more than the few attributes described above; thus, it is a value-neutral medium or media format. The term does not preclude or exclude any one sort of content, just as a pen or pencil has no logical connection to the things people might use them to write. As a technology, there is nothing about the ink pen that makes it more or less capable of producing exquisite literature as opposed to pure drivel. A blog is no different. Thus, blogging is a lot like writing; the way the blog format is used defines blogging as practice.

This chapter is most interested in blogs dedicated to news, information, opinion, and public relations and, therefore, not those devoted to personal events, seemingly private thoughts, and observations from daily life. The practices of good blogging, however, are applicable to all blog formats. The best blogs create for their readers a sort of "targeted serendipity," as pioneering blogger Rebecca Blood has called it, or a shared point of view and information and sources a reader perhaps did not even know he or she wanted to

**FIGURE 7.1**
*The blogroll at the Bleeding Yankee Blue blog
(bleedingyankeeblue.blogspot.com/)*

read. Blogging can be understood as an expression of community, as well, allowing individuals to communicate and congregate around shared ideas and interests.

## HOW TO BLOG

There are at least three hallmarks of good blogs. First, they are updated frequently, often very frequently. The reason blogging software was developed in the first place was to make it easy to publish to the web. So the format is ideally suited to fast-developing news stories or public relations crises; the reporter, writer, or corporate official can frequently, serially update information as it is made available. Good blogs are timely. Second, and related to the first, is the fact that virtually all of the popular blogging platforms automatically place the most recent posts at the top, or in reverse chronological order. This reverse-ordering has become a convention of many digital media, thanks primarily to blogs. Twitter, Facebook feeds, and social mobile media have since embraced this chronological sequencing of posts so that readers do not have to scroll or hunt for the newest information. Lastly, good blogs make good use of tags, or key word identifiers that can be used to find related posts and that search engines use to index the blogosphere. A post on the soccer's World Cup might be tagged with the key words "World Cup," "soccer," "futbol," and "FIFA." Twitter's hashtags are a derivative of the blogosphere's tags.

As they have been discussed so far in this book, the principles of good writing for digital spaces all apply when writing for blogs: Writing a compelling headline, layering content, making that content scannable, breaking information up into easily read chunks, and linking to relevant material elsewhere on the web. Let's say your organization has completed and published an in-depth report on a complex topic. The report is, say, 50 standard print pages, or the rough equivalent of a magazine. In your organization's blog, you could summarize that report's key findings and provide a link to the full report, which could be made available in .pdf or .doc form and/or perhaps in formats for e-readers and tablets (.xml, .epub, and .mobi, among others). You could then tweet out links to both the blogged summary and the full report, using hashtags that will facilitate a conversation about the report's findings. Any or all of these communications could include links to the Facebook pages and websites of organizations doing something about the problems your report describes or charts, connecting your audience with action and involvement.

To promote scanning and layering, blogs should use lists whenever possible, such as when presenting:

- product features;
- requirements for submitting or applying for something;
- aspects of a candidate's background or bio;
- details of a legal decision;
- supplies needed for a project;
- ingredients for a recipe;
- subsections of a long or multi-page article; and
- directions on how to create or complete something.

## Choosing a Platform

With more than 82 million users, the most popular blog software is Wordpress, which offers a free, self-hosted version (wordpress.com) and a paid version (wordpress.org) that can scale and expand into a very complex website or content management

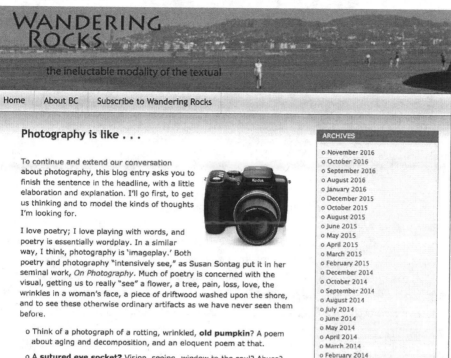

**FIGURE 7.2**
*The author's blog, at WanderingRocks. wordpress.com*

system. Wordpress's flexibility and ease of use are the big reasons it has become so favored. The number and variety of plug-ins and add-ons Wordpress has spawned also is an advantage over the many competitors. The free version lets you choose from a vast and ever-growing catalog of themes, and the software's open source, code-driven environment means you can tinker around with enhancements and customizations to the extent you wish. Wordpress is also superior when it comes to social media integration. Automatic post-and-share features include connecting to Facebook, Twitter, LinkedIn, and Tumblr. Wordpress bloggers can also facilitate sharing via Stumble-Upon, Pinterest, and Reddit by adding buttons to their Wordpress blog posts and pages.

Probably the easiest to start up and begin using is Google's Blogger.com. Like Wordpress, it is free, hosted in the cloud, and almost fully automated and template-driven. The learning curve is short and shallow: You can be blogging in minutes. One of the leaders, even pioneers, of the blogging movement, Meg Hourihan, co-founded Pyra Labs to develop the software now known as Blogger, which Google acquired along with the rest of Pyra in May 2003. Blogger.com's software is one of a number that automate the blog publishing process and, therefore, eliminate the need for users to write any code or install any sort of server-side software or scripting. Once launched, Blogger.com's blogs employ templates and a Word-like toolbar to make writing and submitting posts a simple exercise. Because it is owned by Google, you also have access to Google tools such as AdSense, Analytics, YouTube, Gmail, and Google+. This integration is either a positive or a negative, depending upon your pre-existing relationship with Google and its many services. Google has not been bashful in favoring its own products and services and, therefore, Blogger offers less flexibility with non-Google add-ons. Thus, Blogger isn't as flexible or customizable as Wordpress, but the platform is so easy to use, it is worth trying, even if you intend to go with another software longer term.

Perhaps the platform most integrated with social mobile media is Tumblr. While also easy to use, Tumblr is not a blog as they have been traditionally understood. A sort of hybrid of a blog and a Twitter feed, Tumblr is best suited for short blasts of multimedia, in particular if you are trying to reach an exclusively iPhone- or Android-using market or audience. Tumblr posts are automatically optimized for smartphone delivery. Really short posts, GIFs, Spotify tracks, videos, mp3s, artwork—these are the raw materials of a good Tumblr feed. Also free, with 1,000 themes to choose from, Tumblr is most valuable to those who are a part of the Tumblr community. Starting up an account comes with a built-in community. So if your organization or brand has a recognizable Tumblr sub-community, get in there, but if reaching more general audiences is the goal, this isn't the blog platform with which to start. If you are interested in customizing, Tumblr tumbles down the list of options; its environment is less flexible, with far fewer add-ons and plug-ins than Wordpress allows. Other blogging platform options include Typepad, WIX, Medium, and Movable Type.

## Ten Steps to Better Blogging

Once you've made your platform choice, designated a URL, selected a theme, and created an "About Me" page, you are ready to begin blogging. Here are ten practical steps or, more accurately, good habits that will help you write a better blog:

1. **Write every day.** In arguing for frequent, regular blogging, Rebecca Blood wrote, "It's easy to write poorly, but it's hard to write poorly every day. . . . It's hard to write every day." Write frequently and regularly, and your writing will grow stronger with the practice, and it will keep your blog current.
2. **Schedule your blogging time.** Like establishing any new habit, blogging requires planning and commitment, so determine when in the day or night you can consistently blog, then stick to that time. Some will prefer to write early in the morning, coffee in hand, with energy reservoirs at their maximum. Others prefer the calm reflection of late evenings, after the day's events have played out.

3. **Be authentic.** A jazz music deejay in Greensboro, NC, daily signed off his broadcasts with the call to, "Be yourself so you won't be by yourself." The best blogs have an authentically human voice that is distinctive, even idiosyncratic. Don't worry about pleasing everyone from the start. Instead, write for an audience of one—yourself. This will help you to cultivate the authenticity, transparency, and voice you need. The networked and Google-searched web will connect your area of interest or expertise with readers who share a similar point of view and/or interest, as will your activities on Twitter, Facebook, and other referral systems. Sites like Google, Storify, Technorati, Digg, Reddit, and Stumbleupon will pick up on what you are posting and make your writing known to ever larger audiences.

4. **Carve out a niche.** The best bloggers focus on specific interests—the narrower the topic, the better. This focus leverages your expertise and experience in the area and establishes credibility. It also discourages rambling.

5. **Be curious and take lots of notes.** Not every thought is blog worthy, so keep a notebook or temporary file of your musings, thoughts, ideas, links, and articles of interest—anything that might inform your blogging. When you keep your daily appointment to write, you can relax knowing you have a file or folder of goodies to get you going rather than having to stare at an empty template postbox and write from scratch a pithy or provocative post. This is a really useful tip for writing in general, and many if not most good writers practice this (just look for their Moleskine journals tucked inside a pocket or backpack).

6. **Engage.** When you get comments, tweets, and Facebook "likes," respond to them. Encourage them. Affirm your readers and continue the conversations your posts have begun. This is about community building. Participate on other people's blogs, include their blogs on your blogroll, and link to other posts when appropriate. Share their content. The blogosphere operates on the principle of reciprocity, so make sure you are creating plenty of social capital by being interested and engaged with the ideas of others in your blog circle or community. If you are not prepared to engage at this level, there really is no point to starting up a blog.

7. **Learn the software.** You don't have to become an expert coder, but you can devote an "upgrade day" every few weeks or so to learn more about the software you're using to power your blog. Experiment with its newer features and play with the settings. Learn more about what your blog can do. You could also use this planned time to tag or retag posts to better organize your content and to make it easier to find specific posts. This is a good time to check for broken links, as well.

8. **Promote yourself.** Don't be shy. Market your blog. Tweet out. Integrate it into your Facebook activity. Register your blog with Technorati, which indexes and provides blog search. Register with the major search engines. Set up RSS and email feeds of your site to have your content delivered to anyone who wants to subscribe. Google

Analytics is a free tool any blogger can use to see how people are finding you and what terms they used to locate your blog, which can inform how you tag content and the kinds of headlines you write.

9. **Break up the text.** Though your writing may be Pulitzer Prize-worthy, your readers will still need some visual relief. Follow the basic graphic design and layout principles covered in previous chapters, and use boldface, lists, photos, graphics, cartoons, breakout diagrams, and illustrations to elaborate your post and break up what otherwise might be an overwhelming storm of words.

10. **Be ethical.** Think through and hold to a code of ethics. An old adage advises that the best time to plan what you would do with a lot of money is when you don't have any, because when you are flush with cash, your values will likely change based on your appetites. Similarly, planning ahead for ethical challenges by adopting a code of ethics will allow you to have a set of carefully deliberated priorities, goals, and values to turn to in times of crisis, when decisions about content need to be made quickly and resolutely. Tell the truth, acknowledge and correct mistakes, link to your sources, and when you disagree, do so respectfully.

To this list, integrated marketing company Razorfish adds the following, a list of guidelines issued to its blogging employees:

- Be personal. Write as "I." Let people know who you are and your background.
- Be clear. If you blog, state the purpose of your blog up front.
- Be relevant. Are you contributing to a blog about technology? Keep your comments focused on the topic.
- Be interesting. Have an opinion.
- Be credible. Write about what you know.
- Be responsive. Has someone posted a question for you? Follow up.
- Do not restrict access to your blog by specific individuals or groups.
- Do not self-censor by removing posts or comments once they are published unless they are inappropriate under these guidelines (e.g., comments that reveal confidential information).
- Maintain your blog. Don't blog just for the sake of blogging, but try to post at least once every few weeks.

## LIVE BLOGGING

The simplicity and low or even no cost of blogging and the spread of wifi connectivity have made live blogging a popular genre or category of blogging and an important addition to reportage of crises and events. Live blogging is simply blogging in real time, while a news event is taking place. As a form, live blogging provides a visceral account of the event, usually from the unique point of view of the individual blogger. As such, live blog accounts typically include the personal opinions and observations of the blogger, making these accounts highly idiosyncratic, personal, and qualified.

Given these qualities, it makes the most sense to live blog where no video of the event will be made available. Because it is "live," there is typically a higher tolerance for error; live bloggers are trading accuracy for timeliness. Live blogging is an important, relatively new weapon in reporters' and public relations practitioners' digital arsenals. After all, journalism has been called the first draft of history, so a good journalistic live blog can serve as the first draft of journalism.

One of the first high-profile examples of live blogging was by the *Virginian-Pilot* newspaper in its coverage of the Lee Malvo-John Allen Muhammad sniper trials in Virginia during October 2003, one year after the series of killings the year before. The newspaper's Kerry Sipe live blogged from the media room in the Virginia Beach municipal center, tracking everything from jury instructions and testimony to his impressions of Muhammad's mood. Connected to the courtroom through closed-circuit video and to the rest of the world through a wireless Internet connection, he published on the *Virginian-Pilot*'s website, and his minute-by-minute updates gave readers the closest thing they had to real-time news because the trial's judge barred video coverage of the proceedings. At the time of the trials, Sipe was the *Virginian-Pilot*'s online news coordinator and one of only a relatively small number of writers using blogs to report the news. Along with Sipe's unfiltered copy came an unfiltered experience, one that left the burden of assessing the news to readers. These readers rose to the challenge, passing along corrections to the record and forming something of a community around Sipe's accounts. It is also important to note that Sipe's blog was just one part of the *Virginian-Pilot*'s trial coverage, and not even that coverage's centerpiece. Other *Virginian-Pilot* writers covered the story in more traditional ways. Thus, blogs have not replaced other forms of journalism but have added a new, unique layer of coverage.

## Time to Live Blog

Once you have decided that a live blog is the way to go and have committed to doing it well (there are few things worse than a live blog badly done), here's how.

First, live blogging requires preparation. Find out whether you will have Internet or mobile access at the event, which often means getting in touch with the venue. If they do, will you have to pay? If mobile is all you will have, you might need to verify signal strength and reliability. In short, find out what options you will have for connectivity.

Depending upon what you find out about how to connect, you can then decide from which machine or device to write and post—a laptop, netbook, tablet, or phone.

Factoring into this decision is whether you plan to include other media in your posts, such as photography and/or video. For photo-heavy live blogs, a smartphone might be the best option. For largely textual accounts, a laptop and its full-size keyboard is likely the better choice. Of course, a laptop presumes a seat and a surface, like a table or desk, while a smartphone or tablet does not. (A note from experience: Make sure you take a charger and/or a backup battery for whatever device or machine you will be using.)

When determining where to publish, you might default to an existing blog, or you might set up a new blog or blog feed for the event. Free blogging services like Blogger. com, Tumblr.com, and CoverItLive.com are options. Tumblr works particularly well with smartphones, while Posterous.com can be done via email. Both Tumblr and Posterous have apps for both the iPhone and Android, as well.

Proper preparation can take a lot of the stress out of what can be a pressure-packed experience, because there are so many demands on your attention. Know up front that you will probably annoy or distract those near you. Clacking away on a keyboard really can be obnoxious. Planning where you sit can help, as can congregating with other bloggers and keyboard clackers. You should also turn your phone to "vibrate" and avoid flash photography. Once you are plugged in, powered on, and connected one way or another, you are ready to blog. In your first post, you will want to set up the rest of the account. Where are you? Why? What exactly are you covering? What aren't you covering, and why? Why is this event important, and what do you hope to accomplish or convey in your live blog? What does the venue or room or site look like? Who else is in attendance? Place the event into a broader context.

In short, you want to take your readers there. To do this, leverage the live blog's capacity for immediacy and vicariousness, and provide in your account detail, texture, and reflection. Give readers a sense of what happened and what you thought about what happened. This is visceral, immediate, onsite reporting from a particular point of view—your point of view. So you can and even should use first-person voice. Hyperlink where appropriate. Include a photo where you think suitable, especially in the scene-setting stage.

Following these tips will save you time and worry once you begin:

- Relax. Key in your notes as unfinished sentence fragments, then go back when you have time and flesh out the narrative.
- Provide a transcript if you are covering a speech or panel discussion, if possible. Though tedious for most, for a few who could not attend, this transcript will be a valued resource.
- Write a short blurb about a part of the event you couldn't get to and link to someone who did.

- Post a retrospective or more comprehensive commentary piece once the event is over. Put the event, or your take on the event, into context.
- Know that the biggest challenge is paying attention to the event while writing at the same time. You can take advantage of this challenge by allowing the activity to focus your writing and your attention, placing you in the middle of the stream of events washing over you. What you live blog today can become the basis for a more analytical piece tomorrow.

## BOX 7.1

## Live Blog

The following are excerpts from a live blog account of a Republican Party rally in northwest Georgia. The blogger, John Druckenmiller, did what a good live blogger should:

- He introduces readers to the event and what is about to take place. He brings readers in with description, and he introduces the participants.
- Druckenmiller then provides a near real-time account of what takes place, with plenty of rich detail and some of his own reactions throughout.
- He sticks with it to the end, then provides closure with a wrap-up post.

The live blog's posts are presented in reverse chronological order:

**Senate Candidates Make Their Pitches at Packed GOP Rally**
**Hometown Headlines** spent midday Saturday at the Floyd County GOP's annual rally at the Tillman Hangar. Our speaker-by-speaker coverage is below. We're about to add a photo gallery from the event. Please check back by 3 p.m.

1:22 p.m. Speeches end. Time for the straw poll results. Gingrey wins the poll by 34.4% followed by Handel at 26.7, Broun at 18.3, Kingston at 13.7, Perdue at 5.3, Grayson at 1.5 and no votes for Yu.

1:16 p.m. Eugene Yu: Vote for Yu—for you. That's what Yu says his pitch is. Says do you want a senator who's one of 100 or one of a kind. Says he's one of a kind. Says he might look and talk a little different but "I am proud to be an American. . . I will deliver your voice in Washington." Says the American dream is slipping away; he wants to save it for his children and grandchildren. Says once elected, leaders forget what got them to Washington and what reasons. Talks about the balanced budget and whips out his wallet as an example. Says common sense will solve budget woes.

1:07 p.m. Paul Broun. Very rousing speech including a call to "close down the EPA." Talks about making any legislation pass his four-way test: is it fair? Is it constitutional and can we afford? among the key points.

12:57 p.m. Phil Gingrey. Thanks those who have supported him here. Says he will serve the state with the same heart and intensity as he did with the old 11th Congressional District (and current one). "We don't need a senator who is sort of conservative. . . we need someone who will stand on Georgia values." Says Gingrey: "The Constitution doesn't adjust to the times, the times need to adjust to the Constitution." Key issues: Jobs, jobs and jobs. The debt. And Obamacare. Calls Obamacare the "worst piece of legislation ever enacted" by Congress. Adds Gingrey: "We Republicans are not working to shut down the government. . . that ball is in their court" (Democrats/administration).

12:53 p.m. David Perdue next. Says we watched the Soviet Union collapse and wonders if we'll watch the United States crumble as well. Cites $17 trillion in national debt. Says federal debt is a huge threat to our national security. Says there is a critical need to fix tax code and healthcare. "We have an opportunity to dig out of this mess."

12:50 p.m. Karen Handel talks about her success in local and state offices (including secretary of state). Wants a meaningful plan to fix government, to "get moving on the Fair Tax now." Says the state needs fresh leadership to make needed changes. "I will not resign myself to an America of mediocrity."

12:38 p.m. Wait. David Pennington goes first as gubernatorial candidate. No straw poll on governor's race today. He chides Deal—not by name—for not being here (hence, no poll). Talks about Dalton's ranking as a fast-growing community in terms of city incomes. Preaches limited government on the state level, citing how it has worked in his city. (Applause from the Tea Party's Mike Morton.) Pennington says the state has great resources. "If we put those type assets with true limited government principles," the state's economy will take off, he says. Gets a warm response and a few stood as well.

12:35 p.m. Finally, the Senate candidates.

Now hearing from others involved in the party representing different groups. Nice touch but this crowd is anxious to hear the Senate candidates and perhaps David Pennington, who's challenging Deal in the GOP primary.

11:37 a.m. First speaker is U.S. Rep. Tom Graves. The District 14 congressman comes in low-key dress, oxford shirt and blue jeans. He jumps into Obamacare and how it is being delayed by the administration. "It's too dangerous for American people. . . . It's time to defund Obamacare." Graves talks about "29ers," those working less than 30 hours a week to avoid rolling into Obamacare worker mandates. He asks the crowd, "Are you ready to stop the train wreck?" Rousing support from this partisan crowd.

11:34 a.m. Floyd County GOP Chair Layla Shipman greets the crowd following the presentation of the colors by the Boy Scouts. She introduces local elected officials.

11:23 a.m. Some of the side conversations are on the "general purpose" SPLOST issue to be on the Nov. 5 ballot. If we were taking bets right now, you'd have more in the "won't pass" category. The main issue: The Tennis Center. And those are comments from more moderate Republicans, not the Tea Party members. Big miss not having some of pro-SPLOST push here today.

11:15 a.m. Lots of networking but no candidates at the mic yet. But the candidates are working the crowd, including Senate hopeful Karen Handel.

11:01 a.m. The candidates and officeholders make the rounds. Insurance Commissioner Ralph Hodges is here as is U.S. Rep. Tom Graves. Also on site: County Commission Chairman Irwin Bagwell and Commissioner Rhonda Wallace. Tax Commissioner Kevin Payne. State Rep. Christian Coomer. Lots of side issues on display including a big turnout by Fair Tax supporters.

10:54 a.m. Earl Tillman is greeting guests as they arrive at this hangar for the rally. Lots of campaign paraphernalia, from signs to paddles. It looks like primary season. The barbecue from Duffy's is drawing the biggest crowd so far.

**THE ORIGINAL REPORT TODAY:** And we're off. On a mid-morning that feels more like the final month of the campaign rather than 10 months out,

**Floyd County Republicans** are welcoming the most impressive list of political hopefuls the state has seen this year.

Among those likely facing Democrat **Michelle Nunn** in the November 2014 general election are: **Paul Broun, Phil Gingrey, Derrick Grayson, Karen Handel, Jack Kingston, David Perdue and Eugene Yu**. All flooded the still-forming GOP primary ballot after U.S. Sen. **Saxby Chambliss** surprised most by declining to seek a third term.

Also attending are gubernatorial hopeful **David Pennington**, Dalton's mayor and the perceived Tea Party favorite, as well as Kingston resident **Dr. John Barge**, currently Georgia's school superintendent and rising political rival of **Gov. Nathan Deal**. Barge had yet to formally enter the race; expect an announcement soon. Citing scheduling conflicts, Deal did not attend today's rally but did send a campaign team. Also not attending: Lt. Gov. **Casey Cagle**.

The undercard, if you will, includes just about every other statewide official up for a new term next year as well as local and regional Republican officeholders—and perhaps some potential future rivals.

This is the ninth year the Floyd County GOP has staged the summertime rally at Earl Tillman's hangar at Richard B. Russell Airport/Towers Field. It has grown from around 200 guests to perhaps nearly 300 today. The event, from 11 a.m. until 1 p.m., is free.

Reprinted with permission.

## BLOGGING JOURNALISM

A blog launched by the *Seattle Post-Intelligencer* and written by technology reporter Todd Bishop showed the field of journalism how blogs could enhance reporting. Bishop's blog quickly became a daily extension of an important Seattle beat—covering the software giant Microsoft, which is based in the Seattle area. The newspaper's print edition and traditional website remained the places or spaces to break news, but Bishop said the blog gave him space to follow up on print stories with information that perhaps did not require a full story. His blog also became a place to give readers valuable context for the print stories, expanding and extending coverage for those who wanted to read (much) more about Microsoft. "After writing a story about liability for software flaws," for example, Bishop said, "I posted an entry that gave readers access to a lot of the material that helped me understand the issue and put the story together."

Bishop's blog posts also helped him collect sources for future stories, identifying people who, he says, he would not have found without the blog. One reader emailed him in response to a post about Microsoft's software patching strategy, a reader who turned out to be the person responsible for patching his own company's PCs. The next time Bishop covered the issue in print, he contacted this new source for comment.

A journalist's blog can also be a useful repository for information that has been edited or cut out of a story to fit the available space in print or on the broadcast, such as an observation, anecdote, or extended quoted material. Long, unexpurgated interview notes shouldn't be simply dumped online, obviously, but addenda and sources such as interview notes or excerpts can extend the coverage. *The Daily Show*, for example, routinely posts full interviews with prominent guests after editing down those interviews for the show's 30-minute TV format.

Because blogs typically favor conversational voices, they leverage digital's unique capacity for interpersonal communication, or communication very different and much more personal than any mass medium can provide. Delivered digitally, the potential reach of this otherwise interpersonal communication is paradoxically global, and immediate, matching the capacity of traditional mass media. The more informal, personal nature of most blog writing is due to the fact that most blogs are by a single author, which places priority on voice.

A journalist's blog can also be used to aid reporting by soliciting information. If a reporter cannot make it to a public meeting or event, a post (or a tweet or Facebook post) can notify your readership community of that event and let them know why it might matter. Perhaps someone in your readership can attend the meeting, ask questions, and even provide some reporting on what happened. Hopefully several can. Asking readers to post their reactions to the event or meeting gives them ownership of the coverage and can strengthen the bonds of the community. Of course, the obligation to check facts remains that of the journalist, even when—especially when—presenting news gathered by interactors.

A journalist's blog can also be used to pose questions to a readership. Open questions that identify concerns about a particular issue or event can build community and inform reporting over the long term. Using a blog in this manner can also help the journalist to gauge the readers' interest in certain issues and to determine which stories to continue reporting on and, therefore, to resist the daily print impulse to write and publish a story and then move on without following up. Finally, blogs give reporters and writers, who by nature love to write and to express themselves, another avenue for that expression, one not bound by the finitudes of space and physical distribution.

## What to Do About Corrections

One of the recurring ethical concerns for bloggers, regardless of their profession, has been how to handle corrections. The ease of publishing and the absence of editors have combined to yield a high rate of error relative to that for print media. The imperative for print journalism has been to write, edit, vet, and then publish. In the blogosphere, the paradigm is turned on its head: Publish, then let readers do the vetting. But print journalists typically don't have the option to make a correction directly in the article they've published, instead relying on editor-written corrections that get published in subsequent issues of the newspaper or magazine, often in a small "Corrections" box toward the front of the publication. There is no way to ensure that readers of the first erroneous article will see or read the correction.

In digital spaces, however, a writer has the option of making a correction or change directly to a story he or she has posted, with or without noting the fact that a change has been made. The option to effectively "erase" mistakes has caused concern for blog writers and their readers. Changing or correcting the record without alerting readers to what has been changed threatens a writer's credibility by undermining the very transparency the media format is so good at facilitating. How corrections or changes should be handled, therefore, is an important question. In the blogosphere it is considered bad form to delete anything, including and especially reader comments, but particularly when it is done without notice or explanation. The exceptions would be when published statements or comments are libelous, illegally invade a person's privacy, or infringe on someone's intellectual property rights. These comments should be taken down. If something has to be corrected, however, a blogger has several options. He or she could:

- Include a note at the bottom of the original post with the new information.
- Include the new information in the post while striking through the old or incorrect information (and displaying the strikethrough). This isn't an aesthetically pleasant option, but it does demonstrate maximum transparency.
- Write a new post with the updated or corrected information, a post that links to and refers to the original post.
- Delete the problematic post and replace it with the updated, corrected information, with or without notice that a replacement has been made.

When deliberating over these options, remember that interactors have repeatedly demonstrated that they will reward even a willingness to be transparent. Digital writers who are forthcoming, candid, and open earn their readers' trust as interactors place more trust in those whom they perceive as having nothing to hide. Relative to other online writers and content producers, bloggers very conspicuously took the lead in capitalizing on transparency by disclosing their personal politics and biases, regularly providing links to original source material to allow readers to judge the material for themselves, engaging in public conversations with readers that invite critique, and admitting and correcting errors quickly when they made them. It is these demonstrations of transparency that build and maintain credibility online.

So, after something has been posted, editing should be limited to fixing typos, smoothing out grammar, and modifying unfortunate word choices, but no more. The most conservative or safe way to edit, and a method that bloggers typically use if they find an actual inaccuracy or fact error, is to leave the incorrect text, cross it out, and add the new corrected version. If the correction is more substantial, a line or two explaining what the changes are and why they were made is typical, perhaps with a label of "Updated" or "Correction" above the explanatory note.

For a different point of view, Robert Stacy McCain, a career journalist and a late convert to blogging, quotes an old adage of English teachers: "Writing is re-writing." He questioned "the blogger concept that the first draft—the version of the post as it existed when you initially hit the 'publish' button—must be preserved inviolate." He publishes, then corrects typos. He corrects a more substantial error when learning of it from readers, but seldom acknowledges the error, the correction, or the reader who alerted him to the error, because to do so would "detract from the reading experience." He writes that his object is "to present the clearest expression of my thoughts to the reader, not document the writing process. Not only is the latter messy and potentially confusing, almost nobody will care about it."

McCain's position is not typical in the blogosphere, and it is not the recommendation here. Transparency is a peek behind the veil to see the writing (and reporting and editing) process, to acknowledge errors and how they were handled, and to credit those who help produce a fuller, more accurate account, all of which marks the blogosphere as a place different than mainstream media and that points to a very different paradigm for credibility of information in digital spaces.

## THE BLOGGER VERSUS JOURNALIST DEBATE

Is anyone with a blog a journalist? Is anyone with a camera a photographer? What happens to journalism when every reader can also be a writer, editor, and producer? These are but some of the questions long debated in the blogosphere, in journalism, and in the law. The answer has real, tangible effects. If a blogger is legally a journalist, she is eligible for her state's shield law protection of sources, for example. She is eligible for press credentials to, say, a political party convention. But no clear consensus has yet emerged, despite the fact that the blogger-journalist dichotomy is false. Many journalists blog; many bloggers do journalism. Key distinctions, then, include the methods or processes employed and the purpose or goal of the content.

Where an information-gathering process includes what Kovach and Rosenstiel, in *The Elements of Journalism*, call "the discipline of verification," and where the purpose is service to the public interest, then blogging could be said to be journalism. Where one or both of these is absent, the blogger would be hard pressed to claim to be doing real journalism. Original reporting that has been corroborated, fact-checked, and verified, reporting that seeks to inform a self-governing electorate, whether on a blog or anywhere else, must be called journalism.

Most blogs have a different mandate than does journalism, however. Most blogs are dedicated to some form of commentary or opinion. To the extent that a blog lacks original reporting, it should not be considered as doing the primary enterprise of journalism. For most bloggers, a high value is placed on the act of expression, on providing in the aggregate a diversity of voices. Also important in the blogosphere are writing or publishing with speed, offering transparency of sourcing and of the opinions that influenced the writing, and decentralizing information and knowledge. For journalism, by contrast, great value is placed on providing a filter for information, editing the content, fact-checking, ensuring accuracy and fairness, setting the agenda, and centralizing news dissemination. In some cases, then, the value sets of the blogosphere and of journalism are in tension. The vetting and editing process typically used in print, for example, comes at the expense of speed and of single-voice authenticity, hallmarks of the best of the blogosphere. Blogging, then, can be seen as a thoroughly postmodern form of expression and pursuit, and postmodernism rejects objectivity as a goal or ideal. This rejection pits many bloggers against the guild of journalism, which still strives for objectivity, at least in its methods if not always or even ever possible in its products.

The filtering and editing in journalism is possible because of editorial and production staff. The ethos for news and information blogs is based more on values such as immediacy, transparency, interconnectivity, and proximity to the events. As a heterarchy, in contrast to traditional news media's hierarchies, diverse bloggers post, cross-link, blogroll, and track back to interact in a network, pulling ideas and knowledge from the edges.

## Objectivity as a Process Goal

Few journalists or journalism professors today cling to the belief that pure objectivity is possible, at least as an attribute of journalism's products—the news. Striving for as objective a news-gathering process as possible, however, still is widely regarded as noble and good, at least by professional news-gathering organizations. The last presidential election possibly marked a dark and dangerous shift in American life, one that allowed fiction to compete with and, in cases both dramatic and mundane, defeat fact-based reporting. Digital media showed themselves so far unfit to take the mantle of the marketplace of ideas, instead allowing individuals to put themselves at the center of their own media universes. As one commentator, John Herrman of *The New York Times*, put it, "It will be clear, in retrospect, that this was an election experienced from the bottom of a media trough. Votes were cast from the valley between a collapsing media that was, at one time, at least nominally trusted, and a new media that is not yet ready for the responsibilities it is inheriting." News during the election came complete with new and obliterating signifiers of authority and truth, and with opportunistic insinuations by the candidates themselves that the level of deception by news organizations knows no bounds.

According to Friend and Singer, a journalist in American society is someone "whose primary purpose is to provide the information the citizens of a democracy need to be free and self-governing; someone who acts in accordance with a firm commitment to balance, fairness, restraint, and service; someone whom members of the public can trust to help them make sense of the world and to make sound decisions about the things that matter." Journalists, including digital journalists, perform this *sense-making* role. David Simon, a former reporter and a writer and producer of HBO's hugely successful *The Wire*, asked in the *Washington Post*: "In any format, through any medium— isn't an understanding of the events of the day still a salable commodity?" He wondered if the Internet is so profound a change in the delivery model that "high-end news," or journalism that really matters, will become increasingly scarce, rare, even exotic.

An operative term in Friend's and Singer's definition is "trust." To instill trust, journalists historically have agreed to abide by a code of ethics, however tacitly, typically one similar or identical to the Society for Professional Journalists' Code of Ethics. As Friend and Singer write, "A code of ethics does not create ethical behavior." Such a code can provide a compass, or a map of orienting philosophy to govern or guide behavior. Where these codes of ethics have failed to prevent lapses in journalism, bloggers have brought checks and balances of their own, serving as a sort of watchdog of the watchdogs, or a "Fifth Estate" to journalism's so-called "Fourth Estate." (The other "estates" are the judicial branch, the legislative branch, and the executive branch of government.) Bloggers routinely criticize journalism and mainstream news media for what they see as sloppy, erroneous, and incomplete coverage and reporting. Journalism, therefore, provides these blogs with most of the fodder for the blogs' posts. The vast majority of blog content is derivative, or dependent upon journalism's original reporting. One study showed that less than 5 percent of blog content is the result of doing the legwork of journalism— original reporting, the heavy lifting required of the discipline of verification.

Bloggers instead react, commenting on issues, events, and people in coverage, and providing context and elaboration. These distinctions are not to belittle blogging; on the contrary, blogging has assumed important roles in building a vibrant, well-informed democracy. The distinctions are made to help us understand how the information landscape is changing and how interdependent are the digital media and traditional mass media ecosystems.

The last U.S. presidential election showed the great, even awesome power of social networks, and how a majority of the time, the truth simply did not matter. A falsified presidential endorsement by the pope was shared more than a million times; its correction was barely noticed. Fake news outperformed real news on Facebook, a BuzzFeed study concluded, with more shares, reactions, and comments. And the viral spread of incendiary fake news is a public relations problem too, as many businesses discovered during the campaign, a problem the bigger social networks have shown little capacity to meaningfully address. Washington, DC, pizzeria Comet Ping Pong became the target of a meme claiming it was the home base of a child abuse ring led by Hillary Clinton and her campaign chief, John D. Podesta, a socially mediated charge that had absolutely no basis in fact.

What are the responsibilities and even ability of bloggers and social media networks to stop the spread of incorrect information? What is the responsibility of companies such as Facebook and Twitter as private companies to civic society? What is the role of journalism in a new media landscape that seems to favor ideology over even the attempt to seek, report, and publish truth? For bloggers, for journalists, and for social media managers and companies, these are existential questions of the highest order.

## CHAPTER ACTIVITIES

1. Live blog an event, a trip, a conference, or a meeting. Take your readers there. Use several brief posts to give your readers an account of that event. Hyperlink where appropriate. There is no minimum or maximum for the number of posts. Follow the guidelines detailed in this chapter.

2. Find a handful of blogs on a subject of your choosing. Read them over some extended period of time to get a sense of how each of the bloggers "covers" or writes about the subject you chose. Google quietly disabled its Google Blog Search home page in 2014. To filter content based on blog posts using Google, go to Google News, click on Tools, then select "Blogs"; Alltop, a blog directory (alltop.com); or Blog Search Engine (blog-searchengine.org), a blog search and ranking site. Write up a review of 750 words or so describing the strengths and weaknesses of the four or five blogs you chose. Be sure to discuss:

   - voice and writing style;
   - transparency and disclosure;
   - linking;
   - usefulness; and
   - social media integration.

3. Think about your career aspirations, your research interests (senior project, papers for your classes), and your political/religious/philosophical inclinations and interests:

   (a) Search for news/commentary blogs (not social, personal journal blogs) that line up with one or more of your interests or pursuits. To find the blogs, you could use Alltop, a blog directory (http://alltop.com), Technorati (http://technorati.com/), or, of course, Google.

   (b) Identify three blogs you might actually read on a regular basis. This assumes a few things: quality and style of writing, currency, presentation, and point of view, just to name a few.

   (c) Prepare a tip sheet for the rest of the class that will look something like this (one entry per blog, three blogs/entries for the assignment):

   Blog name or title: TalkingPointsMemo
   URL: http://talkingpointsmemo.com/edblog
   Author: Josh Marshall
   Brief description: Left-leaning political commentary with an impressive record for accuracy and for beating the media elites on breaking stories. Widely read and commented on, this blog is among the very best nationally at what it does, which is why it was among the first blogs to sell advertising and make a nice little career out of blogging for its author.
   Why I like this blog: I like to follow politics, and I like the behind-the-scenes perspective that this blog consistently offers. As a blog with a very particular point of view, it offers me a complement to more mainstream media accounts of inside-the-beltway politics and happenings within the major political parties. The Daily Show and John Oliver's Last Week Tonight are fun, and they actually do a good job providing insights into the faults and flaws of the powerbrokers, but they are mostly for fun, for entertainment. Marshall consistently puts meat on bones served up by these satiric news shows. As fellow blogger, Chris Nolan, writes of Marshall's posts, they do exactly what online web journalism is meant to do: Challenge the other guy to go one better, keeping the competition honest.

## Digital Resources

**Bleeding Yankee Blue blog (bleedingyankeeblue.blogspot.com/)**

**Blogging Software:**

- **Blogger.com;**
- **MovableType.com;**
- **Tumblr.com; and**
- **WordPress.com and Wordpress.org.**

**Wandering Rocks blog (wanderingrocks.wordpress.com)**

## BIBLIOGRAPHY

Bausch, Paul, Haughey, Matthew, and Hourihan, Meg, *We Blog: Publishing Online With Weblogs* (Canoga Park, CA: Hungry Minds, 2002).

Blood, Rebecca, "Weblogs: A History and Perspective," (2000), available: www.rebeccablood.net/essays/weblog_history.html.

Blood, Rebecca, *The Weblog Handbook* (Cambridge, MA: Perseus Publishing, 2002).

Branzburg v. Hayes (1972), available: www.law.cornell.edu/supct/html/historics/USSC_CR_0408_0665_ZS.html.

Cassidy, John, "The Online Life: Me Media, How Hanging Out on the Internet Became Big Business," *The New Yorker* (May 2006).

Cook, Trevor, "The Death of Quality Journalism," *Unleashed* (March 12 2008), available: www.abc.net.au/unleashed/stories/s2186777.htm.

Drezner, Daniel W. and Farrell, Henry, "Web of Influence," *Foreign Policy* (November/December 2004), available: www.foreignpolicy.com/story/cms.php?story_id=2707&page=0.

Friend, Cecilia and Singer, Jane B., *Online Journalism Ethics: Traditions and Transitions* (Armonk, NY: M. E. Sharpe, 2007).

Herrman, John, "What We've Learned About the Media Industry During This Election," *The New York Times* (November 9 2016), available: www.nytimes.com/2016/11/09/business/media/what-weve-learned-about-the-media-industry-during-this-election.html.

Jacobs, Joanne, "The Way It Is Today Isn't How It Was: If the Facts Aren't Right Bloggers Are All Over It," *San Francisco Chronicle* (September 26 2004), (URL no longer available).

Kang, Celia, "This Pizzeria Is Not a Child-Trafficking Site," *The New York Times* (November 22 2016), available: www.nytimes.com/2016/11/21/technology/fact-check-this-pizzeria-is-not-a-child-trafficking-site.html.

Kovach, Bill and Rosenstiel, Tom, *The Elements of Journalism: What Newspeople Should Know and the Public Should Expect* (New York, NY: Three Rivers Press, 2007).

Kramer, Staci, "Journos and Bloggers: Can Both Survive?" *Online Journalism Review* (November 12 2004), (URL no longer available).

Lemann, Nicholas, "Amateur Hour, Journalism without Journalists," *The New Yorker* (August 2006).

McCain, Robert Stacy, "Blogging is Re-blogging," *The Other McCain* (blog) (February 11 2010), available: http://theothermccain.com/2010/02/11/blogging-is-re-blogging/.

"Razorfish Employee Social Influence Marketing Guidelines," (July 2009), available: www.scribd.com/document/34058717/Razorfish-Employee-Social-Influence-Marketing-Guidelines.

Salter, Chuck, "Hyperlocal Hero," *Fast Company* (November 2006), available: www.fastcompany.com/magazine/110/open_hyper-local-hero.html.

Silverman, Craig, "This Analysis Shows How Fake Election News Stories Outperformed Real News on Facebook," *BuzzFeed* (November 16 2016), available: www.buzzfeed.com/craigsilverman/viral-fake-election-news-outperformed-real-news-on-facebook.

Sunstein, Cass R., "Fragmentation and Cybercascades," in *Living in the Information Age*, Erik P. Bucy (ed.) (Belmont, CA: Wadsworth Publishing, 2005): 244–254.

*The Today Show*, NBC-TV, September 25 (2013), available: www.today.com/video/today/53101083.

Wapner, Jessica, "Blogging—It's Good for You: The Therapeutic Value of Blogging Becomes a Focus of Study," *Scientific American* (May 2008), available: www.sciam.com/article.cfm?id=the-healthy-type.

# Journalism in a Digital Age

*In any format, through any medium—isn't an understand-ing of the events of the day still a salable commodity?*
—David Simon, writer and executive producer of
HBO television series *The Wire*

*I keep six honest serving men (They taught me all they knew); Their names are What and Why and When and How and Where and Who.*

—Rudyard Kipling

*In times of profound change, the learners inherit the earth, while the learned find themselves beautifully equipped to deal with a world that no longer exists.*

—Eric Hoffer

**CHAPTER OBJECTIVES**

After studying this chapter, you will:

- explore the roles of the digital journalist;
- understand the basics of good reporting;
- appreciate how journalism can tap into social networks to do news;
- be able to verify information, including that of social media; and
- consider ethical approaches to social media use and policies for social media use.

## INTRODUCTION

Digital offers journalists speed, immediacy, interactivity, and a global reach. It also enables new ways to gather, report, and distribute information. Thus, digital journalists have to become adept at, if not master, a wide range of skills. They have to report, interview, research, produce audio and video, do photography, present and publish stories, and connect to their growing networks via social media. And they have to do this in a rough-and-tumble business that hasn't yet figured out what sustainable economic models should look like when monetizing content and fairly paying for labor has proven so elusive. This chapter provides the basics on these many roles. Also covered are the ways social media can be used to do journalism.

## WHAT JOURNALISTS DO

Regardless of what the future will mean for journalism and, by extension, democracy, and despite claims that "facts" are the luxury of a previous era, the need for what journalists do will not go away. In some ways, this need has only become more acute. In a fun-house world where the fake and the factual compete on seemingly equal footing, the skills of gathering and sharing valuable and valid information become even more important, as does applying a discipline of verification in order to maximize truth, minimize harm, and provide a fair and comprehensive account of the news of the day. By this definition, a great number of people who would not necessarily self-identify as journalists are, in fact, doing journalism. The key differentiator isn't what a person is doing, but how and why. How a person goes about gathering and sharing information, and why someone writes and publishes remain key distinctions—in any media, in all media—just as they have always been for older, traditional media.

Professional journalists are called upon to act independently, according to the Society for Professional Journalists' Code of Ethics, and to be accountable for what they write and publish. They are supposed to provide readers with the information needed to be free and self-governing. People have always craved news. As Kovach and Rosenstiel (2014) wrote, people "need to know what's going on over the next hill, to be aware of events beyond their direct experience. Knowledge of the unknown gives them security; it allows them to plan and negotiate their lives. Exchanging this information becomes the basis for creating community."

But today's journalists are being asked to be jacks of many trades rather than masters of any one. *New York Times* reporter Susanne Craig broke a story deep into the 2016 U.S. presidential campaign on Trump's elusive tax records, a story initiated by leaked documents physically delivered to the newspaper. Craig broke the story about the candidate's nearly billion-dollar loss in 1995 on the *Times*'s website and the paper's dedicated app. Next, she pinned her first-person account of the investigation she had conducted for the story at the top of her Twitter feed. A few hours later, she appeared on CNN to talk about the developing story, by which time her initial story, co-written with three other reporters, had gone viral on social media. Journalist Seth Mnookin responded to news of the Boston Marathon bombings by using his smartphone to tweet, to follow law enforcement's activities, to crowd-source his journalism, to geomap where he was and where the news was taking him, and to coordinate with other journalists in order to cover the large and fluid story. He later wrote that he regretted not taking more photos or video, options also possible with even a smartphone. Digital journalists, then, are almost invariably more than simply writers or photographers or graphic designers. They are increasingly tech-savvy content producers familiar with dizzying assortments of software, apps, and tools. They are being asked to learn HTML, RSS, XML, FTP, Flash, video and photo editing software, global positioning system-enabled apps, social media, and a grab bag of software tools and computer languages and protocols. As Eric Hoffer wrote, "In times of profound change, the learners inherit the earth, while the learned find themselves beautifully equipped to deal with a world that no longer exists."

Despite this diversification of skills necessary for digital publishing, the basic competencies that have characterized the guild of journalism remain valuable and important. The inverted pyramid style of presenting information, for example, a style that has so dominated newspapering and that is partially credited with producing objectivity as a goal or news value, remains useful in ordering information for digital presentation. Consider the fundamental roles of journalism's writers and editors; there is much that has not changed for a digital age.

## Researcher and Guide

The sheer amount of information available today is a double-edged sword. Wonderful in theory, all proximal via digital media, and much of it free or low cost, the abundance of information is also a curse, as the 2016 U.S. presidential election put on such dramatic display. How are we to know whether Comet Ping Pong Pizza in Washington, DC, is or is not part of a global sex trafficking ring in cooperation with the very highest levels of the Democratic Party? Most people need help, and that's the job of digital journalists. They sort, filter, curate, verify, and refer. Thus, journalism students should be introduced to research and organization techniques; how to use a feed reader; how to stay on top of a specific trend via email alerts, Twitter, and search feeds; and how to develop source relationships via social media.

## Traffic Generator and Entrepreneur

Digital writers and editors are learning that it helps to think about the bottom line, even though such thoughts are heretical for older generations of journalists more accustomed to "church and state" divisions of editorial and advertising sales. Good content attracts readers, and it is the reader who creates the page views, clicks, shares, and likes. This attention attracts advertisers, who then pay to reach those readers. That revenue provides writers and editors with a paycheck. But the news business is suffering a prolonged period of creative destruction; lots of digital-first news operations are starting up, but few are achieving profitability. Since 2007, more than 120 newspapers and 30,000 new production jobs have been lost. Perhaps most frustrating of all is that news aggregators as a category outperform the traditional news operations on whose content they depend (and some say steal from) to thrive. The generators of the content that nourish the rest of the food chain are getting their teeth kicked in, economically.

Thus, frontline reporters and content developers are being asked to think entrepreneurially and about how to finance the newsgathering. Media entrepreneurship courses have begun sprouting up in journalism and communication programs at colleges throughout the country at a time when thousands of news startups are being launched annually, especially in the area of community news. To be successful today, therefore, journalists need to be conversant in:

- revenue streams;
- team building and project management;
- audience analysis and market research;
- social media marketing;
- mobile strategies;
- business plan development and competitive analysis;
- public speaking, including how to construct and deliver a pitch; and
- legal and regulatory frameworks.

## Community and Social Media Manager

Community is often messy, and in digital realms it is no place for wimps. This third core digital skill, which is largely absent from journalism pedagogy at the university level, has to do with how to lead, moderate, and participate in communities and conversations in intentional ways. A successful forum, blog, Twitter feed, or Facebook group relies upon a robust community. However, these communities do not magically or easily form. They require an enormous amount of time, effort, leadership, and authentic participation. If you are lucky enough to develop a community, the work only gets harder maintaining and growing it. A moderator or social media manager is equal parts discussion leader, party host, and diplomat.

What does any of this have to do with journalism? In digital spaces and places, writers and editors are expected to interact. Audience interaction can yield better stories and more interesting content, but it also opens the door to arguments, mindless debates, and comments so inane, so egregious, that you might want to pull the plug on the whole enterprise, as many have done. (When *Popular Science* shut off its comments sections, the site's editors explained the decision by saying, "Comments can be bad for science.") Moderators and social media managers have to swallow that first impulse, step back, and remind themselves of the benefits. They need to see opportunity amidst the arguments and the story ideas amidst the flame wars. They need to lead the discussion and prod it when it falters.

## Collaborator

Because news is turning into more of a collaboration and much more of an interactive process, the reader has more of a say in determining or at least selecting the big issues of the day. Such a collaborative, distributive ecosystem is inherently more democratic, but that does not necessarily make the more open system better for democracy or for a democratic form of government, again, as the 2016 U.S. presidential election demonstrated. Fake news over-crowded verified reporting. With less powerful watchdogs, with financially poorer independent news organizations less able to fund the expensive enterprise of investigative journalism, government is increasingly able to creep into the shadows.

## Data Miner

The computer-assisted, data mining journalist uses the statistical methods of social scientists, the mapping tools of geographic information systems, and the visualization skills of graphic design to create data-driven presentations and stories. Many are also called upon to do web development and computer programming, database administration, systems engineering, and sometimes even cryptography. What counts as data? Anything you can count; anything a computer can process; any measurable phenomena. In order to tell a story, the data mining journalist brings context to bear on data he or she finds or collects, categorizes and analyzes, then, finally, visualizes for the reader. At the heart of this activity is meaningful comparison. Should an effect be compared across geographical areas over time? Should groups or populations be compared? What are the relationships needed to better understand a phenomenon or event?

## THE BASICS OF REPORTING

The heart and soul of digital journalism is, of course, reporting. And while it's possible, even easy, to overwrite, it is difficult to over-report. If you have limited time, spend most of it reporting. There is no substitute for boots on the ground, asking questions, doing lots of interviews, checking the databases, using the Freedom of Information

Act to get information, even just hanging out and shooting the bull. In fact, with some sources, take some time *not* to ask questions. A cops-and-courts reporter in Anniston, AL, talked of taking cigars to the local sheriff and doughnuts to the county courthouse, with no agenda in mind. When news did hit, that time spent building relationships, learning the names of sources' children, and just relating as human beings paid off with privileged access to information.

## The two best questions a reporter can ask of any source are:

- How do you know that? Show me some evidence. If a source says, for example, that a new government program is "effective," ask for evidence of that effectiveness. How does the person in fact know that the program is effective? What demonstrable proof can be offered? Seek verification and corroboration. What does "effective" even mean in this context? Effective compared to what? As judged by whom?
- What do you mean? Have a source clarify if there is anything confusing about what was said. If you, the reporter, do not understand what is being said or shared, the reader has no chance. For example, if a source says sales are up 15 percent, find out what exactly that means. Up 15 percent over what or when? Up 15 percent for the year? For the week? Compared to the same period a year ago? Compared to last week? Sales are up, but are profits? How much did it cost to get that 15 percent increase? Now more than ever, it is the digital journalist charged with sense-making, or with explaining and facilitating understanding.

As these two questions imply, reporters and editors should seek to make:

- the familiar unfamiliar;
- the unfamiliar familiar;
- the complex somehow understandable; and
- the mundane, like city budgets and environmental impact studies, somehow interesting and worthwhile.

How do you report a story that one side says is a non-story and the other says is one of the biggest in a decade? Talk to as many people as you can and report what you find. Ask along the way, of everyone, "How do you know that?" Reporting is a wonderful passport to go into the world and around the world, meet people you otherwise would never meet, and learn things you otherwise would never get to know. Perhaps the single most important character trait of a good reporter is curiosity. From coming up with story ideas and angles, to identifying the sources to get the story, to writing the questions to pose to those sources, to writing clearly, it is curiosity that is the constant. Good reporters ask why things work the way they do, what's wrong, and how to make things better. They like to learn about all sorts of things, never knowing what might lead to a story or to insights to pass along to readers. They seek to better understand so they can explain things.

In pursuing answers, it is important as journalists to ask, "What do we stand for? No matter the technology, the fads of the day, the pressures from ownership or administration, what are and will remain our core values?" It is of great benefit to define, even for yourself, craft excellence. How will you know tomorrow that what you've done today was a job well done? Some of the values that recur in discussions on this question include integrity, passion, ethics, courage, accuracy, dialogue, authenticity, sense-making, commitment to informing the public, fairness, professional pride, the First Amendment, balance, credibility, inclusiveness, precision, critical thinking, diversity, accountability, truth-telling, and original reporting.

## INTERVIEWING

Though it's a basic reporting skill, interviewing often gets overlooked. Thus, few are very good at it. A good interview typically depends on at least a few things: background research on the subject and topic, carefully thought-out questions sequenced in order of importance, a listening ear, a genuine interest in the person being interviewed, and a comfort level with silence. Good interviewers remember to listen. They ask good questions. In addition to those just mentioned (What do you mean? How do you know that?), here are a few more to consider posing to your sources, if only to think about what good questions for your particular project might be:

- What happened? Then what happened?
- What did you see? What went through your mind? Describe the scene to me.
- What did that experience tell you? What was the lesson in all of that?
- Why did you care about that? Why was that important? How did you feel?
- What picture or image remains most vivid? Imagine that you're back at the scene.
- What did it smell like?
- What are or were the consequences of. . . ?
- What's the best (or worst) possible scenario?
- What do you fear? How did that affect you? How did you deal with that?
- What were your (other) options?
- What have we not talked about that you think might be important?

Common in these questions is a sort of basic curiosity. It is often helpful to simply revert to childhood and to think like an 8-year-old. For example, for a radio story on an epic arctic expedition, a reporter thought to ask, "What did you guys do about underwear? I mean, you were hiking for a month in sub-zero temperatures. You couldn't do laundry. What did you do?" This question led to the best moment of the interview and, subsequently, of the radio broadcast. The expedition's leader recounted the story of gathering around the campfire two weeks into the hike to (quickly) strip down and turn their undies inside-out. "We did a little dance around the fire feeling that soft cotton for the first time in two weeks," the source recounted. What questions would an 8-year-old think to ask?

Remember also that interviewing is a skill; it can be learned and honed with practice. It is a craft that rewards intuition, creativity, empathy, and courage. Like any good reporting, it also requires observational skills. Watch the subject interact with others, go about his or her job or duties, relate to family members. Don't be afraid of silence. It is often these moments of quiet reflection that precede or lead to the best insights and quotes of the interview. For an example of this, watch Henry Louis Gates allow silence to speak volumes when interviewing comedian Chris Rock for the PBS series on genealogy, *African American Lives*: www.pbs.org/wnet/aalives/profiles/rock.html.

The steps to a good interview are these:

1. Prepare. Do the research necessary to generate good questions and to know your subject. What do you need to know to develop smart questions? What questions most need answering? Don't be too tied to your list, however. Be flexible. And don't start off with the most difficult or uncomfortable question. Build up to these more challenging subjects. The better questions are open-ended, not ones that can be answered with a "yes" or "no." During Game 3 of the 2016 N.B.A. finals, when the Golden State Warriors found themselves trailing the Cleveland Cavaliers by 17 points after the first quarter, it was left to Doris Burke of ESPN to ask Warriors coach Steve Kerr what he had seen from his team. "Not a whole lot," Kerr said. That was the sum total of their interaction. A better question (and a happier coach) would have led to a better sideline moment.

2. Get there early to acquaint yourself with your surroundings. If the interview has been scheduled in a coffee shop, for example, you'll want to test your recording equipment to make sure the espresso machine doesn't drown out all of your sound. Be ready to go to work at the appointed time.

3. Make sure everyone understands the ground rules for the interview, such as what is on the record or off.

4. Take good notes, regardless of whatever recording devices you might be using. Describe the scene and what you see, not only what you hear. Use all of your senses. Record your own thoughts. Jot down questions that crop up during the interview.

Because you will probably use only a few direct quotes in your story, don't worry about transcribing everything the subject says. Listen for the good quotes you're likely to use. This takes practice. If you miss part of the quote, simply ask the source to repeat the statement. You might also develop a few throw-away questions you can pose to buy time to catch up on your note-taking on the information that matters.

5. Use email or texting only to set up the interview and for quick follow-up questions or verification. These are not good interviewing tools because they can't register body language, facial expressions, nuance, and gesture.

6. Once the interview is completed, make sure you have permission to contact the subject again for anything you might have missed or to check for accuracy.

7. Look over your notes. Fill them out from memory. As soon as you can, type them up and annotate with your own thoughts, such as, "Great quote to introduce subject."

## THE DISCIPLINE OF VERIFICATION

In their canonical book, *The Elements of Journalism*, Bill Kovach and Tom Rosenstiel identify the purpose of journalism as providing people the information they need to be free and self-governing. To accomplish this noble and perhaps intimidating mission, the authors state that journalism's first obligation is to the truth and that its first loyalty is to citizens. The essence of good journalism, therefore, is a discipline of verification, which is what distinguishes journalism from, say, entertainment, propaganda, fiction, and art. "Journalism alone is focused on the process employed to get what happened down right," they write.

The first step in applying this discipline is humility, or realizing we don't yet know what we don't know. Finding out is one of the intrinsic joys of doing good journalism, because, as was described earlier, we are a curious people. We want to know why and how and who and what. We won't learn these things until and unless we get out there and talk to people—lots of people—and check out the documents, the records, the paper trail. One thing learned will lead to another in what become the stepping stones to understanding.

The second step is to triangulate and corroborate, or to make sure that you do in fact know what you know. A famous journalism maxim is that if your mother tells you she loves you, that's terrific, but check it out. Get another source. In other words, assume nothing. Dedicate yourself to craft excellence. Kovach and Rosenstiel recommend this "accuracy checklist":

- Is the lead of the story sufficiently supported?
- Is background material required to understand the story?
- Are all of the stakeholders in the story identified, and have representatives from all sides been contacted and given a chance to talk?

- Does the story pick sides or make subtle value judgments?
- Will some people like this story more than they should?
- Have you attributed or documented all the information in your story to make sure it is correct?
- Do those facts back up the premise of your story? Do you have multiple sources for controversial or counter-intuitive facts?
- Did you double-check the quotes to make sure they are accurate and in context?
- Have you checked phone numbers, URLs, email addresses, etc. to make sure they are accurate?
- Do your numbers add up or check out?

In these questions you see a commitment to truth, truth-seeking, and service to citizens. Now, if in addition to truth-telling and sense-making your story communicates voice, a sense of place and time, strong characters, energy, and transcendent meaning, and it does so with good pacing and an appropriate structure, all the better.

With social media, verifying information has become yet more challenging. According to the BBC's social media guidelines, the network declares that "The golden rule for our core news, programme or genre activity is that whatsoever is published—on Twitter, Facebook or anywhere else—MUST HAVE A SECOND PAIR OF EYES PRIOR TO PUBLICATION" (emphasis in the original). Editors are needed to verify tweets and, more generally, information being relayed via social media. So many people are generating so much content that news organizations can find themselves overwhelmed, especially during breaking news events. For its part, BBC News created what it calls the UGC (user-generated content) Hub in order to curate and verify social media content. Steps the Hub's editors take to verify video include, according to its website:

- referencing locations against maps and existing images from, in particular, geolocated ones;
- working with colleagues to ascertain that accents and language are correct for the location;
- searching for the original source of the upload/sequences as an indicator of date;
- examining weather reports and shadows to confirm that the conditions shown fit with the claimed date and time;
- maintaining lists of previously verified material to act as reference for colleagues covering the stories; and
- checking weaponry, vehicles, and license plates against those known for the given country.

The screaming need for verification has provided companies like BreakingNews.com and Storyful.com a business opportunity. Calling itself the first news agency of the social media age, Storyful.com helps news organizations and digital publishers "discover, verify and distribute" material moving across social media platforms. Clients include ABC News, CBS News, Reuters, *The New York Times*, and *The Wall Street Journal*. According to its founder, Mark Little, the company blends technology with human judgment, because "algorithms, apps and search tools help make data useful but they can't replace the value judgments (by humans that are) at the core of journalism."

According to Little, the company has some basic steps for verification, including:

- reviewing the uploader's history and location to see whether he/she has shared useful and credible content in the past, or if he/she is a "scraper," passing other people's content off as their own;
- using Google Street View, maps, and satellite imagery to help verify locations;
- consulting other news sources to confirm that events in a video happened as they are described;
- examining key features such as weather and background landscape to see if they match known facts on the ground;
- translating every word for additional context;
- monitoring social media traffic to see who is sharing the video and what questions are being asked about it; and
- developing and maintaining relationships with people within the community around the story.

It should be apparent that most of these steps work for verifying textual information, as well. It should also be noted how necessary collaboration and cooperation are for doing substantive verification. Little describes the process of verification as putting a puzzle together. Most of the pieces can be found in the social media conversations that emerge out of big, breaking news events. By using several tools and checking in with as many people as possible, the pieces come together to give an increasingly clear indication of how likely it is that a source or artifact is the genuine article. Listening is important, but Little's team engages directly, openly, and honestly with the most authentic voices it can find, judging the credibility of a source "by their behavior and status within the community." Little stresses that "there is no secret sauce," that verification is a painstaking process involving real people.

In addition to Twitter and Facebook, Storyful.com monitors YouTube, SoundCloud, Hootsuite, and Audioboo. To track trends on Twitter, the team uses Tweetdeck and Trendsmap.com. To verify URLs and to check ownership of websites and online companies, Whois (whois.domaintools.com/) is a valuable and easy-to-use tool. Whois can tell you who registered a web address and what physical address that person or company has. TinEye (tineye.com/) can be used to perform reverse image searches to identify different versions of an image that may exist. Google Images also offers a version of this. To check the weather in any specific location, among other fact checks, try the WolframAlpha "computational knowledge" search engine (www.wolframalpha.com). A query for the weather on January 11, 1965 found that the high in Nice, France, reached 59 degrees that day, with a relative humidity of 74 percent.

The telephone and Skype are two of the more valuable weapons in the Storyful.com arsenal, tools that would have prevented the errors made in coverage of the Boston Marathon bombings. Errors in the coverage centered on law enforcement sources, like scanners and police reports. Misinformation flows among law enforcement sources, particularly in the beginning stages of an investigation, and a lot of that misinformation airs over scanners. These mistakes then get amplified by social media, where user-generated content often gets distributed with little or no verification.

BreakingNews.com learned that early, anonymously sourced reports carry a higher risk of being wrong, and that news organizations tend to gravitate toward the same anonymous sources in the first few hours after a story breaks. So the company takes its time and exercises caution. When a detail carries a higher risk of doing damage if it's wrong, the Breaking News team moves even more cautiously to separate fact from fiction. "In the end, our audacious goal is to get it right at the speed of light," co-founder and general manager Cory Bergman wrote. "For now, we're content on waiting a beat when accuracy matters most."

## STORY STRUCTURES

You've done the reporting and verified your information. You are ready to write. Next, it's time to consider the story structure most appropriate to your story. As we have described it, **the inverted pyramid** orders information from most important to least, making stories easier to produce, easier to edit or cut to fit or fill a space, and it emphasizes the "who, what, when, where" fact-based approach to presenting information. As an example, let's say there was a five-car accident on a highway in your city. The first paragraph of an inverted pyramid-style news story on the accident would begin by summarizing what happened. The second paragraph might identify the injured. The third could explain how the accident occurred, including weather conditions, etc. The fourth might report any charges filed against any of the drivers. The fifth could quote witnesses, participants, and police and rescue. The sixth might go into descriptions of delays caused by the accident.

The inverted pyramid often is appropriate for digital spaces, where information should be structured to facilitate scanning or drilling down. Historically, the inverted pyramid also accommodated wire service feeds, which came into the newsroom much as blog posts and tweets are published today, in reverse chronological order. The style has been common because it also helps to satisfy the print requirement that stories jump or continue from one page to another. Of course, with reader attention spans becoming ever shorter, providing the key information immediately, up top, will be rewarded with attention, eyeballs, likes, and shares.

The inverted pyramid also facilitates frequent updating because the top of an article can be replaced, pushing older information deeper into the article. Readers can get what they want and bail out, or keep drilling and reading deeper into the coverage. At many news organizations, due to staffing problems or simply a lack of motivation, too often articles are not treated as specifically online content, or content that should

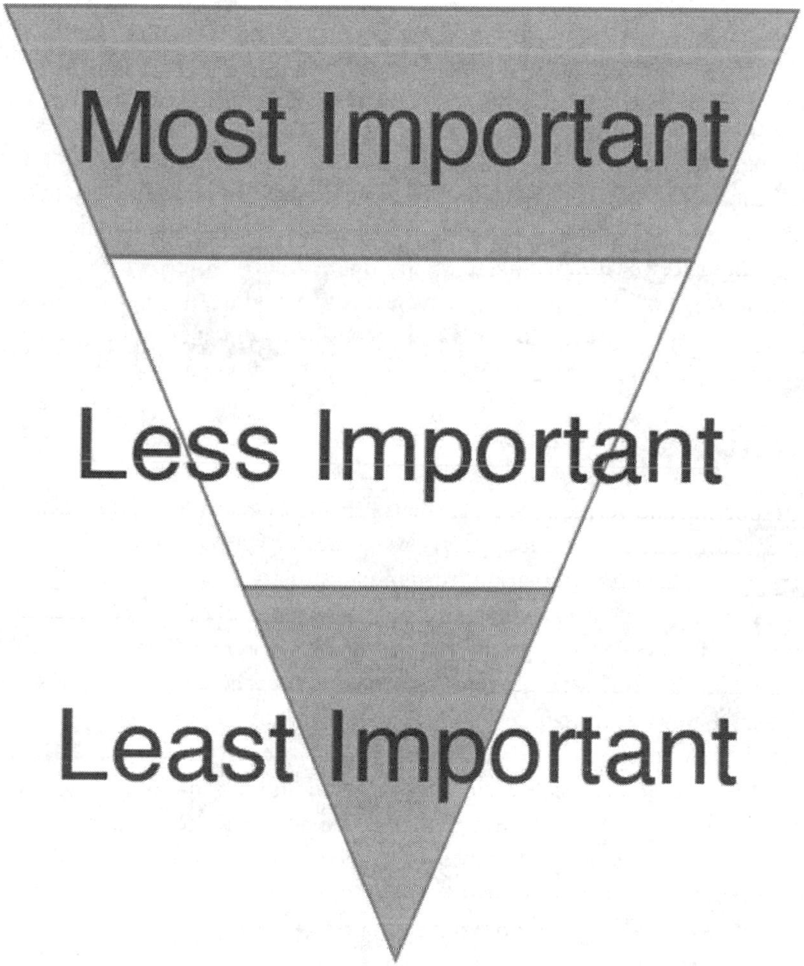

FIGURE 8.1

Most Important

Less Important

Least Important

209

change and develop over time, but rather merely as print poured into a new container. Articles are dumped onto the website and ignored until the next day's dump.

Other common story structures:

- **Chronological stories** are perhaps the easiest to write because they follow a timeline, though often the climax or point of the story is presented first. Live blogging and live tweeting use this structure, one that is ideal for continuing or breaking stories.
- **Narratives**, by contrast, set the scene, then draw readers into that scene. Narratives follow a story arc that unifies a discrete beginning, middle, and end in a way that inverted pyramid stories do not. Narratives rely on vivid description and detail common to the novelistic style. These characteristics make the narrative style problematic online unless sparingly, opportunistically, and expertly employed.
- **The hourglass structure** combines the inverted pyramid approach with a chronological conclusion. After four or five paragraphs stating the central point and supporting facts, this story structure switches to a chronological narrative, using a turn or pivot paragraph to transition to the chronology. This hybrid form is ideal for sports game coverage, allowing for a re-cap of the key developments and moments of a game to begin, pivoting on some aspect of greater import, such as a team's playoff hopes, before turning to a chronological account of the rest of the game.
- **The thematic approach** organizes a complex story by theme or topic, dividing up the story into discrete pieces. For example, in a preview story leading up to the National Football League's Super Bowl, the thematic approach might first compare the two football teams' offenses, then the defenses, then the kicking games, and so on. This sort of chunking makes the thematic approach a useful one online.
- **The focus style or structure** has four main parts: the lead, which focuses or localizes a broader story; a "nut graph," which states the central point or angle of the story in a nutshell; the main body of the story; and a "kicker," or conclusion that brings the larger story back to the focus or local context introduced in the lead. *The Wall Street Journal* typically runs at least one focus style story every day because it is ideal for getting readers interested in a broad topic or larger trend by focusing attention on one event, one family, one business, or one illustration of that larger phenomenon. The nut graph spells out that larger trend. The body of the story explores the bigger story, finishing with a twist or kicker to close out the narrative. This structure is ideal for combining news with narrative.

- **The sidebar**, while not a story structure, is a valuable option to keep in mind even when deciding structure. Sidebars are related to a main story but are presented separately. Typically shorter than the main story, sidebars might give additional information, provide background on the main topic or subject, or explain some key aspect of the main story. For example, let's say the main story is Major League Baseball naming a new commissioner. Sidebars might include one on the incoming commissioner's resume, one on the outgoing commissioner's legacy, and one on how the new commish first fell in love with baseball. Sidebars are like planets orbiting within the gravitational pull of a main story idea, and, thus, they are perfect for layered, drill-down digital presentations. When deciding story structure, it might help to first break off some sidebar possibilities, which will help crystallize the main story. Developing sidebars also creates multiple entry points to the story package as a whole.

## EXPLORING MULTIMEDIA POSSIBILITIES

One of the biggest decisions facing a journalist is which medium or media to use. The type of multimedia produced should depend on the nature of the stories and investigations being pursued. Here are some typical examples of opportunities for adding multimedia to bring an extra dimension to a story:

- **Case studies:** video or audio interviews with someone at the heart of the story, or perhaps a particular instance of something to illustrate a larger trend or story.
- **Reactions:** video or audio interviews with the people responsible, capturing their attempts to explain their role.
- **Explanation and background:** taking something complex and making it accessible to a wider audience. This might be done through a graphic, or through a video or podcast interview with an expert who can explain it clearly.
- **Visual help:** charts, maps, timelines, and infographics that turn data into something that users can more quickly understand. Tools useful here include Google Charts and Gadgets (in Google Docs), Many Eyes, and Tableau for charts; Tagxedo, Wordle, or Many Eyes for word clouds; Google Maps and BatchGeo for maps; and Infogr.am for infographics. These additional layers are opportunities for offering interactivity. Timeline tools, for example, like Dipity and Meograph make developing this sort of content easy and even fun.
- **Re-enactments:** Though re-enactments should never take the place of original reporting, they can help interactors understand a sequence of events or

cause-and-effect. They should be clearly labeled or described as re-enactments, and they should never be used to fake something, but they can aid storytelling.

- **Curation:** bringing together multimedia content by users in a way that adds value, lengthens shelf life, and brings in collaborators. One of the best platforms for aggregation and curation is Storify (storify.com).

## HOW SOCIAL MEDIA CHANGED THE NEWS

One of the more significant shifts wrought by digital media is that the news is now being reported by everyone, however episodic and incomplete that reporting might be. Readers are no longer merely passive receivers; they are actively involved in shaping the news agenda and in sharing and commenting on the news. So-called "we" media, or media in which interactors are participants and contributors, have reshaped the journalistic landscape. Natural disasters such as Hurricane Katrina in Louisiana and Mississippi in 2005, the Myanmar uprising in 2007, and a catastrophic earthquake in southwest China in 2008 were among the first citizen journalism phenomena that showed how socially networked the news could be. In the aftermath of Katrina, CNN.com launched iReport, which solicited and published on the news website's homepage photos and video captured by ordinary people. The *New Orleans Times-Picayune*, which had to go completely digital during and after the storm, also very aggressively sought contributions, reports, video, and photography from Louisiana residents, contributions that helped the newspaper (and website) to win a Pulitzer prize for its hurricane coverage. People throughout the globe relied on participatory (or citizen) journalism to follow China's earthquake and rescue efforts, disaster "coverage" that included widespread use of Twitter to produce a steady stream of on-the-ground reporting from the affected areas. Text messages, instant messages, microblogs, and blogs provided a visceral source of firsthand accounts of the disaster in what was a remarkable development for a country known for its censorship of media and of news reporting.

### Case Study: Boston Marathon Bombings

The Boston Marathon bombings in 2013 revealed the best and worst of a news age in which anyone can contribute. Many *Boston Globe* staffers were runners in the marathon, so some immediately began to live tweet from the scene of the two bombings. These live Twitter feeds the *Globe* integrated into its live blog of coverage of the event and its aftermath, using TweetDeck to monitor the feeds. Bystanders and commentators tweeted freely, as well, adding to what was already a volatile blend of corroborated fact, hunches and intuitions, hearsay, and what turned out to be a great deal of misinformation. The *Globe* monitored readers' tweets, verifying and republishing many of them. The Boston police and other law enforcement also turned to Twitter, which served both to get the official word on the ongoing investigation out, as well as to solicit information, especially during the critical manhunt phase of the investigation.

Journalist Seth Mnookin wrote about his experience with Twitter during the Boston events for Harvard's *Nieman Reports*. In his account, he describes first turning to Twitter for logistics. He saw a student journalist on the scene and used Twitter to connect with the student and a photographer also there. They arranged a face-to-face meeting. Mnookin used a police scanner app on his iPhone to keep track of police activities, and he tweeted through the night. Mnookin's colleague, Hong Qu, used Keepr, a social media monitoring software Qu developed, to capture Mnookin's tweets and to pull in the 100 most recent tweets from Twitter's API (application programming interface). Qu used Keepr to identify reliable sources who appeared to be tweeting from the scene based on four indicators of credibility: disclosure of location, multiple source verification (the tweets cited information from primary as well as other sources), original pictures or video, and accuracy over time.

Mnookin and Qu practiced a then-new form of networked journalism that combined the speed and immediacy of social media with journalism's discipline of verification. Qu described Mnookin's tweets as a sort of "rolling, live-streamed press conference in which he answered followers' questions, corrected misinformation spreading via social media, and distributed important public safety updates from the police." Mnookin also leveraged the wisdom of the crowds by asking for help with his reporting.

Rather than write notes in a notebook, Mnookin turned to Twitter for note-taking, with an added benefit of having all of those notes time- and date-stamped. And as Mnookin describes it, "I knew my notes were going to be public. I spent more time thinking about whether something was important or informative or whether I was simply writing things down because I was nervous or had nothing else to do." He tweeted 483 times between April 15 and 19, and 169 times on April 18, the evening the manhunt ended.

It's also important to point out that Mnookin's reach via Twitter grew exponentially, but principally because traditional news media organizations made note of and reported what he was doing, and re-tweeted his coverage. Mnookin's number of followers went from around 8,000 to 45,000 in only a few days thanks to reports in *The New York Times* and ABC News, to name a few.

## The (Near) Future

An ongoing question for journalists is whether participatory journalism is part of the problem of the decline of traditional news media or part of the solution, and, of course, it is likely a great deal of both. User-generated content raises questions of libel liability, quality standards, and accuracy and fairness, among others. But "pro-am marriages" of professional journalists and regular people armed with phones can produce involvement and participation that get more people interested in the news. Sites and apps such as Pulse, Feedburner, and Reddit give readers the ability to shape a very different news agenda than that of professional news editors, and research has consistently shown that readers have very different definitions and priorities than does the guild of journalism.

"We" media has an underbelly, as the American electorate learned in 2016. The now infamous "Pizzagate" conspiracy claimed that Democratic Party operatives who placed orders at Comet Ping Pong pizzeria in Washington, DC, were actually using code to talk about underage prostitutes and administer a sex trafficking ring. The conspiracy theory was invented and spread because Trump supporters, Reddit users and posters to 4chan. org, and bloggers in the United States and overseas joined for the express purpose of virally spreading misinformation during the campaign.

The misinformation campaign began in late October when a white supremacy Twitter account that presented itself as belonging to a Jewish lawyer in New York tweeted that the New York Police Department was looking into evidence that emails from former

**FIGURE 8.2**
*@DavidGoldbergNY*

**David Goldberg**
@DavidGoldbergNY

⚙  👤 Follow

Rumors stirring in the NYPD that Huma's emails point to a pedophila ring and @HillaryClinton is at the center.  #GoHillary #PodestaEmails23

 **Carmen Katz**
My NYPD source said its much more vile and serious than classified material on Weiner's device. The email DETAIL the trips made by Weiner, Bill and Hillary on their pedophile billionaire friend's plane, the Lolita Express. Yup, Hillary has a well documented predilection for underage girls, and Mr. Weiner just could not bear to see those details deleted. We're talking an international child enslavement and sex ring. Not even Hillary's most ardent supporters and defenders will be able to excuse THIS!

Like · Reply · 👍 6 · 3 hrs

RETWEETS  LIKES
6,369     5,263

12:34 PM - 30 Oct 2016

↩      🔁 6.4K    🛡        ≋        ♥ 5.3K    •••

congressman Anthony Weiner's laptop contained evidence of Clinton involvement in an "international child enslavement ring." Pro-Trump tweeters jumped on the "news," which made its way to YourNewsWire.com and, subsequently, into the blogs of right-wing writers who aggregated and spread the claim that Hillary Clinton was involved in a massive child trafficking and pedophilia ring. No legitimate sources were identified or quoted.

The claims were picked up by at least two pro-Trump websites run by young men in the former Yugoslav Republic of Macedonia, where there were more than 100 of these websites operating in one small town, according to BuzzFeed News. By aggregating sensationalized and often false content, they could attract a U.S. audience and generate revenue from advertising. Back in the States, sites like Red State Watcher and True Pundit expanded the story, introducing additional false information, including conveniently anonymous FBI and NYPD sources. One of True Pundit's versions of the story attracted more than 110,000 Facebook interactions, starting anew the viral spread of the false rumors. All of this occurred in three days, by which time the original tweeter, the invented "David Goldberg," could tweet the True Pundit story as "proof" that "My source was right!"

A few tweets, a couple of message board posts, and some pro-Trump sites and bloggers looking for traffic. What does any of this have to do with pizza? Eventually, the DC pizzeria and bar Comet Ping Pong was falsely named as the hub for the criminal ring, confronting the owner and his employees with waves of threatening social media comments and, ultimately, a vigilante armed with an assault rifle shooting into the restaurant.

**BREAKING BOMBSHELL: NYPD Blows Whistle on New Hillary Emails: Money Laundering, Sex Crimes with Children, Child Exploitation, Pay to Play, Perjury**

*Posted on November 2, 2016 by admin*

FIGURE 8.3 *True Pundit*

**FIGURE 8.4**
*@DavidGoldbergNY*

**David Goldberg**
@DavidGoldbergNY

⚙  👤 Follow

My source was right! truepundit.com/breaking-
bombs    … #LockHerUp #DrainTheSwamp
#Trump2016

David Goldberg @DavidGoldbergNY
Rumors stirring in the NYPD that Huma's emails point to a
pedophila ring and @HillaryClinton is at the center.  #GoHillary
#PodestaEmails23

RETWEETS    LIKES
41    44

11:26 AM - 2 Nov 2016

While fake news might ultimately prove to be great for journalism, showing the need for reporting that debunks misinformation, it has in the meantime further scrambled a news industry that was already on the defensive. Part of the answer must be to intelligently incorporate social media. News sites should make it easy to follow the news on Twitter and Facebook, and perhaps other social media tools and platforms, as well. Readers should be able to easily tweet and re-tweet articles. For larger news topics, news sites should consider setting up specific Twitter accounts for those topics and including a line somewhere on the page inviting readers to "follow us on Twitter for more updates on this story," or the like. The same is true with Facebook. A mobile-first strategy has to supplant web-first approaches. When interactors download an organization's app, they are, in effect, signaling that they want to continue getting that organization's content.

## WHAT SOCIAL MEDIA HAVE DONE TO WORK FLOW

In social media, what formerly was discrete has become fluid, raising interesting questions about labor routines and job duties. Journalists previously have been accustomed to thinking in terms of articles (or stories) as discrete products. Historically, they have also viewed "work" and "play" as distinct and separate activities, or spheres of activity. Digital has changed all of this. From the discrete article, we have moved to a process of knowledge construction, one that could be metaphorically understood as more of a conversation and less of a lecture. So what is meant by "deadline" and "article" is changing as reporters are asked to stay current on Facebook, Twitter, Reddit, the news organization's discussion board, and a raft of other socially networked platforms and channels. The "deadline" as a synchronous chronological fact has become lost in a process that is resisting routinization.

On the other side, social media spaces are growing into virtual newsrooms of sorts, or at least spaces that have, or include, news feeds and conversations about the news, newsrooms in which the primary news gatherers and sharers work for free. These interactors expend a lot of effort to inform others in their community, but they do so in exchange for social capital. What the reporter traditionally has understood as "work" has become in socially mediated spaces something that interactors regard as something other than work: civic duty, hobby, leisure activity, perhaps volunteerism, but not work. So the division that is breaking down is between those who have privileged access to events and participants in order to report on and communicate them, on the one hand, and, on the other, the majority of audience members who do not directly participate in events, who have no expert knowledge about them, and who have no privileged right of access to information.

For interactors, the news is more of a flow, one that should find them. This news should be accurate, transparent, and immediate, and it should, above all, be relevant—relevant to them where they are at that moment. This news should be something interactors can and want to share, and it should be presented in ways that facilitate drilling down, digging deeper, and getting more. It's a different definition of news, therefore. Interactors see news "products" as connecting people and communities, and as something that can be customized and shared. It matters less who wrote or published it than it does how "shareable" it is.

A prime example of many of these shifts is Snapchat's Stories, a format for crowdsourced news being replicated widely among other social media platforms. If a lot of Snapchat users are at an event, such as a concert or sporting event, they are snapping what's happening. Snapchat, which in 2016 surpassed Twitter in terms of number of users, hired producers and journalists—curators—to assemble the best of these clips into a narrative compilation, which Snapchat sends out as part of its Live Stories feature. From football games to natural disasters, Snapchat's Live Stories are presenting news in a way few other platforms can match. For example, in summer 2016, during the massive flooding in Baton Rouge, LA, Snapchat users crowdsourced the news by providing video from inside people's homes, from relief shelters, and from the communities hardest hit, rather than positioning a talking head with a live shot from the state capitol building. Snapchat's editors created the larger narrative of the disaster from the bevy of content its users were collecting, combining coverage of the government's response, for example, with stories of real people directly affected by loss. This ground-level reporting fills a gap in national coverage, and it has the power to produce empathy in ways traditional media struggle to do.

## SOCIAL MEDIA ETHICS

In the wake of the 2016 U.S. presidential election, fundamental and even existential questions were raised about journalism, news, and fact-based reporting. Have we entered or created a "post-fact" world? Does the truth matter when shocking numbers of voters conspicuously avoid credible reporting, preferring instead views and accounts more consistent with their own assumptions and predilections? Who has ultimate responsibility, and who is or should be in control of the information in this new "journalism as process" environment and ecosystem? There is little settled on these questions.

At the same time that news organizations are asking their editorial staffs to take on additional responsibilities for monitoring and participating in social media on behalf of the organization, they are issuing rules for social media use on private time. For examples of approaches to providing this guidance, see Reuters's policy guidelines (handbook.reuters.com/index.php?title=Reporting_From_the_Internet_And_Using_ Social_Media) and those of National Public Radio (ethics.npr.org/tag/social-media). Even a casual reading of each policy identifies several issues that organizations should discuss to prevent problems caused by employees using social media, problems that are often exacerbated by social media's wide reach and un-erasable memory or cache. These issues can be summed up as accuracy, honesty and transparency, accountability, civility (or respect), and legal questions about defamation and privacy. NPR's introduction acknowledges the "new and unfamiliar challenges" posed by social media use and that this use tends "to amplify the effects of any ethical misjudgments you might make. So tread carefully." Here's an excerpt from NPR's policy:

> Conduct yourself online just as you would in any other public circumstances as an NPR journalist. Treat those you encounter online with fairness, honesty and respect, just as you would offline. Verify information before passing it along. Be honest about your intent when reporting. Avoid actions that might discredit your professional impartiality. And always remember, you represent NPR.

This is good advice for any organization's employees and representatives. Even, and perhaps especially, in social media, employees should be transparent about what they are doing and why. As the policy asks its readers to think, employees should ask themselves, "Am I about to spread a thinly sourced rumor or am I passing on valuable and credible (even if unverified) information in a transparent manner with appropriate caveats?"

### Never Off Duty

NPR's policy also recognizes that National Public Radio employees do have private lives, or lives outside of work, lives that exist, in part, in social media. In those cases, the guidance is to follow the conventions of those platforms, but to recognize that "nothing on the Web is truly private." What is shared, even when completely personal and not identified as coming from someone at NPR or having to do with NPR in any way, could reflect on NPR. This makes it of concern to the organization. Thus, even in their personal lives, employees shouldn't write or do anything that could undermine the organization's credibility with the public or harm its standing as an impartial source of news. "In other words, we don't behave any differently than we would in any public setting or on an NPR broadcast," the policy reads.

> To dramatize the risks, the policy includes this hypothetical:

> Imagine, if you will, an NPR legal correspondent named Sue Zemencourt. She's a huge fan of Enormous University's basketball team and loves to chat online about EU. She posts comments on blogs under the screen name "enormous1." One day, an equally rabid fan of Gigormous State ("gigormous1") posts obnoxious comments about EU.

> Sue snaps. Expletives and insults fly from her fingers on to the webpage. They're so out-of-line that the blog blocks her from submitting any more comments—and discovers that her IP address leads back to NPR. The blog's host posts that "someone at NPR is using language that the FCC definitely would not approve of" and describes what was said. Things go viral.

> The basically good person that she is, Sue publicly acknowledges and apologizes for her mistake. But that doesn't stop *The Daily Show* from satirizing about the "NPRNormous Explosion."

> Damage done.

A recurring question for news organizations, especially in the digital age, is when or even whether employees can take political positions, even in their personal lives, for the reasons alluded to above. The safest policy is, of course, to prohibit it, including using an individual Facebook page to express personal views on controversial issues. As the NPR policy states, "In reality, anything you post online reflects both on you and on NPR." Even participation in an online group might be perceived as endorsement. This might seem draconian, but in a business in which impartiality and, more generally, reputation are critical differentiators, such caution is wise.

## Speed v. Accuracy

As the Reuters policy acknowledges, "The tension is clear: Social networks encourage fast, constant, brief communications; journalism calls for communication preceded by fact-finding and thoughtful consideration." These very different priorities are in some ways mutually exclusive: speed, on the one hand; caution and a discipline of verification, on the other. Or as Reuters puts it, "Journalism has many 'unsend' buttons, including editors. Social networks have none." Everything Reuters employees write, say, or post online could be used against it in a court of law, in the perceptions of its audiences and sources, and, perhaps most dangerously, by people who want to harm Reuters.

Also worthy of note is NPR policy's acknowledgement that it is a work in progress and that it will likely change over time. Employees are encouraged to send in questions of interpretation and suggestions for changes or improvements. An editor of standards and practices and an ethics advisory group at NPR have been charged with considering these suggestions for revisions of the policy. The stakes are too high not to routinize this important function.

## An Ethics Case Study: Reddit

The false identification by a Reddit user of Sunil Tripathi, a 22-year-old Brown University student, as a suspect in the Boston Marathon bombings in 2013 and the subsequent treatment of that ID by mainstream media illustrate in stark terms how messy the media ecosystem has become. The interaction and intermingling among mainstream or traditional news media and individuals participating with social media has blurred and perhaps erased once-important distinctions between verified fact and (tweeted and re-tweeted) rumor, and between published reporting and simple speculation. These dangerous trends were magnified by the 2016 U.S. presidential election "coverage," both real and fake, as well.

Reddit burst on the national digital media scene in summer 2012 with the Aurora, CO, movie theater shooting spree. Threads on Reddit opened up for breaking news about the shooting, most of it coming from individuals. One "Redditor" shot in the theater posted a photo of himself from the emergency room. Some of what got posted proved accurate, including its timeline of events; much of it turned out to be unsubstantiated rumor.

Sunil Tripathi disappeared on March 16, 2013. Because his photo was juxtaposed with video surveillance images of what turned out later to be Dzhokhar Tsarnaev, the man eventually apprehended in connection with the bombings, Tripathi became, as far as the public was concerned, a suspect. Tripathi's false identification effectively ended his family's efforts to get the public's help in searching for him, and it led to angry phone calls, death threats, and hateful posts to a Facebook page his parents had set up to facilitate the search. A Twitter user who tweeted using the handle @ghughesca reported that he had heard on a police scanner that Tripathi had been identified as "Suspect 2." Without confirming this with Boston Police, the tweet was reported by Kevin Galliford, a journalist with a TV station in Hartford, CT. Galliford's report was then re-tweeted

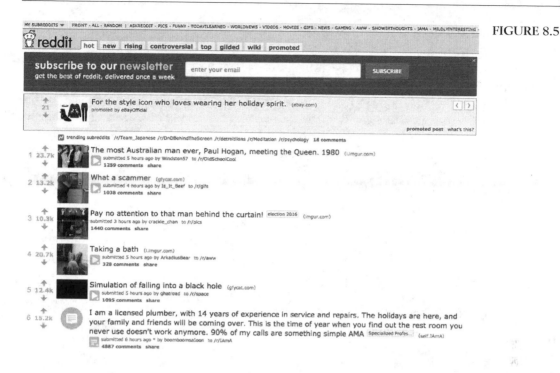

FIGURE 8.5

more than 1,000 times in a matter of minutes, according to *The New York Times*. Next it was BuzzFeed's turn, which sent out the false scanner information along with the confirmation, "Wow Reddit was right about the missing Brown student."

Reddit's role in this new media ecosystem was unprecedented, especially in terms of reach. For some, it is a "haven from the propaganda of the mainstream media. . . the world's most important vehicle for democratized, crowdsourced journalism," according to the *Times*. For others, it's a messy, busy mix of rumor, chatter, and trivia. Among its most popular categories are those for videogaming, computer programming, and pornography. Its bare bones homepage is determined or configured by "upvotes," or popularity of content as determined by its users, which as of late 2013 numbered nearly 100 million unique users. An upvote generates "karma," which is a salute to the pre-existing Slashdot online community, and karma pushes content on toward the homepage. Downvotes do the opposite. Together, these votes organize and prioritize the thousands of posts going up in Reddit's more than 6,000 categories, called subReddits. The homepage is, of course, the Holy Grail, representing perhaps hundreds of thousands of page views and the kind of attention news media, advertisers, marketers, and individual "Redditors" covet. Reddit generates more traffic than either *The New York Times* or Fox News, though primarily among users 25 years old and younger.

## Reddit's Moral Responsibility

On April 23, 2013, police pulled what turned out to be Tripathi's body out of the Providence River. His family's search, which had been complicated by accusations that Tripathi and his family were Muslim terrorists, was mercifully over. (They are neither Muslim nor radicals of any kind.) Some journalists apologized to the family, while others claimed that they were merely passing along information they were receiving without making any sort of truth claim. For its part, Reddit, which saw record-breaking hits, page views, and users, declared itself "content-agnostic," unwilling to intervene except in the most unusual of circumstances.

This amalgamation of public and private expression creates, as the Tripathi case study dramatically, even tragically, shows, a sort of fractal in the national conversation, a sort of hyperbolic geometric folding in on itself, to borrow a description from rubber-sheet geometry. Fueling this is the fact that people form attitudes toward the issues important to them in largely private or interpersonal conversation, even gossip.

Thus, a challenge at both theoretical and practical levels presented by much expression online is that it can be seen as having the qualities of both mass (or public) communication and interpersonal (or private) communication. Much of digital expression, particularly communication in and through social media, can be described as being fleeting or evanescent, as if it were spoken in conversation, a description that fits much of what takes place in digitally delivered social networks. In practice, much of online expression does the work of interpersonal communication, and it has been extensively studied just this way by several disciplines.

## CHAPTER ACTIVITIES

1. Develop the online content you outlined and prepared for in Chapter 6. For this news story or press release or feature, you should report, source, write, edit, and post it online, then share it with whatever social media you are familiar. This article must have or rely upon at least three *human* sources, people you ideally spoke with face-to-face or, as a fallback, on the telephone. But know that this is a bare bones **minimum**. The more reporting you do, the better the story will be. Seek timeliness; ask yourself why the story needs to be done NOW. The story should also demonstrate impact or consequence.

   Do not procrastinate. Do not wait to begin identifying sources, generating sequences of questions to ask those sources and, most importantly, to begin attempting to contact those sources. Procrastination results in sloppy, harried work, and with scarce time you risk being unable to contact sources. Build in time for callbacks, for failure to reach people. Sources are best reached early in the morning and just after 5 p.m., or after most people are gone and the phones are relatively quiet. (Do not use email for your interviews, but only to arrange interviews and for follow-up questions and fact-checking.)

Think about the journalism you've read. Have you ever seen a note like this? "This journalism is not as good as it could have been because I couldn't reach some important sources. They were out of town. I just missed them. They were really busy. Sorry." No, you haven't. Don't wait, and develop contingency plans.

Beware of conflicts of interest, making sure to avoid using friends, family members, and business associates as sources. Avoid stories that could materially affect those companies and entities with which you are affiliated.

Post with the story the questions you asked your sources, a list of the facts you checked and verified, and a list of the sources you attempted to contact (not merely those you were able to include in your story). Also identify your intended audience(s).

As you are completing this assignment, think about what might be added to your main story for publication online, including multimedia and interactive features. Because online you would have all the space you would need, consider the range of added features that could be developed, including fact boxes, an FAQ list, a video extra, interview notes and transcripts, maps, charts, a glossary, a slideshow, animated graphics, a poll, related stories and opinion, and perhaps an area where readers could contribute reactions, story ideas, photos, and comments. No need to do any of these things, but consider what might make a strong story package online.

Look also for publication opportunities. For non-journalists, if you need guidance getting started, Poynter offers a good source through its "NewsU." Look for Hot Courses on its left panel (www.newsu.org).

The five basic journalism questions:

1.  WHO is involved in what you're covering?
2.  WHAT are they doing—and accomplishing?
3.  WHERE are they doing it?
4.  WHY are they doing it in the first place?
5.  HOW do they make it happen?

You can also consult the appendix to this book: "The Core Values of Digital Journalism."

2.  In this hypothetical, you propose doing a story on a local sportswear shop owner's quest to run in the Boston Marathon. He has just qualified to participate in this year's running. For this activity, generate a list of questions for your sit-down interview, organizing them in terms of priority, clustering them by topic, and sequencing them to ensure you get as much of the information you need as you can. Also begin thinking about sidebars, multimedia, and features you could produce to create a more winsome digital package, such as an interactive route of the marathon run, a short biographical sidebar box on the shop owner, etc.

3.  You are working on a story on a dorm fire on your campus. You begin seeing photos of the fire while it is still raging, from presumably residents of the affected dorm, on Facebook, Instagram, and Snapchat. One in particular you believe best captures the situation, and you would like to run it online, tweet it out, and otherwise include it in

your campus news site's ongoing coverage. Apply a discipline of verification. What will you want to know about that photo before you run it? Outline how you will verify the validity of the photo and detail the information you will need to collect.

4. Create a Storify "story" about a current news topic of your choice. Storify (storify.com) is a social storytelling platform that lets you bring together media from social networks like Twitter, Facebook, YouTube, and Instagram. Storify stories begin with a headline and summary. Next, start typing text in your story by clicking anywhere in the white space. Write a summary of your news topic of about 150 words, which will focus your Storify. By combining information and media already published on your topic, you will be creating an informational package to expand your coverage.

- Find at least six social media elements but make sure each one is both credible and relevant. If your social media elements need explanation or clarification, write that in the space above them that Storify provides as part of its template. Storify lets you easily drag and drop media elements from social networks into a post to help tell your story. To get started, click on the Twitter icon on the right and then the magnifying glass icon to search.
- Find at least two visuals, video or images or both. Each visual must be directly relevant to your topic.
- Write two short paragraphs to help present the information about your news topic. The paragraphs should help connect the social media elements you have gathered.
- When you're finished with your story, click "publish" to make it visible on your Storify user page. Storify stories are embeddable, meaning you can also post them on other sites and platforms.
- If you don't like your presentation, re-order any element by grabbing it and moving it around, or deleting it to make room for something else. Readers will see the latest version of what you've published.

   For more help with this activity, see Kelly Fincham's "how-to" on Storify: storify.com/kellyfincham/the-updated-guide-to-storify-for-journalists.

5. The website Reddit, which gets its name by adapting "read it," advertises itself as the "Front page of the Internet." (A case study on Reddit's role in the coverage of the Boston Marathon bombings is in Chapter 8.) Registered users can add links and opinions in more than 6,000 categories (or "subReddits") and make comments about what others have added. Comments determine whether a post gets a high ranking on Reddit's main page. Your assignment: Post your reporting project done for the previous chapter to Reddit:

- Register for an account at reddit.com.
- Decide on a page title and select a "subReddit" category for your reporting. You will want to browse the subReddit categories. SubReddits you might choose from include Advertising, Journalism, Public Relations, News, or Photojournalism. Subscribing to some subReddit categories will order or organize your homepage and cut down on the clutter.
- Add your story.
- Click the "subReddit" you selected to see your article. (Be patient: It can take several minutes.)

Once posted, you can use Reddit to monitor opinions about your work and see it move forward in the content. You could also integrate Reddit into a blog, website, or press release to show the number of comments received from other Reddit users. This takes time, of course, so the purpose of this assignment is simply to become acquainted with the Reddit interface and ecosystem. You might also generate attention by tweeting out a link to your article.

## Digital Resources

**Best Practices for Newspaper Journalists (slowburn.com/clients/fais/journalism/best practices.pdf)**
Written by Bob Haiman and published by the Freedom Forum, this PDF download was developed to help journalists achieve fairness in their reporting.

**Poynter Guide to Accuracy (poynter.org/2003/getting-it-right-2/12036/)**
A collection of articles by Poynter writers to help journalists in the area of accuracy, including help in fact-checking, grammar, punctuation, and quotations and attribution.

**Principles of Citizen Journalism (kcnn.org/learning-modules/principles-of-citizen-journalism)**
Published by the Knight Citizen News Network, this guide provides the basic principles and covers the fundamental values of good journalism.

## BIBLIOGRAPHY

Bender, John R., Davenport, Lucinda, Drager, Michael W., and Fedler, Fred, *Reporting for the Media*, 10th edition (New York, NY: Oxford University Press, 2011).

Bergman, Cory, "Factoring Risk and Uncertainty into Real-Time Coverage," *BreakingNews.com* (September 20 2013), available: http://blog.breakingnews.com/#about.

Carroll, Brian, "Culture Clash: Journalism and the Communal Ethos of the Blogosphere," *Into the Blogosphere: Rhetoric, Community, and Culture of Weblogs* (Summer 2004), available: www.intothe blogosphere.org.

Ferrier, Michelle Barrett and Batts, Battinto, "Educators and Professionals Agree on Outcomes for Entrepreneurship Courses," *Newspaper Research Journal* 37, no. 4 (2016): 322–338.

Friend, Cecilia and Challenger, Don, *Contemporary Editing*, 3rd edition (New York, NY: McGraw Hill, 2014).

Friend, Cecilia and Singer, Jane B., *Online Journalism Ethics* (Boston, MA: M. E. Sharpe, 2006).

Gelman, Lauren, "Privacy, Free Speech, and 'Blurry-Edged Social Networks'," *Boston College Law Review* 50, no. 1315 (2009): 5.

Gomes, Lee, "Why We're Powerless to Resist Grazing on Endless Web Data," *The Wall Street Journal* (March 12 2008): B1.

Hacker, Scot and Seshagiri, Ashwin, "Twitter for Journalists," *kdmcBerkeley blog* (June 23 2011), available: http://multimedia.journalism.berkeley.edu/tutorials/twitter/.

Horrigan, John B., "Seeding the Cloud: What Mobile Access Means for Usage Patterns and Online Content," *Pew Internet and American Life Project* (March 2008).

Joan Shorenstein Center on the Press, Politics and Public Policy, "Creative Destruction: An Exploratory Look at News on the Internet," *Joan Shorenstein Center* (August 2007).

Journalism.org, "The Latest News Headlines—Your Vote Counts," *Journalism.org* (September 12 2007), available: http://journalism.org/node/7493.

Kang, Jay Caspian, "Should Reddit Be Blamed for the Spreading of Smear?" *The New York Times* (July 25 2013), available: www.nytimes.com/2013/07/28/magazine/should-reddit-be-blamed-for-thespreading-of-a-smear.html.

Kovach, Bill and Rosenstiel, Tom, *The Elements of Journalism: What Newspeople Should Know and the Public Should Expect* (New York, NY: Three Rivers Press, 2014).

Li, Charlene, *Social Technographics: Mapping Participation in Activities Forms the Foundation of a Social Strategy* (Cambridge, MA: Forrester Research, 2007).

Little, Mark, "The Human Algorithm," *Storyful.com* (May 20 2011), available: http://blog.storyful.com/2011/05/20/the-human-algorithm-2/#.UjxIJyR4NMo2.

Manjoo, Farhad, "While We Weren't Looking, Snapchat Revolutionized Social Networks," *The New York Times* (December 1 2016): B5.

Massing, Michael, "Digital Journalism: The Next Generation," *New York Review of Books* (June 25 2015), available: www.nybooks.com/articles/2015/06/25/digital-journalism-next-generation/.

McAthy, Rachel, "How To Verify Content from Social Media," *Journalism.co.uk* (April 3 2012), available: www.journalism.co.uk/news-features/how-to-verify-content-from-social-media/s5/a548645/.

Mnookin, Seth and Qu, Hong, "Organize the Noise: Tweeting Live from the Boston Manhunt," *Neiman Reports* (Spring 2013), available: www.nieman.harvard.edu/reports/article/102885/Organizethe-Noise-Tweeting-Live-from-the-Boston-Manhunt.aspx.

Morris, Merrill and Ogan, Christine, "The Internet as Mass Medium," *Journal of Communication* 46, no. 1 (1996): 39–50.

Murray, Alex, "BBC Processes for Verifying Social Media Content," *BBC* (May 18 2011), available: www.bbc. co.uk/blogs/blogcollegeofjournalism/posts/bbcsms_bbc_procedures_for_veri.

Najmabadi, Shannon, "How Can Students Be Taught to Detect Fake News and Dubious Claims," *The Chronicle of Higher Education* (December 12 2016), available: www.chronicle.com/article/How-Can-Students-Be-Taught-to/238652.

Rogers, Simon, "The Boston Bombing: How Journalists Used Twitter to Tell the Story," *Twitterblog* (July 10 2013), available: https://blog.twitter.com/2013/the-boston-bombing-how-journalists-used-twitter- to-tell-the-story.

Silverman, Craig, "8 Must-Reads Detail How to Verify Information in Real-Time, from Social Media," *Poynter Institute* (April 27 2012), available: www.poynter.org/latest-news/regret-the-error/171713/8-must-reads-that-detail-how-to-verify-content-from-twitter-other-social-media/.

Silverman, Craig, "How the Bizarre Conspiracy Theory Behind 'Pizzagate' Was Spread," *BuzzFeed News* (December 5 2016), available: www.buzzfeed.com/craigsilverman/fever-swamp-election.

Straumshelm, Carl, "Who Gets It First: Twitter or the Editors?" *American Journalism Review* (February/March 2012), available: www.ajr.org/Article.asp?id=5271.

Tavernise, Sabrina, "As Fake News Spreads Lies, More Readers Shrug at the Truth," *The New York Times* (December 6 2016), available: http://nytimes.com/2016/12/06/us/fake-news-partisan-republican-democrat.html.

Zinsser, William, *On Writing Well* (New York, NY: Harper & Row, 1976).

# Public Relations in a Digital Age

*It takes 20 years to build a reputation and five minutes to ruin it. If you think about that, you'll do things differently.*
—Warren Buffett

*A squirrel dying in front of your house may be more relevant to your interests right now than people dying in Africa.*

—Mark Zuckerberg, Facebook founder

*We're all naked, so we better be in good shape.*
—Diana El-Azar, World Economic Forum

## INTRODUCTION

The definition of public relations according to the Public Relations Society of America is that of a "discipline that ethically fosters mutually beneficial relationships among *social* entities" (emphasis added). The definition seems to predict or accommodate social media. Notice also the absence of the word "media," which is prescient considering how far beyond traditional media the social syndication of digital content has gone. Social media are re-wiring society, undoing traditional marketing advantages like advertising, de-stabilizing and replacing old-line institutions and norms, and circumventing mainstream media. The focus of this chapter is on how digital writers and editors in the context of public relations can think strategically about social media in service to a message and to the mutually beneficial relationships the PRSA definition identifies. Also covered are how to develop interactive and multimedia press releases, how to earn media mentions, how to measure effectiveness, what to do in crisis, and how to use social media to listen to our publics.

## WATCHING THE GAME, NOT THE BALL

If you have ever watched pre-school children play soccer, you may have noticed their obsession with the ball. So focused on that 27-inch sphere, heads down, eyes looking at their own feet, that quite often—in fact, most of the time—they lose sight of where the goal net is, even of its general direction. This is perhaps the biggest challenge facing public relations practitioners in a digital era—not being so focused on the ball (the product, the event, the message) that they risk losing sight of the larger game. So, instead of putting on a show, we should meet people where they are with an attitude of benevolence and largesse, an attitude that sincerely wants to help our publics find answers to the problems they have. This attitude should be communicated in our webpages, our Facebook posts, our tweets, our FAQ lists—all of our external communications.

To build on the soccer game metaphor, consider the travel experience of Dave Kerpen, founder and CEO of social media software company Likeable Local. After a challenging journey from New York, trying to check into his hotel in Las Vegas, he found the line an hour long. Not surprisingly, he turned to Twitter, tweeting out, "No Vegas hotel could be worth this long wait. #Fail." The nearby Rio Hotel saw his tweet and, playing the game and not merely the ball, tweeted right back, but not the message you might expect. Playing the ball would mean a tweet along the lines of, "Hey @Dave, we've got no waiting. Come on over! We're just a few blocks away." This would be thinking about your own organization, your own products, your own services. The Rio tweeter instead considered Dave's plight and tweeted, "Sorry about the bad experience, Dave. Hope the rest of your stay in Vegas goes well."

The Rio's tweet didn't result in a new customer that day, at least not directly. But where do you think Dave stayed the next time he went to Vegas? What do you think he began talking about and sharing on Twitter with many friends and followers? The Rio listened and used social media to reach concentric circles of potential guests and customers in a way that people want to share and pass along.

Next, a negative example, and one representative of so much of what is called public relations. Take a look at a press release plucked virtually at random from PR Newswire (prnewswire.com); it was the first hit for a search of the site using the key words, "information technology":

PASADENA, Calif./PRNewswire—Vertical Management Systems Inc. (VMS), Envestnet | Retirement Solutions (ERS), a majority-owned subsidiary of Envestnet, Inc. (NYSE: ENV), and United Retirement Plan Consultants (URPC), announced today an innovative strategic partnership designed to help financial advisors, retirement plan sponsors and participants navigate new Department of Labor (DOL) conflict-of-interest regulations, and streamline their fiduciary, recordkeeping and compliance services on one scalable platform.

The seamless integration of these services on VMS's Retirement Revolution platform provides a retirement-plan solution with choice, flexibility, complete transparency and cost-effective pricing. Further, it leverages the combined expertise of leading firms in the financial-services marketplace to offer optimal outcomes across the spectrum of retirement-plan needs—from plan design and set-up to full recordkeeping and administration, wrapped with fiduciary protection that specifically addresses the new DOL rules.

"We are very excited about VMS's partnership with retirement-industry leaders like ERS and United Retirement," said Kevin Rafferty, Chief Executive Officer of VMS. "The combination of Retirement Revolution's cutting-edge retirement platform with top-notch fiduciary and third-party administrator (TPA) services establishes a new gold standard in the retirement industry. At a time when the heightened regulatory environment requires better solutions, we feel this comprehensive offering is just what advisors need to drive operational efficiencies and better serve their clients."

The comprehensive Retirement Revolution® platform offers both "off the shelf" and customizable solutions, providing advisors and their clients with highly flexible retirement plan alternatives to meet their specific needs.

"United Retirement is proud to be part of such a robust retirement plan solution and partner with VMS and ERS," said John Davis, Chief Executive Officer of United Retirement Plan Consultants. "Together, we believe our joint offering provides our advisors and clients with a holistic, yet customizable, retirement plan solution geared at helping them manage and mitigate their fiduciary risks."

This press release and its host of semantic problems is precisely what watching the ball at one's feet looks like. By negative example here, we learn a few important principles applicable well beyond the crafting of a press release:

1. Announcing something doesn't make it news. The value isn't in the announcing.
2. No one cares *who* is making the announcement or that person's title. Lead instead with the news, or information that people will care about. In this release, the internal politics of giving each CEO a quote were likely more important than any sense of service to their respective publics.

3. How excited or proud you or your company is about something—anything—isn't news, either. No one cares. Again, focus instead on how the information actually matters in the real world.

4. Alphabet soup is a barrier to understanding. The many acronyms in this release's lead create a thicket of confusion few readers will even attempt to plow through. The corporation's own style conventions get in the way of clarity and meaning.

5. Don't write about how awesome your services or "solutions" are, as this press release generically puts it. Avoid empty, clichéd claims such as "world-class," "best-of-breed," "cutting edge," or "revolutionary." (For a great parody of this style of corporate gobble-dygook, see: fastcocreate.com/3028162/this-generic-brand-ad-is-the-greatest-thing-about-the-absolute-worst-in-advertising). Write instead about real people and how your organization is helping them.

6. Finally, this release fails to take advantage of the hypertextual possibilities of digital, even of email distribution.

To the last point, online news releases differ in a few important ways from their traditional print counterparts. Chief among these differences are length and hypertextuality. Digital news releases run shorter, or about 250 words or so, and they feature hyperlinks and ways for the reader to take immediate action, such as joining an email distribution list, adding a social bookmark, or posting a comment. Often news releases written for digital distribution will include multimedia, as well, such as a video clip or link to video or a high-resolution photo. Though as a form it has been around since at least 1906, the press release still is a staple of public relations, digital or otherwise. Journalists and bloggers continue to rely heavily on them.

Press releases are written much like the news stories they hope to inspire, or at least they should be. Before you write yours, think about these basic questions:

1. What is the purpose? What is the news here? Think in terms of the values that are found in good journalism (impact, conflict, novelty, timeliness, prominence, a twist or surprise element, proximity, human interest, the bizarre or unexpected).

2. Who is the audience or public for this message?

3. Why should this audience care? How will it benefit them? Why will this public be interested?

4. What is the communicative goal of your organization? How does this release fit into a larger purpose or strategy?

5. How will this news release aid in accomplishing the greater goal or purpose? What will success look like?

6. What are the key points or aspects or messages the release needs to communicate?

7. Why now? Why are you releasing this information now? What's the timeliness?

**FIGURE 9.1**

*An example of a multimedia-rich digital news release for the Great Food Truck Race on the Food Network, at multivu.com/players/English/58431-the-great-food-truck-race*

The mechanics of reporting, or gathering information, and writing the release are much the same—in fact, nearly identical—to those of developing a journalistic news article, including the application of the inverted pyramid story structure and Associated Press style. News releases follow the same rules and format of a news story (headline, dateline, lead, body). These mechanics and basics were covered in last chapter. They also include extensive contact information and an "about us" section.

## EARNING MENTIONS

Though direct-to-consumer communication has never been more possible or more abundant, the research shows that "earned media," or "word of mouth," is still dominant. The prevalence and durability of the press release is evidence. And this earned media is still more valuable than paid coverage. In a study conducted by Outsell, earned media was rated as more effective than either owned or paid media by 81 percent of senior marketers because it results in higher levels of engagement and trust. The earned media tactics such as seeding stories, monitoring social and other media, sending press releases, pursuing speaking opportunities, and managing communities are, therefore, still necessary to be effective. You need mentions, shares, re-posts, reviews, and recommendations, and your content picked up by third-party sites. You want strong rankings on the search engines, and you need good brand content to generate those rankings.

Owned media is any digital form that you can control and is unique to your brand or organization, such as a website, blog, e-book, webinar, podcast, or social media account. The more owned media your organization has, the more channels it has to extend its presence and get attention. Paid media is simply media you pay for or buy, such as advertising, sponsorships, and paying bloggers or YouTubers to refer to or otherwise promote your organization.

What many organizations and companies are learning is that to get mindshare in digital realms and the social sphere, they need valuable, informative, engaging content. Thus, their communications teams are increasingly doing what is essentially journalism, and their perspectives on providing their publics with information are more often those of a publisher. For example, the public relations team at a large, regional hospital in eastern North Carolina routinely brainstorms ideas for connecting with its publics in ways that matter to those publics. One of this team's more recent initiatives was to develop a series of short videos introducing its emergency medical technicians and medivac helicopter pilots. The result were engaging, even thrilling videos of these frontline healthcare givers in action, providing a large, bureaucratic institution with several thoroughly human, even heroic faces. These videos, posted and delivered in multiple channels, including YouTube, were widely shared and used by the hospital in a number of ways.

The idea was only possible because someone on that hospital's public relations team figured out how to think about the organization's publics and what matters to them rather than thinking only about products, services, and surgical procedures. Implicit in this shift of attention was a move away from slick, printed, minted media productions and publications and toward authentically, meaningfully engaging real people. To do this, the hospital's communications team had to overcome their fears—none had produced any video before—and learn by doing. Instead of holing up in the office and pumping mediocre content onto Vine, Periscope, Tumblr, Vox, Twitter, Facebook, and Snapchat, they thought like publishers serving an audience that has particular information needs.

According to data from eVariant, 80 percent of web users look up health information online and more than 75 percent use the web to make healthcare decisions. Despite this, more than 60 percent of hospital marketing departments devote less than a quarter of their marketing budgets to the digital and less than 30 percent of their staff time to creating content for digital. What are they doing instead? Producing brochures, TV ads, and newsletters, which is throwing time and money into the trash, in many cases quite literally so.

**Inova Health Systems** in northern Virginia, a healthcare system with more than a million patients per year, instead thinks like a digital publisher. The communications team there produces compelling journalism focused on real people. Inova has spent a lot of time and money understanding its patients and then developing lots of rich content for those publics, which include referring physicians, as well. In a heavily regulated industry afraid of publishing too much information, Inova stands out all the more. The team that puts this content together has full-time writers, editors, and content producers, and it is led by a director of digital marketing and communication, who draws on a host of freelancers, as well. Two of the full-timers are former reporters. The team also has a full-time social media manager making sure all of this content is interwoven into the conversations Inova is having with its publics.

When **Boeing** overhauled its website, the company shifted from a Boeing-centric approach that touted its technology and aircraft to one focused more on people,

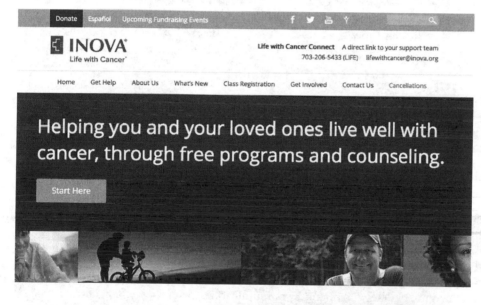

FIGURE 9.2
*Inova's Life With Cancer subsite, Lifewithcancer.org, pulls together information for patients and families and introduces visitors to real people like Phil Gilbert, who is the subject of a video on recovering from hip replacement surgery*

Boeing 747-8 performs ultimate rejected takeoff

including and even especially those who make the planes. The new site relies heavily on well-crafted stories—on good journalism. A centerpiece of this new strategy is the "One of its Own" series of features on employees. One of these stories is "Rocky Earns His Rest," about a Belgian Malinois who served Boeing for 56 dog years as an explosives-detection dog. Another piece of good journalism was the "Freezin' in Florida" feature article about the testing the company does for the 787 Dreamliner in the largest refrigerated hangar in the world, a hangar that can go from 65 degrees below to 165 degrees high. Instead of a news release that perhaps you can imagine ("The Boeing Corp. announced today that . . ."), Boeing's communications team took you inside the hangar to show what real people have to do to freeze a jet airplane. The team produced a feature story and a video of the experience, and all of this great journalism at boeing.com is supported by the @Boeing Twitter feed.

## HOW TO USE BLOGS

Chapter 7 taught that to effectively use blogs in a larger public relations strategy, you are wise to be authentic, transparent, interesting, and at least at some level an expert on something, however focused or narrow that expertise might be. Creating useful content that helps your publics, that eases their pain, that shoulders their burdens, that enriches their lives, that is honestly communicated in human language is not only the right thing to do, but it will be rewarded by the search engines, particularly Google. A sweeping overhaul of Google's algorithm has ensured that gaming gets punished and that empty language gets punished.

The sweet spot for blog post lengths is about 1,500 words, which might sound long. Though you shouldn't write to hit a particular word count, this length underlines the fact that the search engines are looking for and indexing that which is substantial and meaningful. Longer posts have a better opportunity to indicate their relevance, so Google sees these longer posts as more likely to contain the answer to a searcher's question. The 1,500 threshold isn't a magic number, obviously; you shouldn't pad a post. If 300 words is all you need to get the job done, stop there.

Especially in public relations, broadly defined, it is thought leadership that is finding traction in digital realms. Identify some topic relevant to your organization's mission and begin planning and researching a series of posts on that topic. This sort of thought leadership can contribute to your institution's or brand's credibility. The best blogs are actually useful, and they open up a window into the humanity of an organization.

## A Few Examples

The blog for the **City of College Station, TX**, written by Colin Killian, public communications manager, gets so many things right. Killian writes in the first person, with his byline and email address. He uses humor, writing about, for example, what city maintenance crews have found in muddy trenches over the years, as well as about the tough subjects, like the shooting of a police officer. He live blogs city council meetings. Killian's consistent supply of useful information creates trust, reduces rumors, creates goodwill, and seeds media interest. And most people in Killian's position would avoid blogging, saying it is fraught with too much legal risk or might generate too much negative comment.

Killian wisely includes his byline on all of his posts. Most people want to know who wrote the story. If you are in a specialized field, this becomes all the more important. A byline also:

- shows that the organization has thought about accountability;
- offers a name to go with the content;
- communicates that a human being is alive somewhere in the organization, someone thinking about the things the interactor might be thinking about;
- invites feedback and follow-up, especially when combined with an email address and a Twitter handle;

FIGURE 9.4
*The College Station, TX, blog, at blog. cstx.gov/*

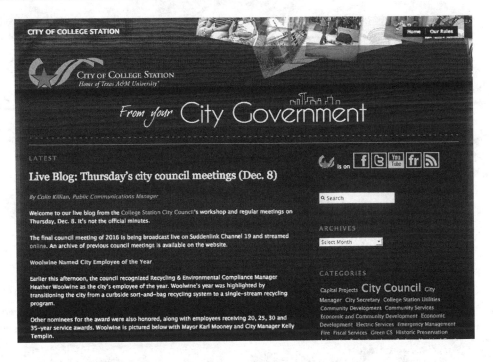

- contributes to credibility, especially in combination with other bylines; and
- offers another way for content to be searched and cached.

Like College Station's blog, the Seattle Police Department's blog—**SPD Blotter**—is a model for how to mix great journalism with personality for a consistently compelling supply of shareable content. For example, SPD Blotter published "Marijwhatnow?", a guide to the legal use of marijuana and an extraordinarily practical guide to how SPD interprets Initiative 502, which legalized the use of marijuana in the state of Washington. One FAQ reads, "Can I legally carry around an ounce of marijuana?" The answer: Yes, for personal use. Another question reads, "What happens if I get pulled over and I'm sober, but an officer or his K9 buddy smell the ounce of Super Skunk in my trunk?" The answer explained probable cause.

SPD Blotter's content comes from SPD employees, including detectives and beat officers, as well as from professional journalists. The result is more than 300,000 Twitter followers, which is remarkable for a government agency.

Both College Station and SPD are progressive if for no other reason than they didn't allow a conversation about metrics prevent them from forging ahead into the blogosphere. How does an organization know what is working? What is worthwhile? The

FIGURE 9.5
*SPD Blotter,
at spdblotter.
seattle.gov*

answer is, of course, complicated, because it isn't as simple as counting sales, page views, or shares. Engaging publics, exercising thought leadership, and developing trust are more difficult to quantify. And these activities are absolutely essential in a crisis, when it's far too late to switch strategies from short-term, imminently quantifiable results and metrics to the attributes and assets that save your organization's standing in a crisis. Thus, you may not be able to deliver the traffic numbers or other metrics that the executive suite thinks represent success if you are instead working on the longer term, on the relationships. Some executives have to be educated on this shift and on the less quantifiable successes related to mission. They have to be persuaded to consider digital content strategies more holistically and with a longer horizon.

## CORPORATE BLOGS

Public relations practitioners might find themselves responsible for a corporate blog or perhaps an employee blog. Corporate blogs typically are "written" by an executive of the company ("written" in quotations, because often that executive doesn't actually write the blog, even though his or her name and image appear on the blog). Corporate blogs are routinely sub-contracted out to public relations firms, which use them to paradoxically give the impression of increased transparency on the part of the client.

The best corporate blogs communicate a thoroughly human, authentic voice. Bill Marriott, founder of the self-named hotel chain, is one of the better corporate bloggers (blogs.marriott.com/marriott-on-the-move/). Well-written, with posts about much more than the hotel business, Marriott's frequently updated blog puts a human face on a global brand. His posts read much like weekly columns by a newspaper editor who knows everyone in his community. Marriott celebrates "unsung heroes," notes the deaths of long-serving Marriott employees, shares his summer reading lists, and notes and lauds community service.

Not surprisingly, tech companies have a disproportionate number of the best corporate blogs, including Cisco, Dell, Google, IBM, Intel, and Microsoft. But non-tech companies, such as Coca-Cola, Delta Airlines, and Walmart, also understand the power of a well-written blog, creating with these blogs a digital meeting place for employees, customers, and partners. This is a corporate blog's biggest benefit: engagement. Like Bill Marriott's blog, Walmart's (blog.walmart.com/) includes human interest stories, seasonal news, and stories that show and demonstrate the company caring about its employees and the communities where it has stores. Notably, the posts are written by real employees, including floor level associates.

The better corporate blogs understand the ingredients for building readership and community:

- high quality, interesting, engaging content;
- a recognizably authentic human voice;
- good writing;
- timeliness;
- engagement with readers and stakeholders;
- share-ability (or virality); and
- alignment with corporate objectives.

Among employee blogs, perhaps the best known is the one maintained by Sun Microsystems. More accurately put, it would be the family of thousands of employee blogs this company uses to reach its global workforce. By one count, Sun publishes 4,000 employee blogs. Employees are obviously encouraged, even financially incented to blog, so they do, including Sun's top-ranking executives. These blogs recognize employee achievement, publicize incentives, discuss leadership, facilitate project development, and make training and development options known, among many, many other topics.

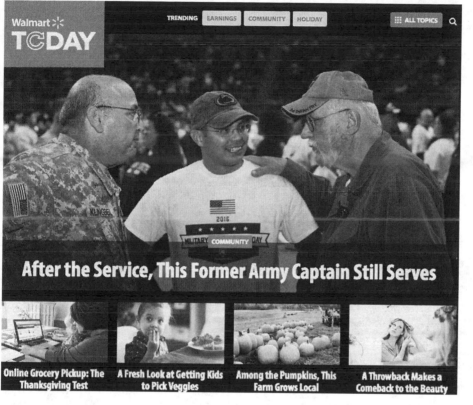

After the Service, This Former Army Captain Still Serves

Online Grocery Pickup: The Thanksgiving Test

A Fresh Look at Getting Kids to Pick Veggies

Among the Pumpkins, This Farm Grows Local

A Throwback Makes a Comeback to the Beauty

**FIGURE 9.6**
*Walmart's blog, at blog.walmart.com*

For both corporate and employee blogs, transparency and disclaimers are critical. When a client or affiliate is mentioned, those corporate relationships should be identified. Individual employees should make it clear they are expressing their own views and not those of their employer, and they should identify themselves, including their role or title with the company. Many if not most companies who allow blogging require a standard disclaimer that the writer is expressing only his or her own views. If material is borrowed or used, it should be appropriately credited; intellectual property has to be respected. And bloggers should be careful not to share trade secrets or proprietary information. In fact, to prevent insider trading, the Securities Exchange Commission prohibits this.

Most large companies have policies that cover how to blog, or even whether an employee can blog. Some of the key points of these policies are:

- To remind employees to be professional at all times, including on a blog. They represent the company.

- To assert the right to request that certain subjects be avoided, that problematic posts be removed, and that inappropriate comments be taken down.
- To remind employees of their employment agreement and any policies included in the company's employee handbook.
- To remind employees not to disclose information that is confidential or proprietary to the company and to abide by financial disclosure laws.
- To identify themselves as employees whenever commenting on an aspect of the company's business.
- To include a disclaimer that the views expressed on the blog are the writer's, that they do not necessarily reflect the views of the company.
- To remind bloggers to respect copyright, privacy, fair use, financial disclosure, and other applicable laws.
- In some cases, to require approval of posts before they are published.
- To avoid sharing internal communications, including email, which by law is proprietary to the company.
- To avoid posting anything defamatory, threatening, hateful, harassing, or obscene.

## HOW TO USE TWITTER

Twitter co-founders Jack Dorsey and Evan Williams have said that the microblog's appeal is its ease of use and near-instant accessibility. In addition, the learning curve for using Twitter is relatively low for anyone familiar with texting, compared to other platforms and networks. Twitter combines the attributes of radio with those of the telegraph. Like radio listeners, Twitter users can "tune in" to specific feeds, individual tweeters, and trending topics. Like radio broadcasters, tweeters can send out messages one-to-many. And like telegraph operators, tweeters can send out short messages quickly and over any distance.

Twitter calls itself a microblog rather than a social network, though Twitter can, of course, be used socially. (Other microblogs include Jaiku, Tumblr, Plurk, and Squeelr.) Twitter isn't inherently social, or designed to be primarily a social network. Tweeters are typically individuals, which leads to a great deal of, in Dorsey's and Williams's words, "incessant chatter." This capacity has led many to discount Twitter as simply another gathering place for nattering nabobs and self-involved online diarists. Such dismissal is a mistake.

Both Twitter and the telegraph have been blamed for an erosion of language. Email, texting, Facebooking, and chat, too, have had a corrosive effect on writing. The informality of writing for these online environments has seeped into professional, business, and educational contexts. Nearly two-thirds of 700 students surveyed by the Pew Internet and American Life Project, in partnership with the College Board's National Commission on Writing, acknowledged that their electronic communication style found its way into school assignments. About half said they sometimes omitted proper punctuation and capitalization in their schoolwork, while one-quarter said they used emoticons. No one is offended when something is punctuated correctly, regardless of character counts; many are offended when you get it wrong, particularly if it is a first impression you are making. So use full stop periods and commas, put apostrophes in the right place, and use quotation marks and parentheses. Studies have shown that re-tweets contain *more* punctuation than original tweets.

## Ready to Tweet?

You know you have only 140 characters, so whatever you tweet, it will need to be short and ever so sweet. A character can be a letter, number, punctuation mark, or symbol, so employ all of these to make the space count. Use as few words as possible, and substitute words with easily intuited symbols whenever possible. This means editing, pruning, revising, and shortening. The steps you take to be clear and concise on Twitter will inform and help you in other media and formats, as well. And all that time you spent earlier becoming an expert headline writer will pay off on Twitter, where headlines can make all the difference. Many tweets *are* essentially headlines.

Write a short message, click "Tweet," and you're done. To build a following, however, you must demonstrate your value and perhaps a discernible informational role. Some Twitter users focus on re-tweeting "found" articles and information on a topic or range of subjects. Others provide witty commentary. Still others prod and provoke. So find or decide your role, but be yourself. Twitter is powerful in removing or preventing noise, in connecting you fairly directly with your audience. If you're having fun, that sense of engagement will rub off on others.

Using Twitter means using hashtags, which are strings of characters immediately following the "#" character. Any words preceded by this hash sign are used in Twitter to note a subject, event, association or group, or trending topic, and these hashtags make it possible for Twitter to thematically link conversations together. It is this "structure" of hashtags that facilitates impromptu interactions of individuals and brings them into these conversations, and it is this dynamic that perhaps explains why Twitter has been viewed as useful, even critical, in social movements like Occupy Wall Street, #BlackLivesMatter, and the grass roots political campaigns in 2016 of Trump and Bernie Sanders. Hashtags are an attempt to aggregate tweets in such a way as to develop or facilitate conversations in a natural, or seemingly natural, way. Because Twitter encourages association, users often think about what hashtags to include in their messages while writing their posts, and perhaps who should be "@-sign" mentioned in the post.

Twitter recognizes the # hashtag and automatically turns the character string into a search query link. In the long run, these hashtagged conversations become *de facto* Twitter groups, but unlike groups on Facebook, there is no registration process and, therefore, no actual group ownership. All it takes to create a hashtag and, therefore, the potential for a group or community organized around a subject or event is adding the # to a string of characters. Hashtags also make a topic easily searchable, like naming a tributary, however small, that flows into the larger Twitter river in such a way that it can be tracked to its source.

A question for public relations practitioners, depending upon the event or subject, is whether or when to set up a separate Twitter account or to create a hashtag (or set of hashtags) on an existing account. Of course, existing hashtags should also be used to tap into the interest that's already out there. For big events, such as sporting events, conferences, and conventions, it might make sense to use both a new Twitter account to communicate event information and assistance, and a hashtag that can be used for conversations about the event or ongoing story. The next question for the editor responsible for the account is how long to keep the account going once conversation has died down or the event has ended.

Here are a few tips on creating and using hashtags:

- Determine whether to create your own hashtag(s) or simply to use those people are already using, or both.
- Search Twitter for key words related to your topic when creating your own hashtags.
- Be careful with hashtags that already are widely in use. It's more difficult to break through the clutter.
- Encourage re-tweets (or tweets shared by other Twitter users) by using both a hyperlink and a hashtag. The link should point to your content; the hashtag will keep the conversation about that content going.
- Keep your hashtags short (#reallylongtagsreallydonotworkwell); make them fairly obvious and direct (#occupywallstreet).

If you tweet, you will inevitably re-tweet and share hyperlinks. Given the 140-character limit, this means you will want to use a link shortener, such as TinyURL, bit.ly, or Twitter's own shortener linked at the bottom of any Twitter post. Another implication of re-tweeting and sharing is the need to credit others with their full Twitter handle, such as "from @newshound." A re-tweet, commonly abbreviated as "RT," allows people to forward tweets to followers, and they provide a way to facilitate the distribution and redistribution of tweets outside one's immediate network to broader audiences.

When starting out with Twitter, public relations practitioners (and journalists and marketers) should remember a few key facts about Twitter and its users:

- First, reciprocate. Approximately 70 percent of those you follow will follow you back, so begin by following a lot of people. But be discriminate. Don't follow anyone, only those who will genuinely add to your nascent online community and who share your mission, interests, activities, or affiliations.
- Second, interact and engage. Many PR practitioners mistakenly use Twitter as just another distribution platform. You should reply to posts, engage in conversation, and recognize your own responsibility to the community you are trying to build (or join).
- Third, make a good first impression. Your headshot should be accurate (a friendly face boosts followership), your bio should be accurate (transparency!), and your first tweets should be meaningful. An accurate biography rich in key words also facilitates you being found in searches.
- Fourth, tweet often. In the tributary-and-river analogy, your contributions should stream in on a regular and frequent basis.
- Finally, resist the erosion of language to which Twitter and social media platforms seem to be contributing. Use proper grammar, syntax, and punctuation. Mistakes will cost you followers.

To these "do's," Scot Hacker and Ashwin Seshagiri add a few "do not's," including:

- tweet just headlines;
- when a story breaks, wait until you have the whole story;
- go it alone;
- auto-pump your tweets to Facebook;
- overdo your hashtags; and
- make it all, or even mostly, about you.

It's important to see that a person doesn't have to tweet to reap many of the software's benefits. For example, simply monitoring how Twitter's vast information network is being used can open a window on news and events and what they might mean to millions of people. Think of Twitter as a searchable human index updated in real time, much like GoogleTrends's reporting of what (and how) its users are searching. By simply having an account, doing some basic research via Twitter, and subscribing to some relevant feeds, public relations practitioners and journalists can use Twitter to:

- generate content ideas;
- do background research;
- identify sources and partners; and
- track news and events, and their coverage, in real time and throughout the world.

Of course, there are advantages to using Twitter to publish, as well. PR practitioners and journalists can use Twitter to:

- conduct interviews with sources (or set up face-to-face interviews);
- promote a news release by tweeting headlines and hyperlinks;
- collect feedback from publics and continue the conversation;
- cover a live event;
- network with other organizations, bloggers, and journalists; and
- provide the organization with a human face and a personal touch.

And they can do all of this on the move, via a smartphone or tablet. It is no accident or coincidence that the demographic identified by one study as the fastest-growing group of Twitter users also is the fastest-growing group of users of smartphones—Millennials aged 18 to 24. Twitter has recognized its own utility to journalists and, in response, has published a suite of search tools to help journalists find what they're looking for, tools every bit as valuable to those doing PR. These search tools include:

- Twitter Search: a query-driven tool to quickly identify information on a certain topic or about a specific person (twitter.com/search).
- TweetDeck and Twitter for Mac: applications that automatically stream breaking news by topic into a person's Twitter feed and good tools for monitoring an event, story, specific subject area, or person. These applications can also be used to monitor readership and the re-tweeting of one's own tweets (backtweets.com).
- Archive Search: a tool for finding older tweets.
- Twitscoop.com: a tool to track the most popular topics on Twitter (Twitscoop.com).
- TweetLater: this app schedules your tweets, posting them when you wish. You can also automate responses to new followers (tweetlater.net).

Another very powerful tool for making the most of Twitter is Twitterfall (twitterfall.com), a powerful interface that can turn Twitter's simple feed into a sophisticated source of specific, granular information. Twitterfall enables:

- Geopositioned customization: by entering your location, tweets can be filtered for those from that location using the key words you specify.
- Key word and topic tracking: enter the key words and/or hashtags you wish to follow, and Twitterfall will filter tweets accordingly.
- Monitoring: using the Twitterfall interface, you can adjust the speed at which tweets scroll and select a user or group of users to track.
- Filtering: screen out re-tweets, filter by language, save your frequently used searches, and mark individual tweets as favorites.

One often-repeated criticism of Twitter and of spending much time with the platform on behalf of an organization is the relatively low adoption by any one demographic. For example, a group of physicians' insurers in North Carolina reported that less than 5 percent of their physicians were on Twitter, a number perhaps closer to 2 percent. This group wasn't at all interested in learning how to leverage Twitter on behalf of the large, multi-national company. When asked to describe this 2–5 percent minority, the company's PR team realized that this small, even elite group of physicians were the thought leaders for the field, for the rest of this insurers group's client base. They are the alpha dogs everyone else looks to for cues, the influencers. Is a communications strategy that incorporates Twitter a wise move? The potential power of tapping into this small but premium minority suggests that it is.

## LIVE TWEETING

Twitter's immediacy, ease of use, and reach via both the web and mobile devices make it a powerful tool for live coverage of events. Longer-term benefits of live tweeting from an event include building the tweeter's or organization's following on Twitter and building community among readers and visitors. Another capacity is giving followers an immediate, visceral connection to the event. But good live tweeting, like most everything else, requires planning and preparation. Before heading out, some key considerations include:

- identifying the public(s);
- promoting the Twitter feed, perhaps with a news release and initial tweet letting existing followers know of the live feed that is coming;
- researching the event;

- contacting the event organizer or contact person to learn more of what to expect in the field;
- beta testing with the equipment or devices to be used in the field to troubleshoot, to get used to the tools, and to become comfortable with the 140-character limit;
- making sure that batteries are charged and that wifi or cell connectivity is available on site; and
- thinking through whether to set up a separate Twitter account and deciding on hashtags so people can easily follow the coverage during and after.

Once the live tweet feed has begun, writers should:

- set the scene and provide followers with a sense of place;
- identify key players and preview readers on what to expect;
- identify the lead of the "story," or the most important 140 characters of the day;
- write tight and develop a rhythm and pace;
- pass along what is seen, heard, perhaps even smelled, because good reporting depends on all five senses;
- answer the basic reporting questions of who, what, when, where, and why;
- track trends, surprises, critical moments, and emerging themes;
- quote key actors or subjects;
- interact with followers who begin replying to the tweets by answering questions and acknowledging comments;
- perhaps include photos and/or video; and
- identify others who are live tweeting or live blogging the event.

As with any form of writing, live tweeting requires some practice to figure out how active to be and to discover or determine voice and style.

## HOW TO USE FACEBOOK

With more than nearly 2 billion people using Facebook, or more than one out of every four on the planet, it is a communication force with which to be reckoned. Nearly half of all Americans get their news from Facebook, and as the fact-free U.S. presidential election of 2016 showed, they aren't very discriminating about the origins of that news. By using Facebook's unprecedented reach and through it building engagement, organizations, brands, and companies can use Facebook interactions to influence behavior, including buying and reading decisions. Word of mouth, after all, is still the strongest form of advertising, and Facebook interactions are a virtual equivalent.

Using "Like" in Facebook is quite simple, and users do not have to visit Facebook to "Like" or to become a fan or follower of a site, page, Facebook group, or area of interest. The alternate method of attracting "fans" is to link to a page on Facebook, where the user can click a "Like" button displayed at the top. The obvious benefit of a direct "Like" is that the user is connected in one step, without the danger of failing to click on the Facebook page "Like" button. The biggest drawback is not being able to control the call to action or its appearance. Linking to a Facebook page, therefore, is similar to linking to a Twitter profile, and it provides the opportunity to closely associate following on Twitter and becoming a fan on Facebook.

What optimization methods can be performed at the page level depends, though both a direct "Like" button and a linked call to action can be used on the same page. Their performance, then, can be compared for future planning. When using the "Like" button directly, it is important to separate this from any other "Like" buttons on the page, and to identify for the user what it is they are about to "Like." When linking to a Facebook page, the same positioning considerations apply as with a Twitter-linked call to action. Content gets three to five times more clicks if:

- thumbnail photos of people are included;
- people can add comments;
- "Like" appears at both the top and bottom of articles; and
- "Like" appears near visual content, such as videos or graphics.

The "Like" box is a sort of extended version of a "Like" button for pages, and it displays a "Find us on Facebook" header, the number of users who "Like" the page, recent posts from the page, pictures of profile photos, and, of course, a "Like" button.

The "Like" box takes up a fair of amount of real estate with all of its functions enabled, but it can be pared down and employed as a beefier call to action than the "Like" button. For active sites with large numbers of users and good content, the "Like" box may serve as an enticement by showcasing the page's usefulness and popularity.

As for all digital writing, think carefully about your "Like" requests. For example, which of these prompts would you be more willing to respond to:

Option A: Like us on Facebook at FB.com/ReallyCoolCompany
Option B: Ask us your questions about local government at FB.com/collegestationTX.

Option A is a brand- or organization-centric approach. Option B is about your public, from that public's perspective. Why would anyone like you if they don't yet know you?

No trust has yet been built. The second option is a tool or road toward building that trust, so think about where in the pipeline of trust- and relationship-building you are with your publics as you think about how to use various media and how to craft messages in those media. Some other first-step options:

- share your feedback with us at ADDRESS;
- join the conversation at ADDRESS;
- connect with other WHATEVER YOUR PUBLIC IS at ADDRESS;
- win a prize (or a subscription or whatever) at ADDRESS; and
- free healthcare advice at ADDRESS.

When someone uses the "Like" function on Facebook, that person subscribes to your updates and allows you to have a conversation with them until or unless they unsubscribe. As importantly, if not more importantly, a "Like" introduces and endorses you to every one of that user's friends, and the average user has 350 friends. Twitter works in a similar fashion. It has a rippling out or exponential influencing effect. According to CoTweet and ExactTarget, the top 10 reasons consumers like Facebook fan pages are:

1. To receive discounts and promotions
2. To show support for brands and friends
3. To get a freebie
4. To stay informed about company products and activities
5. For updates on future projects
6. For updates on upcoming sales
7. Just for fun
8. To get access to exclusive content
9. To learn more about the company or brand
10. For education about topics related to the organization's focus

Entire books have been written on how to incorporate Facebook into an organization's public relations, marketing, or business plans, so here we are only scratching the surface. Fortunately, Facebook has collected a vast number and diversity of resources at facebook.com/business/. And remember that Facebook owns Instagram, so integration of these two platforms has been made quite simple.

## Measuring Success

One of the tools at facebook.com/business is Insights, which helps users measure any one page's performance and track interactions. By organizing anonymized demographic data about any page's visitors, Insights has taken some of the mystery out of the question of knowing when and what to post to attract the most attention. Among the types of demographic information Insights provides on even an hour-by-hour basis going back two weeks are gender, age, and geographic location of "fans." So if, for example, you are targeting males 18 to 25 on the East Coast, the data will show over time how you are doing with that demographic post by post. Average reach, "Likes," comments, and shares are tracked, making it relatively easy to experiment with different types of posts at different times on different days. Compare this data with when your fans are on Facebook, which Insights also tracks, and you have at least a snapshot of your potential in terms of attention. One national healthcare association, for example, found that ideal times to reach its "fan" base are between 5 p.m. and 9 p.m. on weeknights and about noon during the day, or at lunchtime and just after work.

Another lesson the healthcare association learned: Post judiciously. Amidst a debate among its social media team about how many times to post, Insights gave evidence that "fans" hid, reported as spam, or "unliked" the association's page most often when the association posted more than twice per day. Insights generates "scorecard" data on these metrics as part of a section Facebook calls "People Talking About This" (PTAT). Data include:

- number of "Likes," including new "Likes";
- number of "Unlikes";
- number of friends of fans;
- number of people "actively talking" about and commenting to your page; and
- total weekly reach.

In addition, you can sort posts by type to compare which is reaching your fans more effectively, effectiveness that Facebook calls "virality." Insights post types include photos, links, videos, platform posts, and questions. The data so far described are accessed fairly easily using the Insights dashboard. Selecting Page Level Data and exporting it as a Microsoft Excel file will provide a great deal more, perhaps even an overwhelming amount. But analysis at this tabulated data level can go beyond the graphs and charts that the dashboard generates.

## APPROACHES TO ENGAGEMENT

Tweeting, liking, following, and becoming a fan are not the only social engagement conversions organizations can encourage, but given the reach of Twitter and Facebook, they are arguably the most important. Fortunately, many if not most of the optimization techniques used to encourage Twitter and Facebook engagement can be applied to other social networks and bookmarking sites, as well. When combined with or integrated into page and site structures that encourage user-generated content and subscribing to syndicated content, these social media platforms can be powerful in generating traffic and building community. To systematically convert casual visitors into active partici-pants, consider these first steps:

- **Keep share options manageable.** There are dozens of sharing mechanisms available, but that doesn't mean all or even most need to be utilized. The more options that are presented, the less likely an interactor will be to click on any one, so include only those networks and services you think interactors will actually use. As usage statistics become available, you can drop those that see little use.
- **Let history be your guide.** Take some of the lessons learned from email campaigns, landing page testing, and page optimization to guide the crafting of new messages that can maximize social conversions. Specifically:

  - What wording has resonated with your interactors?
  - What calls to action have proven the most effective?
  - What mistakes can help you avoid similar ones going forward?
  - What subject lines were most effective?

- **Be truthful and transparent.** As in everything, be transparent in the presentation and use of social media. It should be obvious whether clicking will share the content or lead the interactor to a Twitter profile or Facebook page. This is especially true for Facebook, where identically styled "Like" buttons may reference either the resource the interactor is viewing or the site's Facebook page. Interactors are less likely to click where there is uncertainty about what will happen next.
- **Adjust and adapt.** Give more visual weight to the network that is most commonly used by your interactors. *The Huffington Post*, for example, places the "Like" button above its Tweet icon. Mashable, on the other hand, puts Twitter on top. The result? *HuffPo* gets more "Likes," while Mashable gets more tweets.
- **Do a practice run.** Even a little testing is better than no testing.

Next, think about some **concrete ideas** for leveraging social media with an emphasis on news you can use and delivering a tangible benefit. The importance of providing something tangible might be one of the more important lessons taught by the success-ful apps in what is a brutal, survival-of-the-fittest marketplace. To begin brainstorming, consider the following:

1. Sponsor a competition, game, or contest.
2. Ask questions.
3. Respond to user questions and posts quickly and meaningfully.
4. Offer a "top 10" list or a "5 ways to. . . " list (or link to one that is online).
5. Interview experts and provide their answers to compelling questions.
6. Introduce your leadership team to a broader audience.

Brands and organizations err when seeking engagement by thinking of "heavy things," like developing media-rich experiences that people will want to share with their friends, when they should instead be thinking of "lightweight interactions," like those most people have with most other people most of the time, Paul Adams, Google's former head of social research and Facebook's global director of brand design, told *Fast Company* magazine. "You meet the first time, chitchat. You're not suddenly best friends," Adams said. This type of interpersonal conversation is what drives social media use. A corollary is that brands can't use social media primarily to pitch or sell.

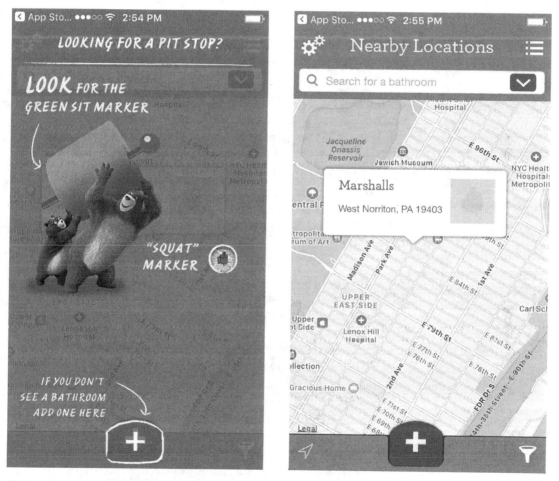

**FIGURE 9.7 and FIGURE 9.8** *The SitOrSquat app from Charmin.*

Some brands have learned that their products simply aren't conducive to conversation, online or anywhere else. Examples include toilet paper, gasoline, and paper. Makers of these commodities can still participate in social and mobile media, but not in the ways that, say, clothing or electronics brands can. Charmin, for example, realized that few people wish to have a conversation about toilet paper, but that a mobile app that helps people to find a public toilet can lead to a positive brand relationship. **SitOrSquat** is Charmin's response to the question of how to provide something tangible in order to build loyalty.

## LISTENING

So far, the discussion has centered on sending out information, networking, and building community. The other side of the social media coin is listening. Companies that aren't at least listening to what people are saying about them via social media, much less moderating and participating in those media, are taking a huge gamble. To cite one example of the potential rewards, Dr Pepper built an 8.5 million-strong fan base on Facebook that the soft drink company carefully tracks and tests. Sending out two messages daily via its Facebook fan page, the company also listens to its "fan" reactions, and software tools help the company to measure how many times a message is viewed, how many times it is shared with other Facebook users, and what fan responses are. Using these tracking tools, Dr Pepper learned, for example, that diehard fans like smart one-liners ("If liking you is wrong, we don't want to be right"), but that they do not like messages that focus on prices and special offers. Social media, therefore, offer platforms for targeted, niche, or specialized experiences.

At Delta Airlines, in a control room outfitted with monitors streaming social media mentions of airlines, Delta customer service agents scour for traveler complaints. One of the objectives is to prevent problems from going viral and turning into public relations crises. These agents use a computer program to search for terms such as "Delta sucks." The monitors show Delta mentions on Twitter and other sites, and when bad weather creates delays and missed connections, agents can monitor the tweets. Agents then respond with information about the causes of delays. "You are there with their emotions, good or bad," Allison Ausband, vice president of reservation sales and customer care for Delta, told *The Wall Street Journal*.

Delta hopes to avoid the kind of backlash United Airlines faced in 2009 when musician Dave Carroll funneled his rage over his guitar having been broken by United Airlines staff into a viral YouTube video viewed more than 16 million times and eventually turned into a book; United's stock fell 10 percent as a result of Carroll's meme.

The lesson for the airlines, and everyone else, is clear: Disgruntled customers are turning to social media with complaints once handled in relative privacy with a desk

**FIGURE 9.9** *Dave Carroll's meme, "United Breaks Guitars," youtube.com/watch?v=5YGc4zOqozo*

agent. Millions are posting their experiences, both good and bad. Delta told the *Journal* that it sees social media as a chance to offer better customer service, creating a channel on Twitter called @DeltaAssist and telling workers in its social media lab to offer customers quick fixes. If one person is complaining, it's likely another hundred or so are facing the same troubles.

Social gives you an array of means by which to listen, to get social signals, to do temperature checks on your organizational profiles with your publics. Here are a few questions to ask your publics via social media, and not just once, but often:

- What can we do better?
- What were your best experiences with us?
- What were your not so great experiences with us?
- What do you think of _____?

The answers to these questions will also generate good content, such as blog posts and contests. Asking questions publicly communicates to your publics that you genuinely care, that you are partnering with them toward some larger, missional goal. Social helps you understand what your publics can get excited about, and what they aren't excited about at all. At IBM, as part of its "MobileFirst Digital Strategy," social media campaigns and programs must be what the company labels "SMART," or "specific, measurable, actionable, realistic, and time bound." In other words, each campaign must identify specific, measurable objectives, and they begin and end at predetermined times in order to be measured for effectiveness. They must also be accountable in terms of delivering the results "business leaders" determined were desirable before the campaign was executed.

## USING SOCIAL IN CRISIS

A mature social media network and followership are game changers when it comes to crisis communication. When crisis hits, people will be talking about your organization anyway. If you're already connected and engaged, if you've built trust, if you've paid social capital into a metaphorical account, you will have social capital to spend when you need it most. In crisis, you need to be able to write some checks and draw on that account of goodwill. Consider the Flint, MI, water crisis. Imagine that you are the Flint Utilities Department responsible for all water services. You've been active in social media for a long time, building social capital, abiding by the law of reciprocity, liking the posts of your consumers, re-tweeting their good news, blogging honestly about water quality for years. All of a sudden, no one in your municipality can drink the water, and everyone is looking at you. What are you going to do? For starters:

1. Have a plan NOW, a plan that has buy-in all the way up the ladder.
2. Learn from the very costly, painful mistakes of those who have gone before, such as Tylenol, Volkswagen, CBS News, General Motors, Takata airbags, Chipotle, etc. (There is no shortage of case studies.)
3. Appoint a (very) visible spokesperson with real access up the ladder, with good information, and authorize that person to speak.
4. Allow, even demand, that that spokesperson be honest and forthright.
5. Having gathered the facts, communicate them. When you don't know something, say so. Your worst possible response is silence.
6. Leverage your mature social networks, which will be lighting up.
7. Patrol and monitor. Allow a robust discussion, but not a profane or hurtful one. You can and should block people. Ironically for a scenario about Flint, the apt metaphor here is a lifeguard keeping the water clean and the swimmers safe. You can and should blow the whistle.

8. Acknowledge the damage, the hurt emotions, the inconvenience—whatever the lived reality on the ground happens to be.

9. Stay active. These networks are real-time, which is powerful, but powerful both ways. They can help; they can hurt.

10. Your fans and sometimes even your competitors will have your back if you've been honest, transparent, responsive, and human.

## A FINAL NOTE

This chapter focused on blogging, Twitter, and Facebook, but there is a seemingly endless parade of social media platforms and services from which to choose. From Instagram, Snapchat, and Pinterest for photography; to Vine, Vimeo, Periscope, and YouTube for video; to WhatsApp and WeChat for conversation; to Tumblr and Reddit for amalgams of socially and non-socially mediated content, the social media landscape is overwhelming. No one can do it all; certainly, no one can do it all well. Just get started. Make some mistakes. Work some new tools and approaches into your PR mix over time, because the goal is continual improvement.

## CHAPTER ACTIVITIES

**1** Live tweet an event, a trip, a conference, or a meeting. Create a hashtag for your coverage or take advantage of hashtags already being used. Hyperlink where appropriate. Use either a laptop or a smartphone, and experiment with a live tweeting app, such as CoverItLive. There is no minimum or maximum for the number of tweets.

**2** Develop a multi-pronged social media strategy to "End the 'R' Word." Your objective is to create and promote a campaign to excise the word "retarded" from common vernacular. Your public relations team will collaborate with the Special Olympics to create compelling content and utilize social media. Map out a content strategy for articles, images, events, videos, and slideshows. Plot out how you will utilize Facebook, blogs, and Twitter, among other social media, to raise awareness. Think about enlisting celebrity tweeters and YouTubers, setting up narrowly focused blogs, and developing Twitter, Facebook, and Snapchat events. How will you garner media attention and raise awareness of the damaging effects of using the word "retarded"?

**3** Develop an interactive press release for something newsworthy related to the women's volleyball team or women's soccer team on your college campus. Use the questions on **page 232** to guide your planning for this assignment. In addition, write a series of tweets to support the news release's digital distribution.

**4** For the next big game or match for the team you chose for the previous activity, develop a fact sheet and a media advisory (or alert). Fact sheets are one-page backgrounders on the event formatted in an outline form. They are often included with a news release on the same subject. (The fact sheet for the PRSA: http://media.prsa.org/about+prsa/fact+sheet/.) An alert is a summary of the "who, what, when, where, and why" of an event. Here's the standard format for an alert:

### Headline

**What:** The event name
**Who:** Who is sponsoring or holding the event
**Why:** The purpose of the event
**When:** Date, time
**Where:** Location of event, parking, etc.
**Media Contact:** Name, phone, email, website, Twitter handle, etc.

For each of these publicity tools, develop them for digital distribution and consumption, using hyperlinks and including contact information.

**5** Visit the online newsrooms of three major companies in an industry of your choosing. For example, if you chose airlines, you could visit the newsrooms for Delta, United, and American.

- news.delta.com/;
- newsroom.united.com/news-releases; and
- news.aa.com/home/default.aspx.

What emerges in a comparison of these sites in terms of best practices? Develop a list that could inform the development or improvement of your organization's virtual pressroom.

## Digital Resources

**Boeing's Mark Vining (youtube.com/watch?v=_g6UswiRCF0)**

**Dave Carroll's meme, "United Breaks Guitars" (youtube.com/watch?v=5YGc4zOqozo)**

**College Station, TX, blog (blog.cstx.gov)**

**Inova's Life With Cancer subsite (lifewithcancer.org)**

**Bill Marriott blog on behalf of Marriott (blogs.marriott.com/marriott-on-the-move/)**

PR Newswire (prnewswire.com)

Seattle Police Department Blotter (spdblotter.seattle.gov)

Walmart blog (blog.walmart.com/)

Twitter search tools:

- **Twitter Search (twitter.com/search);**
- **TweetDeck (dev.twitter.com/media/newsrooms/report#apps 1);**
- **Archive Search (dev.twitter.com/media/newsrooms/report#archive 2);**
- **Twitscoop.com (twitscoop.com); and**
- **TweetLater (tweetlater.net).**

## BIBLIOGRAPHY

Bradley, Aaron, "How to Convert Website Visitors into Facebook Fans," *Search Engine Land* (March 20 2011a), available: http://searchengineland.com/how-to-convert-website-visitors-into-facebook-fans-70557.

Bradley, Aaron, "How to Convert Website Visitors into Tweeters," *Search Engine Land* (March 20 2011b), available: http://searchengineland.com/how-to-convert-website-visitors-to-tweeters-70516.

Bradley, Aaron, "7 Approaches to Engagement Conversion, 5 Explicit Tactics for Twitter & Facebook," *Search Engine Land* (March 30 2011c), available: http://searchengineland.com/7-approaches-toengagement-conversion 5-explicit-tactics-for-twitter-facebook-70030.

Fowler, Geoffrey A., "Are You Talking to Me? Yes, Thanks to Social Media. and the Best Companies are Listening," *The Wall Street Journal* (June 18 2012), available: http://online.wsj.com/article/SB10 0014240527487041164045762630839709618 62.html.

Hacker, Scot and Seshagiri, Ashwin, "Twitter for Journalists," *kdmcBerkeley blog* (June 23 2011), available: http://multimedia.journalism.berkeley.edu/tutorials/twitter/.

Hutto, C. J., Yardi, Sarita, and Gilbert, Eric, "A Longitudinal Study of Follow Predictors on Twitter," CHI 2013 conference paper (July 2013), available: http://comp.social.gatech.edu/papers/follow_chi13_final.pdf.

Kerpen, Dave, *Likeable Social Media* (New York, NY: McGraw Hill Education, 2015).

McCartney, Scott, "The Airlines' Squeaky Wheels Turn to Twitter," *The Wall Street Journal* (October 26 2010), available: http://online.wsj.com/article/SB10001424052702304173704575 57832116156 4104.html.

Murthy, Dhiraj, *Twitter* (Cambridge, UK: Polity Press, 2013).

"New Study From Outsell and PR Newswire Finds Earned Media Amplifies Marketing Impact," *PR Newswire* (June 29 2016), available: www.multivu.com/players/English/7868451-pr-news wire-outsell-earned-media-marketing/.

Sacks, Danielle, "Can You Hear Me Now?" *Fast Company* (February 2013): 37–43.

Scott, David Meerman, *The New Rules of Marketing & PR*, 5th edition (Hoboken, NJ: Wiley, 2015).

Sullivan, Danny, "By the Numbers: How Facebook Says Likes and Social Plugins Help Websites," *Search Engine Land* (May 22 2011), available: http://searchengineland.com/by-the-numbers-how-facebooksays-likes-social-plugins-help-websites-76061.

"Twitter Use 2012," *Pew Internet and American Life Project* (May 2012), available: http://pewinternet.org/Reports/2012/Twitter-Use-2012/Findings.aspx.

Wilcox, Dennis L. and Reber, Bryan H., *Public Relations Writing and Media Techniques*, 7th edition (Boston, MA: Pearson, 2013).

Yamkovenko, Stephanie, "5 Ways to Increase Engagement with Facebook's New Page Insights," *Poynter* (September 2 2013), available: www.poynter.org/how-tos/digital-strategies/222045/5-waysto-increase-engagement-with-facebooks-new-page-insights/.

# Navigating the Legal Landscape

*He who receives an idea from me, receives instruction himself without lessening mine, as he who lights his taper at mine, receives light without darkening me.*
— Thomas Jefferson, in a letter to Isaac McPherson, explaining copyright, August 8, 1813

*Monsieur l'abbé, I detest what you write, but I would give my life to make it possible for you to continue to write.*
— Voltaire, in a letter to Monsieur le Riche, February 6, 1770

*If all mankind were of the same opinion, minus one, mankind would be no more justified in silencing that one person, than he, if he had the power, would be justified in silencing mankind.*
— John Stuart Mill, 1947

## INTRODUCTION

The law cannot keep pace with technological innovation. Thus, digital forms of gathering, publishing, and sharing information continue to raise new questions for the law. As a result, each

---

### CHAPTER OBJECTIVES

After studying this chapter, you will be able to:

- understand the legal contexts in which digital writers gather and publish information, with an emphasis on the freedoms and protections offered by the First Amendment to the United States Constitution;

- understand Section 230 of the Communications Decency Act and the protections it offers digital publishers;

- know the basics of libel and privacy law; and

- understand the basics of intellectual property law, including copyright, as it relates to digital content.

and every day, decisions from the judiciary, statutes from legislatures and policies and rules from both government and corporate America serve to re-shape and re-define the rights of expression guaranteed by the U.S. Constitution. These rights, somewhat ambiguously articulated in the First Amendment, often find themselves in tension with other imperatives, such as a person's right of reputation, commercial interests, national security, and preventing or punishing cyberbullying. This chapter focuses on digital media law as it relates to writing, editing, and publishing in digital media. In no way is the chapter meant to be a comprehensive survey; it is an introduction.

After exploring the rights of access to information, which is of utmost concern to journalists, public relations practitioners, marketers, and many other professionals, the chapter looks at a few of the more complex legal areas for digital media, including libel, privacy, and copyright. Also of interest are the implications of Section 230 of the Communications Decency Act of 1996 and the takedown notice in the Digital Millennium Copyright Act. Finally, the chapter addresses the implications of methods of publication and dissemination that, because of their potentially global reach, can subject them to the laws of other nations.

*NOTE: This chapter can't be a substitute for legal advice. Only an attorney with knowledge of a particular situation can provide legal advice in the event of a lawsuit. The goal here is to provide a basic roadmap to the legal issues facing digital writers and publishers.*

## GATHERING INFORMATION

*Congress shall make no law respecting an establishment of religion or prohibiting the free exercise thereof; or abridging the freedom of speech, or the press; or the right of the people peaceably to assemble, and to petition the Government for a redress of grievances.*

—First Amendment to the U.S. Constitution

The First Amendment guarantees the right to publish information about government and about public issues, among other rights, but it doesn't help much with access to that information. Since the attacks of September 11, 2001, and the resulting "war on terror," a "war" with no end in sight, access to U.S. government information and records has become yet more problematic. In fact, the U.S. government began removing information from the Internet's web after 9/11 and has since proven less responsive to Freedom of Information Act requests for information. Troublingly, these steps into darkness coincide with an increased willingness on the part of the U.S. government to surveil even its own citizenry.

Among the many revelations in Edward Snowden's release of classified National Security Administration information were the many practices and programs for collecting data on citizens' use of their smartphones and the Internet, including telephone metadata and Internet search and email data, often with the full cooperation of telecommunications companies and Internet companies. The government's aggressive secrecy and surveillance efforts raise profound constitutional questions at a time when print news media have been in decline and, therefore, have been increasingly unable to hold that government accountable. Introduce into this mix the reach and speed of digital communication, as well as the pace of innovation and change in digital technology, and the result is confusion and unpredictability in U.S. law.

Yet, the need for accountability has never been greater. Constitutional law scholar Thomas Emerson said that "a democracy without an informed public is a contradiction." Democracy implies a significant level of transparency in government, and transparency is rarely provided voluntarily. It is more commonly the result of watchdogs interested in holding power accountable. For this reason, when print periodicals first emerged in Europe in the 17th century, they saw their role as principally investigatory. During the English Civil War, when press freedom in England emerged, these periodicals promised that they would investigate what was going on in government and inform their readers. *The Parliament Scout*, a publication that began in 1643, promised to "search out and discover the news." The next year, in 1644, a publication calling itself *The Spie* pledged to its readers that the newspaper "planned on discovering the usual cheats in the great game of the Kingdome. For that we would have to go undercover."

Thomas Jefferson famously wrote that he would rather live in a nation with newspapers and no government than in a country with government but no newspapers, and he wrote this during an age of mostly, if not exclusively, partisan newspapers. He could not have predicted the levels of secrecy and surveillance of the early 21st century. Like any bureaucracy and most institutions, governments seek to do their business behind closed doors and out of the public eye. Sometimes the secrecy is warranted. National security often demands secrecy, to name a fairly obvious "greater good" that since 9/11 has become a national refrain.

Two landmark Supreme Court cases that serve to establish a limited constitutional right to information for all citizens are *Richmond Newspapers v. Virginia* and *Branzburg v. Hayes*. The case of *Richmond Newspapers v. Virginia* (1980) gave U.S. citizens "a right to know" how their government administrates justice. The U.S. Supreme Court ruled that the First Amendment in fact does establish the right for the public to attend criminal trials, where a defendant's "life, liberty, and pursuit of happiness" can hang in the balance. This constitutional right is for everyone, not just or especially for news media, though it is often journalists in courtrooms as the public's surrogates to report on the administration of justice. The *Richmond Newspapers* decision could have been extended by the high court to cover legislatures, council meetings, and review boards, but it wasn't. For access in these other circumstances, statutory law determines the levels and kinds of access. Statutes that provide some guarantees of access include the Freedom of Information Act, state open meetings laws, and state-level open government laws. In short, whether as a communication professional you have the "right" to government information in any particular situation is highly contingent, and it can vary state to state.

Whether reporters should be allowed to protect confidential sources is a recurring question for the law, one with no clear answer under federal law. *Branzburg v. Hayes* in 1972 presented the high court with an opportunity to speak clearly on whether there is or should be legal protection for journalists who promised confidentiality to their sources. More specifically, the case asked whether the requirement that news reporters appear and testify before state or federal grand juries is an abridgement of the freedoms of speech and press as guaranteed by the First Amendment. In a contentious, contradictory 5–4 decision, the court disappointed. Paul Branzburg, a reporter for the *Louisville Courier-Journal* newspaper, had cultivated sources within a drug ring; law enforcement, not surprisingly, wanted access to those sources and sought access through the courts. A grand jury ordered Branzburg to reveal his sources. To protect the identities of those sources and to fulfill his promise of confidentiality, Branzburg argued that the First Amendment's protections of a free press should shield him from government requests for his privileged information. Instead, the Court ruled that the First Amendment does not carry with it any sort of guarantee of protection. Requiring reporters to disclose confidential information to grand juries served a "compelling" state interest and, therefore, did not violate the First Amendment. For Justice Byron White, who wrote the majority opinion, the fact that reporters receive information from sources in confidence does not privilege them to withhold that information during a grand jury criminal investigation.

Complicating the ruling, however, was White's seemingly contradictory statement that "without some protection for seeking out news, freedom of the press could be eviscerated." White argued that "a corollary of the right to publish must be the right to gather news. The full flow of information to the public protected by the free press guarantee would be severely curtailed if no protection whatever were afforded to the process by which news is assembled and disseminated. . . . News must not be unnecessarily cut off at its source, for without freedom to acquire information the right to publish would be impermissibly compromised." White's limited opinion, therefore, has been interpreted since as providing some constitutional protection for both gathering information and protecting confidential sources, but very limited protection. When combined with the various versions of a state-level shield law written to offer some protection for reporters' sources, of which 49 of the states have either by explicit statute or common law, a strong case can be made for such protection. But that case has to be made each and every time a subpoena is issued, requiring a journalist to come to court to be asked for his or her sources' identities in a criminal proceeding. Complicating matters further with respect to digital communication is difficulty determining just who is and who is not a journalist and, therefore, who might be eligible for that state-level shield. Courts have been reluctant to make these sorts of definitional distinctions, relying instead on state statutes that also resist clear definitions.

In short, anonymous sourcing is perilous, and the legal consequences are somewhat unpredictable. Claiming a constitutional right to information, too, is dubious. Despite White's logic in *Branzburg*, journalists historically have had no more right or access to information than the general public, as the *Richmond Newspapers* case demonstrated, and, therefore, no special right to gather information from within government or about government. To put it another way, the government's information buffet is open, so grab a plate and help yourself, but do not expect the government to come to you to wait on your table and take special orders. The buffet has what it has—meat loaf and baked potatoes. There is a public prison tour at 8 a.m. The F.C.C. white paper is posted on its website. These are available to anyone, including media, but no one will be coming to your table, saying, "Hello, my name is Jeff Sessions. I'll be your Attorney General today. I'd like to tell you about a few specials on the information menu."

Without a constitutional imperative for government to open its doors, its records and files, meetings and dealings, often we have to litigate. We have to lobby. We have to plead for legislative relief. One attempt at providing this relief is the Freedom of Information Act (FOIA), initially passed in 1966, amended for the Internet in 1996, and most recently shored up by the Obama Administration in summer 2016. FOIA provides the disclosure of previously unreleased information and documents possessed by the federal government. Its effectiveness depends upon cooperation from government, however, and that cooperation has often proven to be problematic. FOIA covers agency records and information collected, maintained, used, retained, and disseminated by the federal government, and it is available to anyone, public or private, media and non-media. The 1996 amendment expanded FOIA to cover electronic information, including email correspondence. In addition, the Electronic Freedom of Information Act established priorities or rankings for agencies to use when petitioned for information:

- top priority: requests in situations in which life or safety is at risk;
- middle: information requested by news media for the public's interest; and
- low: everything else.

Often, using FOIA is a cat-and-mouse game. A request is made. Government agencies drag their feet, claiming national security interests, or a prohibition in the Health Information Privacy Protection Act (HIPPA), or some other statute to block access to information. The Bush and Obama administrations exercised what could be called reflexive secrecy. Bush's attorney general, John Ashcroft, for example, ordered a more intensive review of requests by agencies already willing to stall requests. After campaigning on promises of transparency in government, Obama became perhaps the most secretive president in U.S. history. In 2012, for example, the secret Foreign Intelligence Surveillance Court established in 1978 to authorize surveillance warrants for the National Security Administration and the FBI granted all 1,800 requests from U.S. intelligence agencies. This court has effectively created a secret body of law, regularly assessing broad constitutional questions and establishing important judicial precedents with almost no public scrutiny. And absent from any of this is any sort of adversarial process, which is a cornerstone of the rule of law.

To bolster FOIA, President George Bush signed into law the Openness Promotes Effectiveness in our National Government Act of 2007, also known as the OPEN Government Act. This law amended FOIA by establishing a definition of "news media," prohibiting an agency from assessing certain fees if it fails to comply with FOIA deadlines, and establishing an Office of Government Information Services in the National Archives and Records Administration to review agency compliance with FOIA. The new definitions are liberal, meaning that most bloggers and digital publishers are eligible for reduced processing and duplication fees available to "representatives of the news media." The law also broadens the scope of information that can be requested.

The OPEN Government Act was the first makeover of the FOIA in a decade, or since it was first amended to account for the web. The Act also brings non-proprietary information held by government contractors under the law, which effectively reverses an order by Ashcroft in the wake of 9/11 to resist releasing information when there was uncertainty about how doing so would affect national security. The legislation also creates a system for the media and public to track the status of their FOIA requests, as well as a hotline service for all federal agencies to deal with problems and an ombudsman to provide an alternative to litigation in disclosure disputes.

More recently, Obama signed into law the FOIA Improvement Act to codify a presumption of disclosure intended to bolster requesters' access and to make it more difficult for government to withhold certain kinds of information. However, FOIA compliance will continue to require the good faith efforts of government agencies and their employees. Battles will continue over what should and should not be released, and federal agencies will continue to struggle with the volume of requests.

## How to Use FOIA

Using FOIA to get information is relatively simple, at least in theory:

1. First, informally ask an agency's public information or FOIA officer for the information you want, a method that is usually faster and less expensive than making a formal

request. It is surprisingly effective. In 2013, for example, a peace activist in Washington State blew the lid on a massive, secret U.S. law enforcement surveillance program operated in conjunction with AT&T by simply asking West Coast police agencies for the information.

2. If making the request in person is either not feasible or unsuccessful, file a formal, written request under FOIA. Each agency must identify a FOIA officer to whom to submit requests, as well as its own FOIA procedures and a listing of the records it releases as a matter of course.

3. Once a request is made, the agency must release the documents or provide a reason for exemption. Exemptions must cover only the information they are applicable to, not the entire record.

4. FOIA gives agencies 20 business days to determine whether to grant or deny a request, except for "unusual circumstances," such as sudden popular demand for a particular record.

5. If a compelling need is demonstrated, such as danger to human life, agencies are required to expedite requests.

6. Agencies can charge for information, including electronic information, to cover the actual costs of getting the information and duplicating it.

7. If 20 days expire without a decision, the person requesting the information can file a complaint in federal district court.

FOIA has several exceptions or exemptions that agencies can cite to deny information. These include:

1. National security, the broadest category and the only one that allows the executive branch to determine the criteria for release of documents, rather than Congress. This exemption covers military plans, weapons and operations, and intelligence activities; programs for safeguarding nuclear facilities; and U.S. foreign relations, among many other categories.

2. Agency housekeeping practices or rules, such as internal personnel rules or sick leave policies. This exemption is meant to avoid swamping agencies with trivial requests.

3. Statutory exemptions, which include documents that Congress has declared by law to be confidential. Examples are personal tax records, patent applications, and Central Intelligence Agency records.

4. Confidential business information, including trade secrets, private commercial information, and contracts or information related to seeking a contract.

5. Agency memoranda, including working papers, studies, opinions, policy drafts, and staff proposals used to make a final report, policy, or decision of some kind.

6. Personnel and medical files in which the release would warrant an invasion of privacy.

7. Law enforcement investigations for which the information released would interfere, invade personal privacy, disclose the identity of a confidential source, endanger

someone's life, deprive a defendant of a fair trial, or reveal protected enforcement techniques.

8. Financial records and bank reports.
9. Geological data and maps concerning oil, gas, and water.

Examples of the statutory exemptions mentioned in No. 3 include:

- The Homeland Security Act, Section 214, which stipulates that the government cannot disclose critical infrastructure information provided by agencies and private businesses, including information about the national electrical power grid, nuclear power plants, or air transportation.
- The Privacy Act of 1974, which states that the government can only use "personally identifiable records" for the purpose for which they were created and for which the information was initially gathered.
- The Family Educational Rights and Privacy Act (FERPA), which protects student records, including student disciplinary records of non-violent crime and violations of institutional rules.
- The Driver's Privacy Protection Act of 1994, which prohibits the release of a driver's license information without that driver's consent.

All 50 states also have public records laws, though they vary state by state. Several state courts have held that federal judicial interpretations of FOIA are at least helpful in interpreting similar language in state public record laws, and many of these laws are similar to FOIA. An excellent resource for identifying and accessing state-level FOI laws is FOIAdvocates, available: foiadvocates.com/records.html.

## Open Records and Open Meetings: Sunshine Laws

The Government in Sunshine Act was passed into federal law in 1976 to open most federal government meetings to the public. In addition, all 50 states have their own "sunshine laws" aimed at increasing openness in government. These state laws offer different degrees of access, making it difficult to generalize, but the purpose of these laws is to hold government accountable. Georgia Supreme Court Chief Justice Charles L. Weltner wrote in a 1992 concurring opinion that "because public men and women are amenable 'at all times' to the people, they must conduct the public's business out in the open" (from *Davis v. City of Macon*).

The purpose of open government and open meetings laws, as was stated in a 1980 Georgia Supreme Court case, *Athens Observer v. Anderson* (1980), is three-fold. State government should provide access so that:

- The public can evaluate the expenditure of public funds.
- The public can evaluate the efficient and proper functioning of its institutions.
- This accountability can in aggregate foster confidence in government.

Open records acts typically apply to documents, papers, letters, books, tapes, maps, photos, and computer-generated information and files, and they cover every state department, agency, board, bureau, commission, and authority; every county and municipal corporation, school district, and political subdivision; and non-profits receiving funding from public monies. Similarly, open meetings acts generally cover meetings of any state, county and regional authority, municipality, school district, and political subdivision, whether appointed or elected. The laws apply to non-profits receiving government funding, but not to advisory groups and quasi-governmental bodies that collect information, make recommendations, and advise government.

## LIBEL AND DEFAMATION

There are two primary forms of communication "malpractice" with respect to legal liability: invasion of privacy and libel. Libel and defamation are the legal claims that most commonly drag journalists into the courts, and it is an area of the law that has become quite active due to the amount and degree of vitriolic anonymous expression enabled by discussion boards, comments sections, social media, and other public forums online. Even the fear of libel litigation can silence people into self-censorship. And while most digital writers aren't typically worth suing from a financial point of view, being poor is not a great legal defense when faced with a libel action. The huge privacy invasion decision won by Terry Bollea, more commonly known as Hulk Hogan, against Gawker Media in 2016 included huge damages judgments against both the company and its editor, Nick Denton. The decision, along with lawsuits from other plaintiffs pursuing action against Gawker, shut the media company down. Digital writers should, therefore, be aware of the law and how to stay out of court.

Libel has three essential ingredients: the questionable material must be printed or published (written or broadcast), erroneous or false, and defamatory. All three must be present for a claim to have any chance of winning. Spoken defamation is termed slander; it is handled differently by the law and, thus, isn't typically a concern of digital writers and publishers. Like medical malpractice, libel is almost always a state-level tort, or civil wrong, and not a question for criminal law. Although about half of the 50 states still have criminal libel laws on the books, criminal libel cases are extremely rare and almost always have something to do with disturbing the peace. Since 1910, there have been no cases in this area of the law in Georgia, to cite just one state. And libel is primarily a question for state law, though the states' approaches are guided and shaped by U.S. Supreme Court precedent.

The premise in libel law is that a reputation has been damaged and that it can be repaired through the awarding of monetary damages. This reasoning is, of course, flawed, but it is the law's attempt at justice and, though not perfect, most agree that it is superior to duelling, which was the way these kinds of disputes were handled in the (even recent) past. Libel can appear in headlines, in a news story or editorial, in a press release or company newsletter, in a blog post or tweet, in advertising copy, on a Facebook wall, or in a letter to the editor. And since 1997, the courts have viewed communication online in much the same way as they have historically regarded or treated material in print (*Reno v. ACLU*).

Allegations of libel are included in about three-fourths of all the lawsuits filed against media, but most libel suits are dismissed before they ever get to a jury. When a suit does make it to trial, media are likely to lose, because juries are unpredictable and are often predisposed not to trust or show sympathy for media. Ordinary citizens often think the media are unfair, manipulative, and exploitative. As CNN reported as part of its Hulk Hogan v. Gawker coverage, "Jurors and ordinary American citizens are fed up with out-of-control media that seem to believe that once the title of 'newsworthy' is arbitrarily attached to an event or a person, the First Amendment will protect the publication of even the most salacious and offensive material that can be dredged up by sifting through celebrity mud." Digital publications are, therefore, challenging traditional definitions of "newsworthy" and "of public concern," and not in a good way. Robert Lichter of the Center for Media and Public Affairs told the *American Journalism Review* that he thinks there's a feeling that journalists have overstepped their boundaries. "People don't look on [journalists] the way journalists like to view themselves—as the public's tribune, speaking truth to power, standing up for the little guy. They don't look like the little guy anymore," Lichter said.

Because libel cases take an average of four years to litigate, and with lawyers typically taking home 50 percent or more of the winnings, making a libel claim and pursuing it through the courts takes fortitude. But, people get mad at how they are reported on and, if their buttons have been pushed, they will want to sue to recover their reputations and make the offending media pay, even though, statistically, they likely can't win. They sue because they are hurt and angry, and because there is always a lawyer who will take the case.

Digital writers and publishers can protect themselves from a libel suit simply by knowing the law and by doing a good, professional job reporting, writing, and publishing. Sometimes doing additional reporting or gathering more information or sources can prevent the problem. Know the law, have a solid story, and follow the evidence—the records or documentation. Libel occurs only where or when what has been published is untrue, so simply stay away from things that are not true or claims that cannot be verified. Do enough reporting to discern the truth from untruth. Be fair and honest. If you are writing negatively about a person, give that person an opportunity to respond.

Michael Hiltzik, a Pulitzer Prize-winning investigative business reporter for the *Los Angeles Times*, said in his career the single most important technique has been "getting the documents." The whole point of dealing with sources is to get them to point to things you can get in black and white, he said. Hiltzik and Chuck Phillips teamed to win a Pulitzer for a story exposing that the Grammy Awards, an event held supposedly for charity, generated huge income but, in fact, contributed almost nothing for charity. Grammy organizers threatened legal action, including a libel suit, but "couldn't lay a hand on us because everything was written down in documents," Hiltzik told The Committee of Concerned Journalists.

In the United States, unlike most areas of the world, when someone sues for libel, the burden of proof is on the plaintiff, who has to prove at least six things:

- defamation;
- identification;
- publication (and re-publication);
- fault;
- falsity; and
- injury.

## Defamation

A plaintiff will have to prove that the published or printed material is in fact derogatory, something that holds him or her up to hatred, ridicule, or contempt. Accusing someone of a crime qualifies, as do accusations of serious moral failings or incompetence in business or professional life. Juries decide what is defamatory, which means that interpretations can vary with the times and even with geography. Tom Cruise once sued for libel after being described as gay. The case was dropped, but had it proceeded it is difficult to imagine that such a "charge" or description would be seen by a jury in southern California to in fact be defamatory. But in southern Mississippi, who knows?

A community would not think less of a doctor or businessperson who makes a single error, unless the single error proved to be fatal, perhaps. This reasoning explains the **single mistake rule**. Journalists making a single mistake aren't typically deemed to be guilty of libelling someone, again, depending on the severity of the mistake. Stories that suggest a pattern of incompetence, however, that go beyond a single error, can be found to be defamatory.

There are three kinds of defamation, according to the courts: libel *per se*, libel by interpretation, and libel *per quod*:

- **Libel *per se*, or libel "on its face**," occurs with accusations that are obviously defamatory, that require no interpretation. A published statement such as "Smith killed the postal worker," is libel *per se* if, in fact, Smith did not kill the postal worker. It does not cover merely embarrassing information, like stating a person's age as ten years older than they actually are or having them earn a PhD from the wrong institution.
- **Libel by interpretation** concerns something published that is or could be libelous depending upon at least one of a number of competing interpretations. At least one of the interpretations must be seen to be defamatory. The plaintiff must prove that the defamatory interpretation is the interpretation that was intended, and that the defamatory interpretation is the one that readers would be expected to hold.
- **Libel *per quod*** concerns something that has been published that becomes defamatory when readers add something commonly known, something that does not appear in the story. The writer may or may not have knowledge of the added fact or element; usually it is the plaintiff who provides this missing piece of information. The lack of real-world examples points to the rarity of this type of libel. Using the film *Chariots of Fire* as an example, imagine that a Jewish runner well known for sitting out of races conducted on the Sabbath is reported by a website to have won a race falsely described as taking place on a Saturday. The story isn't libelous on its face, nor does it report that the runner is in fact Jewish. When the public adds the fact that the runner previously has never run on the Sabbath because of his faith, that same public might hold the runner in contempt for sacrificing or surrendering his standards or religious convictions in order to win glory and, perhaps, a medal.

## Identification

To prove identification, a plaintiff has to prove that at least one other person could read the story and identify the plaintiff as the person referred to or described in the story. Publish the plaintiff's full name, and this hurdle can be easily cleared, unless the plaintiff's name is a common one. Identification can also result from publication of a nickname, because of a physical description, or use of a title or affiliation.

## Publication

If the actionable material was published, posted, tweeted, or broadcast, the plaintiff clears this hurdle. Did the accusation reach a third party? Sending a note to a second party doesn't count, but add just one intermediary and a plaintiff has met what is called the "minimum contacts" requirement in most states. Listservs, Facebook walls, press releases, blog entries, and email can all be found to have been "published." An interoffice memo, faxed or emailed press release, tombstone, Post-it note on a cash register, or bounced check thumbtacked to a restaurant wall also can all qualify as having been "published."

Under what is called **the republication rule**, the person reporting and/or writing the story is fully and legally responsible for the libel. That person's source can be sued for slander, but it is the reporter who is responsible for the published libel. Thus, "I just repeated what they said" is not a reliable defense. Repeating a rumor is not necessarily libelous, but publishing it could be, and anyone who participates in publication can be named in a suit: copy editors, publishers, editors, press release writers, company owners, and discussion board moderators. Plaintiffs not surprisingly go after the money, however, which typically puts media owners in the most jeopardy.

## Fault

The most complicated area in libel law is fault. Briefly, different types or classifications of plaintiffs have to prove different standards or levels of libel, called fault. This hurdle was added in 1964 with the landmark U.S. Supreme Court case, *Times v. Sullivan*, and it dramatically diminished the possibility of a successful libel judgment against news media acting in good faith. Prior to this case, civil libel law had been governed by the doctrine of strict liability. Reporters and their publications were strictly and legally responsible for everything they wrote and published. In *Times v. Sullivan*, however, the Court ruled that plaintiffs had to prove what is known as fault, and for public or government officials, the level of or standard for fault was determined to be "actual malice." By distinguishing public officials and assigning a higher level of fault for them to prove, the Court ruled by implication that private citizens need prove only negligence. All plaintiffs have to clear the hurdle, but different classifications of plaintiffs must clear varying fault levels. *Times v. Sullivan* ended strict liability.

The highest fault level is known as "actual malice," which is defined as showing a reckless disregard for the truth and/or knowledge of falsity. To clear this very high level of fault, a plaintiff will have to prove that the reporter or writer knew the published material was false and went ahead with it anyway, or that the reporter or writer demonstrated a "reckless disregard for truth." The term's definition underlines how good, honest, professional reporting and writing can prevent successful libel claims. If you have three reliable sources, you cannot be guilty of actual malice-level libel. If you have no reliable sources, just the word of an unemployed former insurance salesman with a grudge, as it appeared was the case in a libelous *Saturday Evening Post* story on supposed game-fixing in college football, you could be guilty of actual malice-level libel. Relying on only one discredited source can be interpreted as reckless reporting.

It is important to note from *Times v. Sullivan* that the majority opinion supported an aggressive, free press. Justice William J. Brennan, Jr., wrote for the court that at issue was "a profound national commitment to the principle that debate on public issues should be uninhibited, robust, and wide open, and that it may well include vehement, caustic, and sometimes unpleasantly sharp attacks on government and public officials." It was Brennan's opinion that established the actual malice fault level. In rulings since *Sullivan*, the Court has made it clear that it wants more people to have to prove actual malice when suing for libel. The plaintiff category of "public officials" has been expanded to include "public figures," or celebrities, the well known, and people with power and influence in society. In other words, people commonly in the news. The Court had serious people in mind, but it is this strand of legal reasoning that ultimately evolved to include celebrities, who now must prove actual malice, as well. As libel law has grown more complicated and labyrinthine, the number of plaintiff categories has increased, but all plaintiffs must fall into one. The four are:

- all-purpose public figures;
- limited or "vortex" public figures;
- public officials; and
- private citizens.

Public figures make themselves public by seeking fame or notoriety (media attention), and public people have access to media to refute things said or written about them. They can tweet out to their millions of followers. They can call a press conference, for example, and media will show up to report what is said. Thus, the same media that are allegedly libelling them can be used as a remedy to the libel. Since *Times v. Sullivan*, the courts have sub-divided the public figure category in these ways:

- **All-purpose public figures**, or people with widespread fame or notoriety, such as LeBron James or Beyoncé. These figures are typically household names, people with special prominence in society. They are considered to have persuasive power and influence and are, therefore, continually newsworthy. Consider celebrities who sell their "exclusive" wedding or baby photos to periodicals for millions of dollars. Public figures have virtually no private aspects to their lives, at least in a legal sense, so their lives are fair game, as the TV shows *Entertainment Tonight*, *TMZ*, and *Access Hollywood* demonstrate. Once a person has been classified in this category, that public figure never falls out or lapses back to the lesser fault level category, regardless of how obscure he or she might become.

- **Vortex or limited public figures** are private figures who have been pulled into the public sphere, like an object swirled into a vortex. The key court case for this category is *Firestone v. Time* (1972), which involved the wife and heir to the Firestone tire fortune. She found herself mentioned in *Time* magazine as getting a divorce for cruelty and adultery. The magazine column was in error, however, and Firestone sued. The preliminary question for the court, before it could consider the libel, was, given her fortune and profile in philanthropy, is Firestone a public figure who, therefore, must prove actual malice, or, because the reason for the publicity was a divorce, which is considered to be a private matter, is she a private citizen? The court noted that she was a socialite active in philanthropy, and that she had hired a publicity clipping service. Nonetheless, for the purposes of the lawsuit, she was classified as a private person, because her divorce was deemed by the court to be an essentially private matter, something with no relationship to her activities as a philanthropist. Had *Time* written about Firestone's role as head of a cotillion or charity, she likely would have been classified as a vortex public figure.

Since the *Firestone* case, a test of sorts has emerged from case law to help courts determine a plaintiff's classification for the purposes of establishing a fault level. Courts should ask:

1. Is the published material about *a public controversy or real dispute*, the outcome of which affects a substantial number of people? Firestone's divorce was a real dispute, but its outcome did not affect a substantial number of people. It was not an issue of public concern. (The Court has not defined "substantial number of people.")
2. Did the plaintiff *voluntarily participate* in the public controversy?
3. Did the plaintiff voluntarily participate to *affect the outcome* of the issue, question, or controversy?

Case law suggests that a person cannot lose vortex public figure status over time, at least for anything relating to the issue or event that led to the status in the first place. This principle holds true for former public officials, as well; they don't lose their public status once they retire or lose a re-election.

In contrast to actual malice, the fault standard of **negligence** is defined to be a failure to exercise ordinary or reasonable care. Plaintiffs who are deemed to be private citizens need only prove this relatively low level of fault. To determine if a defendant has in fact been negligent, courts frequently rely on professional standards, calling in editors and academics to testify to standard practices. The courts are interested in the quantity and credibility of sources used, looking for red flags raised about the story's veracity, as well as in the newspaper's or website's policy for sourcing and verifying accuracy. Some courts follow what is known as the "reasonable person standard," which asks how a reasonable person might respond in similar circumstances.

A lack of thorough investigation, failure to verify information from official and reliable sources, and an absence of contact with the subject of the story have all been found to be evidence of negligence. What is deemed negligent, therefore, fails to measure up to what is considered good reporting practice. In other words, the courts are looking for sub-standard reporting, for malpractice, and not merely the absence of professionalism or good practices.

## Falsity

Defamation has nothing to do with truth or falsity. In fact, true statements are often more defamatory than false statements. But to win a libel claim, a plaintiff is going to have to prove that the published story is defamatory *and* false, the latter an element of libel law unique to the United States. Until earlier this decade, truth (or falsity) was not a factor in England, for example, and it still is not a recognized defense in Australia, New Zealand, or Canada, countries that trace their legal systems' origins to English common law. In the United States, the courts require only substantial truth, at least for private citizens, not that each and every word be literally true. Remember, public figures and public officials will have to prove actual malice; media need only prove *the absence* of actual malice, not absolute truth. Careless errors are not necessarily enough to lose a libel suit. If a published report states that a person embezzled $75,000 and the actual amount was $70,000, the error will not likely qualify as "substantially" false, because the "fact" of having committed embezzlement was true.

## Injury

Another relatively easy hurdle to clear is demonstration of injury. A plaintiff need only produce one psychologist testifying to the plaintiff's need for medication as a result of the claimed libel, for example. In this category are three types or classifications of damages:

- **Compensatory (or actual) damages** compensate for harm done or harm proven, and they include damage to reputation and personal suffering.
- **Special damages** are those one might think are "actual" damages. Examples include losing a job and, therefore, income; having to move and sell a home; or requiring psychotherapy.

- **Punitive damages** are meant to punish the defendant. The jury decides these, and no plaintiff eligible to sue for these fails to because it is this classification that promises the big money awards. Juries typically look at the financial status of the defendant and calibrate their judgments in order to punish that individual or organization. The results typically are, not surprisingly, huge damage awards, though almost all judgments are reduced on appeal.

Not all libel cases systematically proceed through the six elements or dimensions. The defense can submit a motion for dismissal at any time, for example, initiating a ruling called summary judgment. If a defendant can persuade a judge that the plaintiff cannot possibly win, summary judgment is a possibility. Second, there is a **statute of limitations** on libel actions, in most states one year from publication or initial broadcast. If the actionable material was published or aired more than a year prior to filing the claim, that claim can possibly be summarily dismissed. If the material was published online, the clock typically begins on upload, or when the site publishes, tweets, or posts the actionable material, as opposed to when someone downloads, reads, or accesses it.

Sometimes, a person or organization uses a lawsuit simply to intimidate. With no intent or likelihood of winning a libel action, plaintiffs in this scenario hope to scare or pressure a defendant into silence. When this is recognized by the court, such a lawsuit is deemed to be a **Strategic Lawsuit Against Public Participation (SLAPP) suit**. More than 20 states explicitly bar or severely limit such lawsuits, and the high cost of defending a SLAPP suit is one of the concerns that is spurring the states to act. As an example of what anti-SLAPP laws are supposed to do, Maine's Supreme Judicial Court struck down a defamation lawsuit filed against a former legislator who claimed that the plaintiff was using the court system to try to stifle free speech in a political debate. The defendant successfully gained dismissal of the lawsuit on the grounds that it violated Maine's anti-SLAPP law, which is intended to protect a citizen's right to directly or indirectly petition the government through public discourse, a right fairly explicitly protected by the First Amendment. Thus, asking a court to recognize a lawsuit as a SLAPP is another potential defense against a libel claim over and above tripping a plaintiff up on any one of the six essential hurdles.

There are other additional defenses, as well, including the following:

- **Qualified privilege (or fair report)**, a defense that shields media when they report on official government reports and meetings. Courts recognize the importance of scrutiny of government proceedings, meetings, and activities as part of news media's watchdog role. Thus, acting as a sort of video camera, media can claim this defense and not necessarily be responsible for the truth or falsity of what occurs in those meetings and proceedings, provided that the reporting is fair and accurate. If, for example, a local citizen at a city council meeting charges that an official took a bribe, accurate reporting of the accusation is protected by this defense. The qualified privilege defense is especially valuable in political campaign coverage, when it is particularly difficult to parse fact from fiction.

- **First Amendment opinion**, a defense that often protects rhetorical hyperbole and fair comment and criticism. Varying from state to state, and based on common law, this defense typically is applied to published opinions, arts and music criticism, and parody and satire. Hyperbole, parody, and exaggerated statements that a "reasonable person" would not read as being literally true are typically protected by this defense, as well. Because political cartoons, parody, and satire are strong vehicles for expressing public opinion, they are generally protected even if they offend or inflict emotional injury. Similarly, statements that cannot be proved true or false are typically protected. The 1984 case *Ollman v. Evans* produced the **Ollman Test**, which is used by lower courts to guide use of this defense. The test asks courts to consider these questions:
  - o   What is the common or ordinary meaning of the words?
  - o   Can the contested statement be proved true or false?
  - o   What is the journalistic context of the remark?
  - o   What is the social context of the remark?

## Section 230 of the CDA

In a 2003 case, *Batzel v. Smith*, the Ninth Circuit Court interpreted into libel law many of the same protections for bloggers that have been recognized as being for traditional journalists, which isn't to say either that journalists don't blog or that bloggers can't be journalists. In *Batzel*, the court ruled that bloggers, website operators, and email list operators cannot be held responsible for libel in information that they re-publish, and it pointed to Section 230 of the Communications Decency Act of 1996, which states that "no provider or user of an interactive computer service shall be treated as the publisher or speaker of any information provided by another information content provider." Section 230 is one of the more valuable tools for protecting freedom of expression in digital space, even though the purpose of the CDA was to *restrict* expression on the Internet. Fortunately, the anti-free speech provisions of the CDA were struck down by the Supreme Court, but Section 230 remains.

In short, online intermediaries that host or re-publish expression are protected against a range of laws that might otherwise be used to hold them legally responsible for what others say and do. These protected intermediaries include regular Internet Service Providers (ISPs) and what the law terms "interactive computer service providers," an elastic term that includes any online service that publishes third-party content. It is the broad protections in Section 230 that have allowed, to name a few examples, YouTube and Vimeo videos posted by users, user reviews at Amazon and Yelp, classified ads at craigslist, and offensive expression at Yik Yak.

Section 230 also protects bloggers who act as intermediaries by hosting comments on their blogs. Under this law, bloggers are not liable for comments left by readers, the work of guest bloggers, tips sent via email, or information received through RSS feeds, and this legal protection can hold even if a blogger is aware of the objectionable content or makes editorial judgments. However, sites run into legal jeopardy or liability when they contribute commentary or substantively change posts in editing, though the courts have yet to clarify what is and is not an acceptable amount or degree of editing. As Karen Alexander Horowitz has found, decisions interpreting or otherwise relying on Section 230 have been wildly inconsistent, from offering blanket immunity to depriving immunity when and where an ISP engaged in even minor editing. And Section 230's protections are unique to U.S. law.

## Anonymous Expression

Section 230 has exacerbated a problem long wrestled with by the courts even in the analog pre-web era: anonymous defamation. The courts are faced with the difficult, sometimes seemingly impossible task of balancing a person's, company's, or organization's right to a good name on the one hand against a speaker's First Amendment right to anonymous expression, even that which defames, on the other. And they're asked to do this for content delivered by media that enable and encourage cheaply, even freely published, globally distributed, cached, and searchable expression. A legitimate state interest exists in the compensation of individuals for the harm done to them by defamatory and false statements, but in making it too easy for plaintiffs to force the discovery of anonymous speakers' identities, states could unnecessarily, perhaps even unconstitutionally, chill online expression.

Typically, the first step in a defamation action against an anonymous speaker is to seek a subpoena on the defendant's ISP in order to obtain that speaker's identity. It is difficult for a plaintiff to sue unless he or she knows who made the actionable statements. By most of the standards issued by district courts and intermediate state courts, once issued the subpoena, an ISP then notifies the accused that his or her identity is being sought in order to give that defendant an opportunity to contest the subpoena. Different ISPs deal with subpoenas for the identity of anonymous speakers in different ways, usually in conformity to their own user agreements and privacy policies. Of course, if the speaker is anonymous or pseudonymous, notifying that person of the action can prove difficult. Conversely, it is impossible to defend against a subpoena to force disclosure if you have not been notified of the subpoena in the first place.

Anonymity is regulated by a multitude of federal and state constitutional provisions, state and federal statutes, and state and federal court decisions. Just how broad a right one has to be anonymous in digital spaces in the United States is unclear and even unstable. Most courts faced with questions that involve a speaker's claimed right to anonymity cite the majority opinion in *McIntyre v. Ohio Elections Commission* (1995), an opinion that interprets into the First Amendment the right to anonymous expression by finding the state of Ohio's interests in "preventing fraudulent and libelous statements" and in "providing the electorate with relevant information" insufficient to justify a ban on anonymous speech that was not narrowly tailored, according to the U.S. Supreme Court decision. Lower courts have applied the precedent set in *McIntyre* to online expression by recognizing that speech on the Internet is entitled to full First Amendment protection, as the Supreme Court declared in *Reno v. A.C.L.U.* in 1997. These courts have, therefore, generally sought to protect the identity of online speakers.

This constitutional freedom protects even speech that is crass, offensive, insulting, or objectionable; in fact, it protects speech that is especially these things. "One man's vulgarity is another's lyric," wrote Justice John Marshall Harlan, in *Cohen v. California* (1971). The Court in *Times v. Sullivan* has made clear that, through the First Amendment, the United States has a "profound national commitment to the principle that debate on public issues should be uninhibited, robust, and wide open," and that, because that debate is sometimes messy, some false speech must be protected in order to ensure that uninhibited debate.

## COPYRIGHT, FAIR USE, AND INTELLECTUAL PROPERTY

William Shakespeare wrote his play, *As You Like It*, between 1598 and 1600, taking as his source for the plot and general outline Thomas Lodge's 1590 play, *Rosalynde, Euphues Golden Legacie*. Lodge, in turn, "borrowed" his play from Chaucer's *The Cokes Tale of Gamelyn*, a 14th-century poem. It is likely that under U.S. copyright law today, Shakespeare could not legally write or, more accurately, publish his play, or that if he did, he would find himself in violation of that copyright law. Now flash forward a few centuries to consider Honore de Balzac, one of France's most prolific authors. He wrote everything for a flat fee. He was the J.K. Rowling or Stephen King of his day, at least in terms of popularity and productivity. In part because of the lack of copyright protection, and in part because of his appetites, Balzac wrote to eat and died a pauper.

In the United States, copyright law has de-evolved since Thomas Jefferson first articulated it in 1790. Intended to foster innovation, intellectual property law in the United

States has been transformed to primarily protect commercial interests. In fencing off vast areas of popular culture, artistic expression, and ideas, the United States's IP regime raises significant First Amendment freedom of expression questions. The situation is so grave that a video posted to YouTube with background music of Beethoven's "Moonlight Sonata" can be forced off the web by multiple companies claiming copyright to the music (see Jaron Schneider, "Ridiculous Copyright Claims Are Smothering YouTube Content Creators"). Fox News, which itself relies on the First Amendment, sued U.S. Senator Al Franken and his publisher for naming a book, "Lies and the Lying Liars Who Tell Them: A Fair and Balanced Look at the Right." Fox sued for use of Fox's trademarked "Fair and Balanced" tagline, arguing that use of the slogan would "blur and tarnish" the network's reputation. Franken was described in the suit as being "unfunny." Fox lost its case, but that the question had to be answered in a court of law points to a problem with U.S. intellectual property law.

Complicating an already complex area of the law is the fact that copyright law protects the expression of ideas, not the ideas themselves or the labor required to create the expressions. To help understand some of these distinctions, consider the last book you read. To whom does that volume belong? It's yours, unless you borrowed it. You own your physical copy of that book, which is why you can sell it to a second-hand bookstore, put it on eBay, give it away, or burn it. But who owns the copyright to the expression inside that physical container? Typically, the publisher. Sometimes, the author. So there are two pieces of property: the physical, or material, and the expression in the physical document, and the organization of facts in that printed book. But the publisher and/or the author of the book own the copyright, protecting the expression of its ideas. The tricky part, then, is how to treat the two very different properties and not to treat them in the same ways. Intellectual property is largely intangible, but it is mistakenly, even tragically, treated by U.S. law more like tangible property, like a piece of land or a lawn mower. And the Internet has put an unprecedented strain on copyright law as a result of the ease with which intellectual property can be copied, downloaded, uploaded, altered, mass-emailed and mass-duplicated, hacked, and stolen. Making matters worse, at least for the copyright owners, is that unlike for analog copies, a digital copy has 100 percent fidelity to the original; the copies (or clones) look or sound every bit as good as the original.

During the 16th century, English law protected only the printers, not authors or painters, or those we would think of as the originators of the intellectual property. This changed in 1710 with, "An Act for the Encouragement of Learning, by Vesting the Copies of Printed Books in the Authors or Purchasers of Such Copies, during the Time Therein Mentioned." Coming too late to help, say, Balzac, this awkwardly named law gave a legal claim of intellectual property ownership to the creator, or to someone who bought the creative rights from the creator, and it is this law that is (or, more accurately, once was) the basis for U.S. copyright law. The U.S. Constitution's copyright and patent clause (Article I, Section 8, Clause 8) charges Congress to "promote the Progress of Science and useful Arts, by securing for limited Times to Authors and Inventors the exclusive Right to their respective Writings and Discoveries." Implied in this verbiage is that people will innovate and create if they are guaranteed protection for their work for a limited time. How Congress has defined "limited," however, has changed over time.

In the nation's beginnings, U.S. law gave the copyright owner the right to protect his or her creation for up to 28 years, or for two 14-year terms. Registering provided the first 14 years; one renewal provided the next 14. In 1831, the timeline lengthened to cover the original 28 years plus an automatic 28-year renewal *and* an additional 14-year renewal, or the potential of 70 years in total. Musical compositions were added in 1831, and photography gained protection in 1865, largely because of the commercial value of photography of the Civil War. Translation rights followed in 1870.

Before 1978, copyright law was an opt-in system, granting protection only to those who registered and renewed their copyrights, and only if they marked their creative works with the © symbol. In 1978 Congress created an opt-out system, meaning that copyright protection no longer need be solicited. Protection is granted automatically to a created work once it is in fixed form, and this protection now extends for nearly a century, whether or not the author or creator needs it or even knows he or she has it. The law once offered protection only to those who wanted it, and for a "limited time." Current copyright law universally grants it, regardless of need, even though according to the government's own study, only about 2 percent of copyrighted works 55 to 75 years old have any commercial value whatsoever. And it protects that copyright for longer than the creator's lifetime.

According to U.S. copyright law, "All works of authorship fixed in a tangible medium of expression" receive copyright protection. This definition applies to writings and online postings, paintings and animated gifs, music, drama, and recordings. It does not protect the ideas themselves, only their fixed expression. How can you know the idea without its expression? You can't. Thus, the two dimensions are in some ways indivisible. Generally, the copyright owner is the author of the created work. Exceptions are works made for hire, such as those routinely published in newspapers and magazines and on the web. Copyrights may also be sold or given away, such as in publication contracts that transfer copyright from an author to the publisher of the work. Re-assigning copyright requires a written statement of transference, and acquiring a previously unpublished creation, such as a manuscript, does not mean that one has acquired its copyright.

In the last 40 years, Congress has extended copyright terms 11 times, each time in favor of private incentive versus the enrichment of the public domain. When the Sonny Bono Copyright Term Extension Act added 20 years to existing and future copyrights in 1998, Eric Eldred and other commercial and non-commercial users of public domain works sued, claiming the CTEA to be in violation of the U.S. Copyright Act and that the extension raised important First Amendment questions. By a vote of 7–2, the Supreme Court ruled in early 2003 that the CTEA does *not* violate the constitutional commandment that copyrights be granted for a limited time. The Bono extension, therefore, locks up or excludes a vast majority of creative works in order to protect the 2 percent with any commercial value. This means, as Kembrew McLeod noted, that we are "allowing much of our cultural history to be locked up and decay only to benefit the very few." Until a judge ruled in February 2016 that the song, "Happy Birthday to You," belongs in the public domain, the song was not set to enter the public domain until 2030. Copyrighted in 1935 by the Hill sisters, the song was sold in 1988 by Birch Tree Group to Time Warner, which claimed and enforced its copyright until a judge ruled the claim invalid. It is this complicated history that explains why restaurants have their own versions of "Happy Birthday," because singing "Happy Birthday to You" in a public place would likely have been regarded as a public performance of a copyrighted song.

Websites, software, and apps typically include in their user agreements an articulation of copyright rights covering content produced for or on those sites, software, and apps. Facebook's user agreement, for example, states that once you have logged on to the social media site, you grant Facebook the non-exclusive, fully paid, worldwide license to use, publicly perform, and display such content on the website or app. This means that essentially all photos and entries, video, and music clips are the property of Facebook the instant they are published there.

Thomas Jefferson was not primarily concerned with protecting the commercial interests of the last known user of the property, but rather with fostering innovation, development, knowledge, and progress. "He who receives an idea from me, receives instruction himself without lessening mine; as he who lights his taper at mine, receives light without darkening me," Jefferson wrote. Supreme Court Justice Sandra Day O'Connor expanded this thinking in her *Rural Telephone Service v. Feist Publications* decision in 1991 that "the primary objective of copyright law is not to reward the labor of authors, but to promote the process of science and the arts."

The danger, as McLeod wrote in his excellent diagnosis of the problem, in his book, *Freedom of Expression*, is in corporate interests wielding intellectual property laws like a weapon and in overzealous owners eroding the expressive freedoms of ordinary Americans. McLeod posits that we self-censor because we might get sued, even where there is no threat. We censor ourselves in backing down from a lawsuit even when that suit is frivolous, often because of the expense of even winning the case. And we are losing freedoms because everything from human genes and business methods to slogans, gestures, and scents are being privatized and commercialized. We should not be required to hire an expert to determine whether we can use Beethoven's "Moonlight Sonata" composed in 1801, or whether a library can display documentary photographs of the Japanese Internment.

Having spelled out some of copyright's protections and contradictions, we should look at what it means practically to own a copyright. There are six permutations protecting a copyright owner's right to granting, limiting, or prohibiting:

- reproductions (such as prints of paintings or limited edition versions);
- derivative works (like a videogame version or website or online encyclopedia);
- public distribution;
- public performance;
- public display; and
- public digital performance of a sound recording.

The above list means that there are several works that are not covered, including:

- trivial materials;
- ideas (remember, it protects only their expression);
- utilitarian goods (like a toilet or, more specifically, how the toilet works);
- book or movie titles and names;
- lists of ingredients;
- standard calendars and rulers;
- methods, systems, procedures, math principles, formulae, equations, and the periodic chart of elements; and
- anything that does not offer its origin to the author (non-original works).

Copyright holders, then, have five distinct rights to a given creation. The holder can copy, distribute, display, perform, and create derivative works from the original creation. These derivations include translations, abridgments, and adaptations, such as making a movie from a novel. Another right, called a *moral right*, entails that one cannot change or mutilate a creation, such as removing an artist's name from a painting. Moral rights were originally recognized by European countries and now are recognized in the United States, as well.

The *Rural Telephone* case proved important for databases, CD-ROMs, and digital anthologies. To instigate the case, Feist Publications combined Rural's telephone directory with others to create a regional phone directory that it then printed and sold for profit. Rural Telephone sued for copyright infringement and lost, with the Supreme Court allowing Feist's alphabetical listing of residents with a telephone. Such public information cannot be copyrighted because there is no "idea" there, the Court ruled. The listing is not novel or unique, in other words, and copyright does not cover purely "sweat of the brow" labor, in Justice O'Connor's words. Since 1991, *Feist* has been expanded, even though it was a relatively narrow ruling when issued.

A related qualification is that facts cannot be copyrighted, only the way in which those facts are expressed. The naked truth cannot be copyrighted. URLs, for example, cannot be copyright protected, meaning a copyright holder cannot prevent or control their publication, including in hyperlinks, even deep hyperlinks. Unique expressions of truth, including facts, however, often can be copyright protected. The copyright protections we normally associate with print also govern the use of audio, video, images, and text on the Internet and the web.

In the United States, copyright terms are a bit complicated because of a series of extensions granted by Congress and upheld by the Courts. Generally, however, works published:

- before January 1, 1923 are protected for 75 years from the date the copyright was first secured;
- from January 1, 1923 to January 1964 were required to have copyright renewed during the 28th year of their first term of copyright, which then covered them for 95 years from first publication;
- on or after January 1, 1964 to December 31, 1977 are protected for 95 years with no need of renewal;
- from January 1978 in their second term of protection automatically have the full 95-year term without requiring renewal; and
- prior to 1906 or published by the U.S. government are in the public domain and require no permission to quote.

These terms and limits are spelled out on a webpage from Cornell University Copyright Information Center, available at copyright.cornell.edu/resources/publicdomain.cfm.

In the United Kingdom and throughout the European Union, copyright terms generally are shorter, and they depend upon who owns the copyright. For a copyright held by an author, the work is protected for 70 years from the end of the year in which the author died. For a copyright held by the publisher, works are protected for 70 years from the end of the year in which the work was first published. If the author is not known, the work still is protected for 70 years, but from the end of the year in which the work was first published. Works published by the British government generally can be reproduced free of charge for uses such as analysis and commentary, provided that use is credited and non-commercial.

## Fair Use

Much of what digital writers and editors wish to do is potentially protected by a provision of copyright law known as "fair use." This provision is the right to use copyrighted material without permission or payment under some circumstances, especially when the cultural or social benefits of the use are clear. Fair use is a generally applicable right, meaning that the law does not have to provide an explicit authorization for the specific use. Digital writers can avoid infringement and legally use copyrighted materials if they understand and comply with fair use guidelines, or after obtaining permission for use from a copyright's owner. Fair use is the most significant limitation on a copyright holder's exclusive rights, but determining whether the use of a work is fair or illegal is not a science; there are no clear, stable guidelines that are universally accepted. It is, however, generally understood that copyright owners' rights are exclusive and monopolistic except in four sets of circumstances:

- where the work is not eligible for copyright protection (government information, for example, generally, is not eligible);
- where the work is not an original (copyright does not cover copies, like a print of Van Gogh's "Sunflowers," for example, only the original "Sunflowers" painting);
- where the copyright has expired; and
- where the work's copying is covered by fair use.

The doctrine of fair use is meant to provide "a rule. . . to balance the author's right to compensation for his work. . . against the public's interest in the widespread dissemination of ideas and information on the other," according to one district court opinion. Fair use generally covers:

- small amounts of copying, generally understood in print to be around 150–500 words or less, depending on the length of the original;
- the advancement of ideas, education, information, and knowledge, such as copies of a journal article distributed to students in a classroom; and
- all intellectual property.

Since the U.S. Copyright Act was enacted in 1976, federal judges typically ask four questions in determining whether the use is, in fact, "fair." The individual who wants to use a copyrighted work must weigh these four factors:

1. Is the use transformative? In other words, what is the purpose and character of the use? If it is transformative, the new work likely is eligible for its own copyright. Andy Warhol's appropriation of a Campbell's soup can is an example.
2. What is the nature of the copyrighted work? A workbook with perforated pages, for example, is obviously designed to be purchased, not photocopied and distributed.

3. How much of the original work was changed? What amount and how much substantiality does that amount represent when viewed as a part of the whole? "Borrowing" a large portion or, perhaps, a small but essential or distinctive portion risks litigation.

4. What is the effect on the market or the potential market for the copyrighted work? This factor gets the most attention, again underlining the commercial interests driving the action in this area of the law.

These questions are implicit in the U.S. Code, Title 17, Chapter 1, Section 107, which reads, in part, "The fair use of a copyrighted work, including such use by reproduction in copies or phonorecords or by any other means specified by that section, for purposes such as criticism, comment, news reporting, teaching (including multiple copies for classroom use), scholarship, or research, is not an infringement of copyright." To better understand this dense language, let's unpack these four factors.

1. **What is the purpose and character of the copying?** What is the copyrighted material being used for? Teaching? Comment and criticism? Scholarship and research? If so, there is a good chance that it is covered. This factor permits a professor to photocopy an article, even in full, and pass it out to students in a classroom. In digital terms, the professor can store a PDF of the entire article behind a password-protected firewall for his or her students to access using their passwords. If the professor copies an article in full, then charges students $15 per copy, it would likely be viewed as an infringement. In general, educational copying must be:

    (a) brief;
    (b) spontaneous (when there is no time to get permissions from publishers);
    (c) labelled with a copyright notice somewhere on the copied material(s) crediting or otherwise identifying the copyright owner(s); and
    (d) equal to or less than the cost to the student of obtaining the original.

Finally, ask whether the new work offers something above and beyond the original. Does it transform the original work in some way? If the work is altered significantly, used for another purpose or to appeal to a different audience, it is more likely to be considered fair use.

2. **What is the nature of the copyrighted work?**

    (a) Is it a workbook intended to be used only once? If that's the case, copying the workbook is probably an unprotected use.
    (b) Is the work out of print? If it is, copying it is more likely to be considered fair use.

(c) Is it informational or creative? If it is a newspaper, your right to copy is probably protected because newspapers are informational. A poem, however, is more likely to be protected. The more a work tends toward artistic expression, the less likely it will be considered fair use to copy it.

(d) Has the work been published? Copyright is meant to protect in order to encourage people to publish. If you are not the author, and it has not been published, be very careful. The courts want to protect the author's right of first publication. Generally, however, unpublished works are less likely to be considered fair use.

3. **How much is used and, just as importantly, what does the use represent in terms of the "essence" or substantiality of the original work?** Using only 150 words, typically, is a fair use, unless those 150 words are the heart and soul or essence of the original work. The more you use, the less likely it will be considered fair use. If the amount approaches 50 percent of the entire work, it is likely not to be considered a fair use of the copyrighted work. If the very small portion used is the essence of the work but it is used in a wholly different way, as in a parody or satire, it is likely permissible. To help us understand this last distinction, consider the Supreme Court case, *Campbell v. Acuff-Rose Music* (1994), which concerned 2 Live Crew's re-working of Roy Orbison's "Pretty Woman." The 2 Live Crew version used the lyrics: "Big hairy woman, all that hair ain't legit; Big hairy woman, Cause you look like Cousin It," mimicking Orbison's lyric, "Pretty woman, walking down the street; Pretty woman, the kind I'd like to meet."

The plaintiff's argument was based on two claims:

a. The parody is a commercial use. 2 Live Crew is making money.
b. 2 Live Crew is using the "heart of the original," or the essence of the song, so the amount appropriated should not be a factor.

The Court disagreed, recognizing that it is the "heart of the original" that makes 2 Live Crew's parody most likely to "conjure up the [original] song for parody." In other words, what was copied had to be recognizable to be heard as a parody. In ruling, the Court also suggested that the four provisions or criteria for fair use are not binary. If you fail one or more, you still might not be infringing. Rather, the four exist on a sort of continuum, where an overall balance of fairness is struck between the old work and the new.

4. **What is the effect on the market?** This factor is often the most important, or at least it is often treated as being the most important. It covers direct impact, such as lost sales,

and indirect impact, like that on derivative rights. For example, *Castle Rock Entertainment v. Carol Publishing* in 1997 centered on a book entitled, *The Seinfeld Aptitude Test*. Seinfeld's distributor, Castle Rock, won the case because of the claimed effect on the market of the book in preventing Castle Rock from profiting from a similar work, a "Seinfeld"-based trivia test—a claimed derivative right. In another well-known example, the creator of an online encyclopedia of virtually every character, creature, place, spell, and item in the Harry Potter series, school librarian Steve Vander Ark, ran into trouble when he published the site as a book. A district court ruled that the lexicon was not a fair use, deciding "while the Lexicon, in its current state, is not a fair use of the Harry Potter works, reference works that share the Lexicon's purpose of aiding readers of literature generally should be encouraged rather than stifled."

Generally, then, the more the new work differs from the original, the less likely it will be considered an infringement. If the audience for the new work is the same as that for the original, as was the case for *The Seinfeld Aptitude Test*, it might be considered an infringement. If a new work contains anything original, it is more likely the use of the copyrighted material will be seen as fair use. If it is a reference work, like Vander Ark's Lexicon, it might or might not be a fair use. There are few hard and fast rules, therefore.

This summary of fair use and its provisions isn't comprehensive, and it omits other permissions to use copyrighted material, such as those covered by Creative Commons licenses. Under a CC license, a copyright holder can elect to share his or her work. Some musicians, for example, license others to reproduce, remix, and/or distribute their works at no cost, provided they are credited for the original. Flickr was one of the first major online communities to incorporate Creative Commons licensing options into its user interface, giving photographers the ability to share photos on terms of their choosing. As the Flickr community grew, so did the number of CC-licensed images. As of late 2016, there were more than 200 million on the site, establishing Flickr as the web's single largest source of CC-licensed content. CC licenses, like those offered by Flickr, stipulate the ways in which copyrighted materials can be used. Creative Commons was established as a response to the U.S. Supreme Court upholding of Congress's extension of copyright terms by 20 years, with the *Eldred v. Ashcroft* decision.

## The Internet and Copyright

The prevailing culture on the Internet is that content should be free and freely obtained, even where copyright protected. We live in a cut-and-paste culture. Google, YouTube, and the blogosphere are cut-and-paste, record-and-stream worlds and, as such, they bump up against U.S. law, including and perhaps especially the Digital Millennium Copyright Act. During the mid-1990s, the World Intellectual Property Organization framed digital copyright rules in negotiating two treaties, and from those treaties came the DMCA of 1998. Among its provisions:

- You cannot circumvent copyright protection-using devices or their technologies.
- You cannot use a file-sharing software program to circumvent copyright to copy and distribute content.
- You cannot alter the code in DVDs that prevents copying, or use a descrambler to pick up satellite broadcasts.

The DMCA has been at the center of a storm of litigation, including *MGM v. Grokster* in 2005, a case that echoed the famous 1984 Sony Betamax case (*Sony Corp. v. Universal City Studios*). In the Sony case, it was acknowledged that the VCR can be used to play home movies, and it can be used to illegally copy TV programming. Should VCRs, then, be deemed illegal? The Supreme Court ruled that they should not. The manufacturer of the machine should not be held liable for the use to which it is put by the consumer. VCRs do not violate copyright, in other words; people do.

In *MGM v. Grokster* (and Streamcast), Grokster, an online, peer-to-peer file-sharing service, argued the Betamax defense from the previous Sony case: "Don't hold us responsible for miscreants" who violate copyright by illegally copying and sharing music. The Supreme Court ruled, in sending it back to the lower court for decision, that Grokster (and Streamcast) could be sued because there was evidence that the companies knew their software was being used primarily for illegal uses and did nothing about it. As a result, Grokster shut down on November 7, 2005, agreeing to pay a $50 million fine. Grokster's website was changed to say that its existing file-sharing service was illegal and no longer available. "There are legal services for downloading music and movies," the message said. "This service is not one of them." The *Grokster* decision significantly weakened lawsuit protections for companies that had blamed illegal behavior on their customers rather than the technology that made such behavior possible, which since 1984 had been an effective defense. This weakening helped the recording and film industries in their aggressive campaigns against copyright-infringing file sharing.

In June 2009, a 32-year-old woman from Brainerd, MN, lost her copyright infringement case over downloaded music and was assessed $1.92 million in damages, or $80,000 per song for the 24 songs she was accused of downloading. Of the more than 30,000 suits brought by the Recording Industry Association of America (RIAA) against alleged file-sharers, the Minnesota woman's is one of only a handful to go to a jury. The damage amount underlines the high stakes in downloading and sharing copyrighted digital content, and the lengths to which the RIAA has been willing to go to protect its control regime.

Who, then, can best manage the commons, or the shared public resources, culture, its icons and slogans and intellectual property? The people or private industry? Although it belongs to the people, as a matter of free speech, it is most often litigated as private, commercial property. Corporate interests are most often the winners.

The DMCA has another troubling aspect: A takedown notice. The act subjects online service providers to distributor liability if that provider fails to remove from its service *potentially* copyright-infringing content posted by a third party if that provider knows or has been notified that the content *might* infringe another's copyright. The DMCA's takedown policy has, in effect, criminalized legitimate research, stunted software development, and chilled expression. Merely by threatening ISPs with litigation under the DMCA, intellectual property owners can silence speakers simply because they do not like what the online speakers have to say. This intimidation has on occasion censored First Amendment-protected parody and satire. The Church of Scientology invoked the DMCA in calling for Google to block links to websites critical of the church, claiming that those sites were reprinting copyright-protected content owned by the church. Google blocked the sites, stating that, "Had we not removed these URLs, we would be subject to a claim of copyright infringement, regardless of its merits." It did not matter that the re-publishing was almost certainly protected by fair use provisions of U.S. copyright law.

## Copyright and Image Use

If you need a photo or graphic, can't you just surf the web until you find one you like, download or copy it, then insert it into your blog or Facebook post, webpage, or FAQ list? Everyone does it, right? The answer is that while it is standard practice, lifting other people's intellectual property is to invite a cease-and-desist letter, a DMCA takedown request, litigation, and possibly all three. You have to assume any image you find online is protected by copyright, whether in the United States or somewhere else, unless otherwise indicated, and this applies to Google Images just as it does to any other collection or aggregation of graphic content online.

Copyright protects original works of authorship, and these works can be literary, written, dramatic, artistic, musical, photographic, and graphical. Copyright is granted as soon as an original work is created, and it applies to both published and unpublished works. In fact, just as soon as you key into your computer, click the shutter on your camera, apply paint to canvas, or record a few tracks for your music video, you are granted a copyright. It's automatic.

When you wish to incorporate or otherwise publish an image, illustration, photo, or infographic, if you're not using your own copyrighted intellectual property, you will likely need to seek permission. The general rule is that you cannot use a copyrighted work without express (or written) consent from the owner, except where that use is determined to be a "fair use." When you pay a stock photo service, you are paying for permission or license to use the copyrighted image. Works with creative commons licenses and images from public domain image libraries are also options. Creative commons licenses confer the right to use an image under certain circumstances, while public domain images are not subject to copyright in the first place.

The purpose of the Fair Use Doctrine is to allow for limited and reasonable uses as long as the use does not interfere with an owner's rights. Let's say you are blogging a review of the latest iPhone. To liven up the post, you want to include a photo of that iPhone. After visiting Apple.com and finding one you like, you pull the image down to your laptop to publish in your post. Fair use provisions should cover your specific use of the photo, because your review is for the benefit of the public good. Why you are using the image is, therefore, an important consideration. If it is "for purposes such as criticism, comment, news reporting, teaching (including multiple copies for classroom use), scholarship, or research," you are probably on solid ground. To remove ambiguity, simply seek permission and get that permission in some express form.

Sometimes there isn't time to get permission. In these instances, ask yourself whether the copyright owner of whatever image it is you wish to use is likely to seek damages for your use or re-use of that image. Typically, a copyright owner's first move is to issue a cease-and-desist letter or order, which gives you the choice of taking down the offending image or leaving it up and facing legal action. Most uses most of the time aren't worth litigation. Also keep in mind that providing attribution or credit is not the same thing as obtaining permission, and it offers no protection against a copyright claim.

So, if you need to use someone else's image, get permission for the specific use you intend, make sure your use fits clearly into one of the protected purposes, or seek legal counsel. Fair use may be considered an exception that allows you to use copyrighted images, but you probably don't want to find out that the copyright holder disagrees. Beyond the legal questions are ethical ones. To pay for and acknowledge the intellectual property of others, namely photographers and graphic artists who make their living creating, selling, and licensing their work, is the ethical and right thing to do. Nearly every photo taken gives the person who takes the photo a protectable right to prevent others from using or reproducing that image. The photographer owns the copyright. A few online sources of "free" images (images for which you do not need to either pay or seek permission to use):

- **Flickr Creative Commons Group** (flickr.com/creativecommons);
- **Free Digital Photos** (freedigitalphotos.net);
- **Free Images** (freeimages.com);
- **Morgue File** (morguefile.com); and
- **Photos8** (photos8.com).

Read over the rules so you know exactly what type of attribution or credit you must provide.

## Copyright and Image Protection

Let's flip the script to ask about the options for a copyright owner seeking to stop someone else's infringement. First, ask whether it is worth your time, effort, and possibly expense to fight or stop the infringement. If the infringement is trivial, maybe ignoring it is the best response. If, however, you want to pursue action, here are the remedies:

- Request credit. If you simply want proper credit, write the infringer a letter officially granting the right to use the image but designating the parameters or limits of that use, including as a condition that the infringer post a credit with a copyright notice on or adjacent to the use.
- Send a DMCA takedown notice. If the publishing site is an ISP, it is not liable for transmitting information that infringes a copyright *only* if that ISP removes the infringing content after receiving notice of the potential violation. The notice must be in writing, signed by the copyright owner, and it must identify the copyrighted work that is infringing. Such a notice must include the copyright owner's contact information, a statement that the complaint is made in "good faith," and a statement, under penalty of perjury, that the information contained in the notification is accurate.
- Send a cease-and-desist letter. For the cost of a stamp, this is often all you need to do. Simply contact the infringer to explain that the use is not authorized and ask that the infringing content be taken down.
- File suit and seek damages. U.S. law states that you are entitled to actual or statutory damages for infringement as provided by 17 U.S.C., Chapter 5, specifically Section 504. But no one likes litigation, and you could end up inviting retaliatory legal action. If you are considering this step, it is time to seek legal counsel.

## INTERNATIONAL LAW

The transborder nature of digital media could mean that local laws everywhere, from Australia to Zimbabwe, apply to what we publish and post. And where an article is downloaded and read can be more important than where it was published or uploaded, which makes digital writers and publishers potentially subject to the laws of 190 countries. Not surprisingly, the result is dizzying jurisdictional complexity. With no international consensus to guide how or even where jurisdictional disputes should be resolved, international legal questions are inevitable. For those who write and publish digitally for large media organizations, awareness of potential legal challenges internationally could prevent legal actions that threaten to haul the employer organization into a foreign court. For lone, untethered writers who do not have the benefit of large constituent legal departments, the lack of significant material assets abroad and relative anonymity likely provide ample protection against lawsuits in most cases.

## CONCLUSION

Good, thorough, professional information gathering, writing, and publishing practices should keep you out of court. Corroborate a claim with three credible sources, and you should be fine. Avoid intruding on a person's privacy by publishing what is protected by statute, and you should be okay. Obtain copyright permission to re-publish digital content, and you shouldn't end up in court. But the fast pace of technological innovation and, in contrast, the slow pace of change in the law guarantees that lawyers will have plenty to do for a long, long time.

---

### CHAPTER ACTIVITIES

**1** You operate and manage a website for which many of your writers include graphics and images simply found and "borrowed" from the open web with their submissions. You are charged with drafting a policy that will guide contributors as to what they can and cannot appropriate, basing your policy on the notion of fair use. Write that policy.

**2** In this hypothetical, you are legal counsel to ThePuffingtonHost.com, a news aggregator that faces a libel action. Advise the site as to how to avoid or win the libel action based on the following facts. On September 2, 2017, The PuffHo publishes a story with the following headline: "Six Killed in Pair of Wrecks." The published story includes this paragraph:

Six people were killed Saturday night in a horrifying pair of alcohol-related crashes near Yankee Stadium after a sold-out baseball game. Five of the six victims had stopped to help after the first accident.

The accidents occurred on a congested street near the Stadium at about 11:45 p.m., roughly two hours after the Yankees' victory over the Red Sox. The identities of the victims had not been released by early September 3. New York Police Sergeant Rocco T. Ruggiero said that a white Ford Explorer ran a stop sign and pulled onto East 161st Street. The Explorer was likely coming from the stadium and alcohol was a factor, Ruggiero said.

The Explorer struck a silver Toyota Prius in the intersection. The driver of the Explorer that ran the stop sign was killed. Other motorists and one person riding a bicycle stopped to help.

A green Chevy van heading east then slammed into the good Samaritans and into both the Explorer and the Prius. Ruggiero said that the third motorist was arrested on suspicion of drunken driving and faces "more very serious charges."

The driver was not seriously injured, and he was taken to a local hospital to be treated. Ruggiero identified that motorist as David Simmons, a 19-year-old Brooklyn College student from Queens, NY, whose address is a campus dormitory. Brooklyn College officials confirmed that Simmons is enrolled there as a student. They said he is a soccer player and the vice president of the campus chapter of SADD, Students Against Drunk Driving.

Five victims were pronounced dead at the scene; the sixth died, en route, to the hospital. Five of the six were males. Their ages were not released.

As authorities blocked off streets in the area, bodies lay on 161st Street covered with sheets. Robin Hubier was leaving her apartment on a bicycle when she saw the green van pass her. "I heard a sound and saw something, but that's about all," she said. As she pedaled closer, she saw that the van had hit people. "It's a tragedy," Hubier said. "All I can say is that it's a damn tragedy. Whoever was driving the van was too much in a rush. I think people like that guy are just too stupid to know when it's unsafe to drive."

Simmons sues The PuffHo for libel *per se*, seeking US$5 million in damages. Simmons said the story was libelous because it falsely reported that he was guilty of drunk driving and that it falsely portrayed him as stupid. Simmons said he was not drunk and that he's not stupid. He said he majors in inter-disciplinary studies at Brooklyn College.

In your advice to the site, provide counsel on the following concerns:

- What type of libel plaintiff is the court likely to make Simmons?
- What, then, will be the requisite standard of fault in this case?
- Will Simmons be able to prove the requisite standard of fault?
- Are there other defenses PuffHo might consider?

In the second part of this assignment, rather than being published to PuffHo.com, the coverage is tweeted by a reporter at the scene, the police station, and the hospital. Ruggiero now is suing for libel because of the reporter's live tweets. How might your counsel change?

*This assignment is entirely fictitious; the names, places, and events were invented to create the above hypothetical.*

## Digital Resources

**ADLAW (adlawbyrequest.com)**
A good source of legal information for advertising and marketing researchers.

**Art of Public Records Searches (archive.virtualchase.justia.com/articles/public_records_research.html)**
How-to site with help in finding and searching public records repositories.

**Digital Media Law (dmlp.org/)**
Legal resources for citizen media from the Berkman Center for Internet and Society.

**Electronic Frontier Foundation (EFF) (eff.org/)**
The EFF is a donor-supported membership organization that works to protect citizens' rights regardless of technology and to educate the press, policymakers, and the general public about civil liberties issues related to technology.

**EFF Legal Guide for Bloggers (eff.org/bloggers/lg/)**
A guide developed especially to inform bloggers of their legal rights in publishing online.

**Electronic Privacy Information Center (EPIC) (epic.org)**
Established in 1994, EPIC is a public interest research center in Washington, DC, that tries to focus public attention on emerging civil liberties issues and to protect privacy, the First Amendment, and constitutional values.

**Federal Communications Commission (FCC) (fcc.gov/)**
FCC is charged with regulating interstate and international communications by radio, television, wire, satellite, and cable. This site offers links to regulations, news, complaint forms, bureaus within the FCC, and licensing information.

**Federal Communications Law Journal (www.repository.law.indiana.edu/fclj/)**
Published by the Indiana University Maurer School of Law.

**Federal Trade Commission's Privacy Page (ftc.gov/tips-advice/business-center/privacy-and-security)**
Protecting consumers' personal privacy is a duty of the FTC. This page outlines how the agency attempts to do this.

**First Amendment Center (firstamendmentcenter.org/)**
A non-partisan foundation dedicated to free press, free speech, and free spirit for all people, founded by the Freedom Forum.

**Freedom of Information Act (FOIA) (foia.state.gov/)**
Site explaining the FOIA and how to use it, at the U.S. Department of State.

**Free Expression Policy Project (FEPP) (fepproject.org/)**
Founded in 2000, FEPP provides research and advocacy on free speech, copyright, and media democracy issues.

**How to File a FOIA Request (fcc.gov/reports-research/guides/how-file-foia-request)**
**JDSupra (jdsupra.com/)**
Source for all sorts of legal documentation, cases, briefs and the like, a sort of WebMD of the legal profession.

**Journal of Information, Law and Technology (www2.warwick.ac.uk/fac/soc/law/elj/jilt/)**
Electronic law journal covering a range of topics relating to information technology law and applications.

**Jurist Legal News and Research (jurist.law.pitt.edu/)**
Published by the University of Pittsburgh School of Law.

**Landmark Supreme Court Cases (landmarkcases.org/en/landmark/home)**
Site developed to provide teachers with resources and activities to support the teaching of landmark Supreme Court cases.

**Law.com (law.com/)**
A daily news website for practicing lawyers, with search.

**Media Law Resource Center (medialaw.org/)**
A non-profit information clearinghouse originally organized by a number of media organizations to monitor developments and promote First Amendment rights in the libel, privacy, and related legal fields. The "Hot Topics" section is especially useful.

**Politech (politechbot.com/)**
A blog by Declan McCullagh, an investigative journalist with *Wired* magazine. Topics include privacy, free speech, the role of government and corporations, antitrust, and more.

**The Privacy Place (theprivacyplace.org/)**
Site for news on privacy-related policy developments.

**Privacy Times (privacytimes.com/)**
A subscription-only newsletter covering privacy and freedom of information law and policy; it is primarily for attorneys and professionals.

**Reporters Committee for Freedom of the Press (rcfp.org/)**
A non-profit organization dedicated to providing free legal assistance to journalists since 1970. Excellent source of news on free speech issues.

**University of Iowa Library's Communication and Media Law Resources (bailiwick.lib. uiowa.edu/journalism/mediaLaw/index.html)**
The content here is precisely what the name suggests. Excellent search functionality by topic.

**U.S. Copyright Office (copyright.gov/)**
The Copyright Office advises Congress on anticipated changes in U.S. copyright law; analyzes and assists in the drafting of copyright legislation and legislative reports and provides and undertakes studies for Congress; offers advice to Congress on compliance with international agreements; and is where claims to copyright are registered. This site has links to copyright law, international copyright treaties, general information, and copyright studies.

**U.S. Supreme Court Blog (scotusblog.com/)**
A surprisingly lively, very current blog and website, richly sourced with links to primary source documents such as briefs and precedent cases.

## BIBLIOGRAPHY

Banisar, David and Davies, Simon, *Privacy and Human Rights 2000: An International Survey of Privacy Laws & Developments* (Washington, DC: EPIC, 1999).

Callan, Paul, "Hulk Hogan Verdict Body-Slams Gawker," *CNN* (March 22 2016), available: www.cnn.com/2016/03/20/opinions/hulk-hogan-verdict-warning-shot-media-opinion-callan/.

Committee of Concerned Journalists, "Reporting Tips from Pulitzer Winners," *Project for Excellence in Journalism* (July 29 2006), available: www.concernedjournalists.org/reporting-tips-pulitzer-winners.

Dash, Samuel, *Unreasonable Searches and Seizures from King John to John Ashcroft* (Piscataway, NJ: Rutgers University Press, 2004).

Farhi, Paul "In the Tank?" *American Journalism Review* (May/June 2008), available: www.ajr.org/Article.asp?id=4516.

Friedman, Samuel, *Guarding Life's Dark Secrets: Legal and Social Controls Over Reputation, Propriety, and Privacy* (Palo Alto, CA: Stanford University Press, 2007).

Frohlich, Anita B., "Copyright Infringement in the Internet Age: Primetime for Harmonized Conflict of Law Rules?" *Berkeley Technology Law Journal* 24, no. 51 (2009): 852–896.

Gardner, Eriq, "Warner Music Pays $14 Million to End 'Happy Birthday' Copyright Lawsuit," *The Hollywood Reporter* (February 9 2016).

Garfinkel, Simson, *Database Nation: The Death of Privacy in the 21st Century* (Boston, MA: O'Reilly & Associates, 2000).

Gleicher, Nathaniel, "John Doc Subpoenas. Toward a Consistent Legal Standard," *Yale Law Journal* 118 (2008): 320, 330.

Horowitz, Karen Alexander, "When is § 230 Immunity Lost? The Transformation From Website Owner to Information Content Provider," *Shidler Journal of Law, Communication and Technology* 3, no. 14 (April 6 2007), available: www.lctjournal.washington.edu/Vol3/a014Horowitz.html.

Lessig, Lawrence, *Code and Other Laws of Cyberspace* (New York, NY: Basic Books, 1999).

McLeod, Kembrew, *Freedom of Expression®, Overzealous Bozos and Other Enemies of Creativity* (New York, NY: Doubleday, 2005).

Packard, Ashley, "Wired But Mired: Legal System Inconsistencies Puzzle International Internet Publishers," *Journal of International Media and Entertainment Law* 57 (2007): 57–96.

Rosen, Jeffrey, *The Naked Crowd: Reclaiming Security and Freedom in an Anxious Age* (New York, NY: Random House, 2004).

Schneider, Jaron, "Ridiculous Copyright Claims Are Smothering YouTube Content Creators," *Motion* (January 19 2016), available: http://motion.resourcemagonline.com/2016/01/ridiculous-copyright-infringement-claims-are-smothering-youtube-content-creators/499/.

Solove, Daniel J., *The Digital Person: Technology and Privacy in the Information Age* (New York, NY: New York University Press, 2004).

Swire, Peter P., "Elephants and Mice Revisited: Law and Choice of Law on the Internet," *University of Pennsylvania Law Review* 153 (2005): 175.

Trager, Robert, Dente Ross, Susan, and Reynolds, Amy, *The Law of Journalism and Mass Communication* (London, UK: CQ Press, 2016).

Worthen, Ben, "Best of the Business Tech Blog," *The Wall Street Journal* (June 3 2008): B6.

# APPENDIX

# The Core Values of Digital Journalism

*A free press can, of course, be good or bad, but, most certainly without freedom, the press will never be anything but bad.*

—Albert Camus, French novelist, essayist, and dramatist

*Were it left to me to decide whether we should have a government without newspapers, or newspapers without a government, I should not hesitate a moment to prefer the latter.*

—Thomas Jefferson

Presented here are definitions and descriptions of the core values of journalism, values that are essential regardless of medium. These values include **accuracy**, **reasonableness**, **transparency**, **fairness**, and **independence**.

## JOURNALISM VALUE 1: ACCURACY

Without accuracy, what would be the point of journalism? The Society of Professional Journalists' Code of Ethics instructs journalists to maximize truth and minimize harm, making accuracy the starting point for good journalism. Get the facts, check and double-check them, then report with enough contextualization that the collection of facts can tell a truth, if not the truth.

### Before Writing

1.  Do your research. Get the background material you need to corroborate facts, avoid misassumptions, and spot inconsistencies and contradictions. With online databases and, of course, Google, doing routine background research has never been easier.

2. Take time to read back to an interviewee the spelling of his or her name. If you need an age, ask for a birth date and year.
3. Avoid using secondary sources to verify facts.
4. If you have to use secondary sources, find at least two and make sure they agree independently; don't simply ask one to confirm what the other said.
5. Verify phone/fax numbers, web and email addresses. Plug the URL (web address) into a browser to make sure it works. Call the phone number.

## While Writing

1. Identify sources. Readers need to know where the information came from so they can judge its credibility for themselves. Online has put an even higher premium on this kind of transparency.
2. Do not confuse opinions with facts. It is easy to jump to conclusions when you are predisposed to believe something.

## After Writing

1. Do your fact-checking. Verify. When describing a financial transaction, a medical procedure, or how a sewer bond works, there's nothing wrong with calling the source and asking him or her to listen to what you've written. Editors at *The Oregonian* in Portland concluded that the three most frequent sources of error are working from memory, making assumptions, and dealing with second-hand sources.
2. Assemble all source materials—notebooks, interview transcripts, recordings, books, studies, photos, everything used to report and write the story. Go over the story and compare it to the original sources.
3. Copyedit. Check spelling. Read your article backwards. Read the copy out loud. Read (at least) once for content and effect. Read (at least) once for the mechanical errors, including those of grammar, punctuation, and keystroke errors. Errors often come with friends, so when you spot one, look just before and after. There may be others.
4. Proofread corrections, too, because error can be introduced even when correcting copy.
5. Do the math. If challenged by the complexity of the math or statistics or, say, how a survey was conducted (confidence level, margin of error, sample size, etc.), get some help. Do not pass along information you do not understand yourself, words of advice valid for much more than simply math.
6. Check maps when providing geographic information, including routes and locations. Be careful with city and county names. The city of New York is in the county of New York, which is, in turn, in the state of New York.

7. Check for balance. Are the major perspectives or voices or points of view represented in the story? This is the Rule of Fair Comment, and it is aimed at avoiding one-sided or one-source stories, which are incomplete and, therefore, inaccurate. Talk to as many people as possible, even circling back and speaking again with previous sources after learning more from subsequent ones. Try not to allow the first source you speak with to frame the entire story.

## JOURNALISM VALUE 2: REASONABLENESS

Digital content that exhibits reasonableness will be even handed and will incorporate as many perspectives as is possible. In other words, the information will have no obvious conflicts of interest, or it will clearly acknowledge where potential conflicts might exist. The information will be consistent in presenting the facts and will clearly identify opinion when and where it is such. Here are a few questions to check a story's reasonableness:

Is the article offering a balanced, reasoned presentation that incorporates the many sides of an issue or question or topic rather than one that is selective or slanted?

Is the tone calm and reasonable? Check also for severe language ("Anyone who believes otherwise has no basic human decency") and sweeping generalizations.

## JOURNALISM VALUE 3: TRANSPARENCY

Chapter 2 described disclosure and transparency, which are crucial to establishing and maintaining credibility online. Blog readers, especially, want to know our motives, our experience and expertise, our background, and, especially, any financial interest we have in the publication or dissemination of the story or article. So reporters and writers should be up front with this information. In addition, linking to source materials; providing brief biographical information somewhere on the page or site; and triangulating facts, figures, and data can communicate thoroughness and transparency. Make it easy to be contacted, document your source material, and include however parenthetically any tie to or interest in these sources you might have. Readers will wonder:

- Where did the information come from?
- What sources did the creator use?
- How well is the information supported? Even if it is opinion, a sound argument will probably have other people who agree with it.

Corroboration uses information to test information. It is most important in cases where information is surprising or counter-intuitive.

Transparency is needed in disclosing motives and potential conflicts of interest, and biases and subjective approaches should likewise be acknowledged. Transparency of process also contributes to credibility, which has to do with linking to documents, sources, and supporting evidence. This transparency of process also serves to place the individual post or article in the collective, connective tissue of the online information space.

Transparency should also be the goal when things go wrong. When mistakes are made, publish an apology, take responsibility, and correct the mistake. In addition to correcting the record, this kind of transparency shows that we all are human and that we are interdependent. We demand transparency in the institutions and organizations we cover; it only makes sense to offer that same transparency of process and product to readers.

## JOURNALISM VALUE 4: FAIRNESS

How many sides to an issue are there? Two? Think again. There are likely hundreds. Are your accounts providing as many of these perspectives as possible? What does balance look like in your story? Have you slanted the facts, or selectively, disingenuously included only certain ones to make a point? If you are attacking someone or a perspective, are you including different viewpoints? Are you giving the subject an opportunity to respond?

Balance and fairness are not about giving "equal weight to two sides." They have more to do with incorporating several different perspectives and giving relative weight to those different perspectives. An exposé on the toxic waste dumping practices of an industrial manufacturer should not strive to give the company's public relations officers equal time or space to tout the wonderful things the company is doing in the community. Balance and fairness are a bit more complicated than that. While giving the polluter an opportunity to respond, the story should maximize truth and minimize harm.

"Take readers to the margins and extremes, but do not dwell there at the exclusion of the 'middle'—report on ambiguity, consensus and ambivalence," the American Society of Newspaper Editors (ASNE) states. Understand that communities have many different layers and dimensions, and that we need to move between and within them to capture the mosaic of voices, viewpoints, events, problems, and solutions that exist.

Balance and fairness also strive to reflect a community's diversity and wholeness, which will include, according to the ASNE, "the good, the bad and the profoundly ordinary." The ASNE also recommends that writers and reporters:

- look beyond conflicts to explore underlying issues and perspectives—this will help to engage people and create a greater sense of possibility;

- avoid falsely creating or over-presenting "sides" or points of view where they don't exist; and
- step back and reflect on the patterns within news coverage and communities—provide balance over time, not just on a day-to-day basis.

## JOURNALISM VALUE 5: INDEPENDENCE

Independence is at the heart of journalism's essential role in a self-governing democracy, and it sets a standard for professionalism and ethical behavior. This value calls for us to guard and defend the role of a free press and to give a voice to as many perspectives as possible without favor and without being unduly influenced by anyone. Independence means avoiding membership in, and associations with, any group or individual who could compromise our integrity or credibility before our readers. The SPJ's "Act Independently" principle includes the following: "Journalists should be free of obligation to any interest other than the public's right to know." The code also states that journalists should:

- avoid conflicts of interest, real or perceived;
- remain free of associations and activities that may compromise integrity or damage credibility;
- refuse gifts, favors, fees, free travel, and special treatment, and shun secondary employment, political involvement, public office, and service in community organizations if they compromise journalistic integrity;
- disclose unavoidable conflicts;
- be vigilant and courageous about holding those with power accountable;
- deny favored treatment to advertisers and special interests and resist their pressure to influence news coverage; and
- be wary of sources offering information for favors or money; avoid bidding for news.

These are guidelines, not absolute rules. They do not preclude tough calls, particularly when one or more of these imperatives are in tension with one another. In those situations, it helps to have a collaborative decision-making environment and a process of ethical decision-making already in place.

## ONLINE NEWS ASSOCIATION

These core journalism values are reflected in the mission and vision statement of the Online News Association (journalists.org/), which is composed largely of professional digital journalists. The association has more than 2,500 professional members whose principal livelihood involves gathering or producing news for digital presentation. Here is the association's vision statement, reprinted with permission:

**MISSION:** Inspiring innovation and excellence among digital journalists to better serve the public.

**OUR VALUES:** We believe that the Internet is the most powerful communications medium to arise since the dawn of television. As digital delivery systems become the primary source of news for a growing segment of the world's population, it presents complex challenges and opportunities for journalists as well as the news audience.

**Editorial Integrity:** The unique permeability of digital publications allows for the linking and joining of information resources of all kinds as intimately as if they were published by a single organization. Responsible journalism through this medium means that the distinction between news and other information must always be clear, so that individuals can readily distinguish independent editorial information from paid promotional information and other non-news.

**Editorial Independence:** Online journalists should maintain the highest principles of fairness, accuracy, objectivity, and responsible independent reporting.

**Journalistic Excellence:** Online journalists should uphold traditional high principles in reporting original news for the Internet and in reviewing and corroborating information from other sources.

**Freedom of Expression:** The ubiquity and global reach of information published on the Internet offers new information and educational resources to a worldwide audience, access to which must be unrestricted.

**Freedom of Access:** News organizations reporting on the Internet must be afforded access to information and events equal to that enjoyed by other news organizations in order to further freedom of information.

## BIBLIOGRAPHY

Haiman, Bob, *Best Practices for Newspaper Journalists* (Arlington, VA: Freedom Forum, 2000), available: www.freedomforum.org/publications/diversity/bestpractices/bestpractices.pdf.

Knight Community News Network, *Principles of Citizen Journalism* (Washington, DC: J-Lab), available: www.kcnn.org/principles.

Magee, C. Max, *The Roles of Online Journalists* (Chicago, IL: Medill School of Journalism, 2006).

*The New York Times Ethical Journalism Handbook* (September 2004), available: www.nytco.com/pdf/NYT_Ethical_Journalism_0904.pdf.

*Poynter Guide to Accuracy*, available: www.poynter.org/content/content_view.asp?id=36518.

Rosenstiel, Tom and Kovach, Bill, *The Elements of Journalism* (New York, NY: Three Rivers Press, 2014).

# Index

Note: Page numbers in *italics* denote references to Figures and Tables.